POSTCARD HISTORY SERIES

Fore River Shipyard

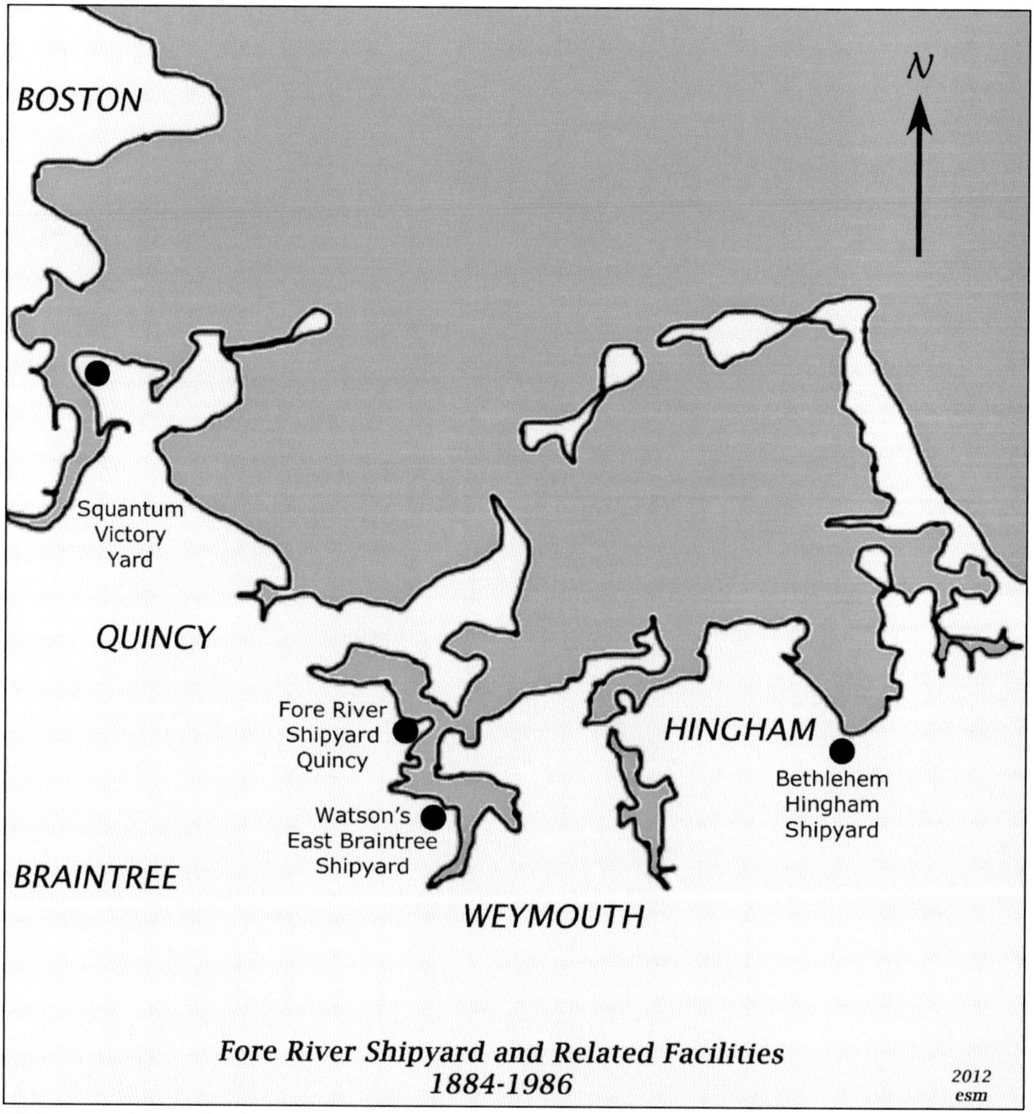

This map shows the locations where shipbuilding activities took place, including Watson's original shipyard at East Braintree in 1884, the relocated shipyard at Quincy in 1901, the temporary facilities used during World War I at Squantum, and additional facilities used during World War II at Hingham. (Courtesy of Ellen Miller.)

On the Front Cover: This grand overview of the shipyard was taken from the top of the 75-ton gantry crane around 1915. It showed almost the entirety of the bustling shipyard. The large building at the right was the machine shop, which had been expanded twice since its arrival in 1900. To the left, the building slips were filled with ships under construction. (Author's collection.)

On the Back Cover: USS *Lexington* was one of the most famous ships built at the shipyard, entering the US Navy as one of its first aircraft carriers in 1927. Known as the "Gray Lady," she was on the way to reinforce Midway Island when the Japanese attacked Pearl Harbor. Tragically, *Lexington* was sunk on May 8, 1942, at the Battle of the Coral Sea. (Author's collection.)

POSTCARD HISTORY SERIES

Fore River Shipyard

Wayne G. Miller

ARCADIA
PUBLISHING

ISBN 978-0-7385-9798-0

Published by Arcadia Publishing
Charleston, South Carolina

Printed in the United States of America

Library of Congress Control Number: 2012942950

For all general information contact Arcadia Publishing at:
Telephone 843-853-2070
Fax 843-853-0044
E-mail sales@arcadiapublishing.com
For customer service and orders:
Toll-Free 1-888-313-2665

Visit us on the Internet at www.arcadiapublishing.com

This book is dedicated to the men and women of the Fore River Shipyard who built the ships that helped win two world wars.

Contents

ACKNOWLEDGMENTS

I am grateful for the advice and help of the following people and organizations: the staff of the Thomas Crane Public Library, especially librarians Mary Clark and Linda Beeler and director Harry R. Williams III; Dr. Edward Fitzgerald, executive director of the Quincy Historical Society; James E. Fahey, director of the Braintree Historical Society; Cole Smith at Atlantic Fleet Sales and George B. Barber of Marine Photos of San Diego for allowing me to use images of their companies' postcards; my editor at Arcadia Publishing, Rebekah Collinsworth, for helping me through the process of writing this book; Kevin Johnson of Penobscot Marine Museum; Stacey Edwards of Wright and Logan, National Museum of the Royal Navy; and the staff of the US Naval Shipbuilding Museum for the behind-the-scenes tour.

The following resources were invaluable in researching the shipyard and the ships that were built there: Quincy's Shipbuilding Heritage Collection at the Thomas Crane Public Library, including *A History of Shipbuilding at Fore River* by Sarcone and Rines, *The Plant of the Fore River Ship and Engine Company* by Rogers Dickinson, and *Fore River Log* periodicals from 1915 to 1920; the Bethlehem Steel Hart Nautical photo album at the MIT Museum; *Three Hundred Years of Quincy* by Daniel Munro Wilson; *Historic Quincy Massachusetts* by William Churchill Edwards; *Exploring Life: The Autobiography of Thomas A. Watson*; Tim Colton's *Shipbuilding History*; Andrew Toppan's *Haze Gray*; *Navsource*; the *Dictionary of American Naval Fighting Ships*; and the General Dynamics Corporation.

Finally, thank you to my wife, Ellen, who put in countless hours providing technical and emotional support, and a belated thank-you goes to Maude Wheeler, my American history teacher at Quincy High School, who instilled in me the joy of studying history.

Unless otherwise noted, all photographs are courtesy of the owner's personal collection.

Introduction

Shipbuilding was not new to Quincy. The ketch *Unity* was built at Ship Cove in 1696. During the 1780s, ships were built in Quincy's Germantown section, including the 160-foot *Massachusetts*, which, at that time, was the largest commercial ship ever built in America. But it had been a quarter century since the last clipper ship was built in Quincy. *Red Cloud* was launched on November 24, 1877, from the shipyard of Deacon George Thomas in Quincy Point. Thomas had been building clipper ships in Quincy since 1854. Now, a new era of shipbuilding had begun at the Fore River with a much larger size and scope of work.

The man who founded the Fore River Shipyard was Thomas Augustus Watson. Most people know him as the person on the receiving end of Alexander Graham Bell's first telephone call. Watson's association with Bell led to the formation of the Bell Telephone Company. At the age of only 27, Watson retired from the telephone business with considerable wealth, looking for a second act in his life. In 1884, Watson began manufacturing small marine engines along the Fore River at East Braintree, Massachusetts. Eventually, the rapidly growing business needed more space, so Watson relocated the company to Quincy Point in 1901. The shipyard was sold to Bethlehem Steel in 1913. They managed it through two world wars, selling to General Dynamics in 1964. Fore River Shipyard's final ship was delivered in 1986 when General Dynamics exited the shipbuilding business in Quincy.

For over a century, the shipyard was a driving force in the local economy. During peak periods, tens of thousands were employed, resulting in a population surge and housing boom. Many small businesses emerged in the shadow of the shipyard and all along the South Shore. The closing of the shipyard in 1986 not only created a severe economic impact but also a sense of loss and a dent in local pride. Today, there is hope for a revival in Quincy Point as the 111-acre site has a new owner, the Fore River Shipyard Redevelopment Project.

This postcard history celebrates the Fore River Shipyard and the ships that were built there. Many are real-photo postcards taken by famous marine photographers like E. Muller Jr., O.W. Waterman, Nathaniel Stebbins, and N. Moser. Some of the scarcer photographs were taken by sailors onboard ships. Back in port, these images would be taken to a dealer who would develop them as postcards, enabling sailors to share their experiences with family and friends. These candid postcards are highly sought after.

There were about 600 ships built at the Fore River Shipyard for a myriad of customers. The first picture postcards were being marketed at the same time the shipyard was expanding at Quincy Point, so they provide a unique opportunity to see the shipyard in its infancy and to follow its growth. In selecting the 200-plus postcards included in this book, every effort was made to give the reader a fair representation of the different types of ships built at the shipyard through the decades.

As one who grew up in Quincy, I have many memories of family excursions over the Fore River Bridge to Nantasket Beach and beyond. My brother and I hoped the bridge would be open so we could see a ship sailing out to sea. It is easy to appreciate the work ethic that produced many of the largest and fastest ships of their day. These postcards will forever remind us of the great achievements of the Fore River Shipyard.

One

The Founder
Thomas Augustus Watson

Thomas Augustus Watson was born in Salem, Massachusetts, on January 18, 1854. He had a knack for working with his hands, and it was while employed at the machine shop of Charles Williams in Boston that he met Alexander Graham Bell. In 1874, Bell came into the shop with his invention, the harmonic telegraph. Watson's subsequent collaboration with Bell resulted in the invention of the telephone. They worked together only seven years, but their time together was magic.

In September 1882, Watson married Elizabeth Kimball and settled down in East Braintree, Massachusetts, planning to be a farmer on his newly purchased 60 acres of land. However, farming did not suit him, as he yearned for work in a machine shop. In 1884, Watson realized his dream by establishing the Fore River Engine Company, producing small marine engines.

In the late 1890s, the US Navy needed to upgrade its fleet of warships. The Navy Department requested designs and bids for a new type of ship, the torpedo boat destroyer. In 1898, the Fore River Engine Company was awarded the contract to build two 400-ton ships, USS *Lawrence* and USS *Macdonough*. The increase in business created a constant need to fund operations until payment came from the government, and Watson underestimated the cash required to build out the shipyard. Eventually he lost control of the shipyard he had created.

Watson was 50 years old, but life was just beginning for him. He studied geology, the speaking voice and elocution, gave public readings of poetry and lectures on the telephone, and became a painter and author. In 1910, Watson went to England to study acting, joining a Shakespearean troupe for a year. He was a true Renaissance man.

Watson died December 13, 1934, at the age of 80. He is buried at the North Weymouth Cemetery on a hill overlooking the Fore River Shipyard.

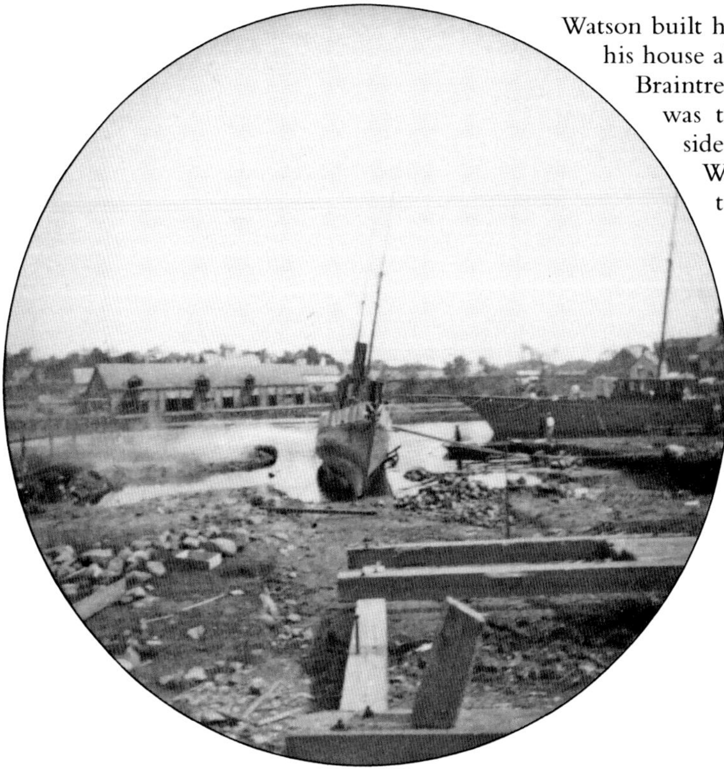

Watson built his machine shop just below his house along the Fore River in East Braintree. This c. 1890 photograph was taken from the Weymouth side of the river showing Watson's property and the types of boats that used his small engines. In 1884, Watson experimented with the wing rotary steam engine. Unfortunately, this engine was a failure, but he hired a young machinist, Frank O. Wellington, to help him. (Courtesy of the Braintree Historical Society.)

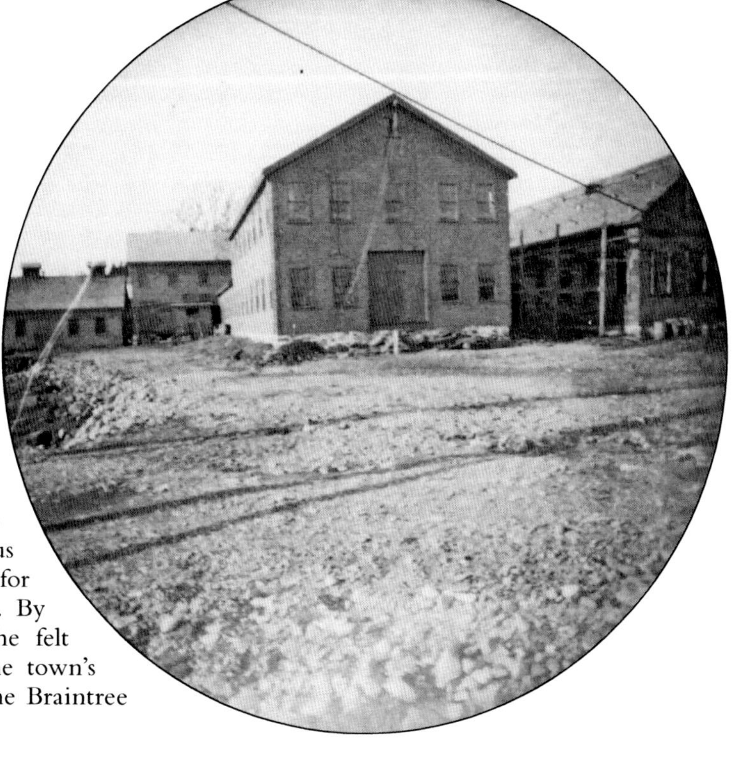

Watson made Wellington a partner in the business. Their marine engines worked so well that customers lined up to buy them. They had to construct another building at the bank of the Fore River to house 25 men. Watson was a generous man, always looking for ways to hire local people. By expanding the business, he felt he was contributing to the town's prosperity. (Courtesy of the Braintree Historical Society.)

Watson and Wellington designed a steam automobile, which would have made them pioneers in the automobile industry. However, they chose to build ships instead of horseless carriages. The Fore River Engine Company used a Weymouth address even though there were never any operations at that location. Most likely, the nearest post office was in Weymouth. This 1896 envelope advertised the company as yacht and machinery builders.

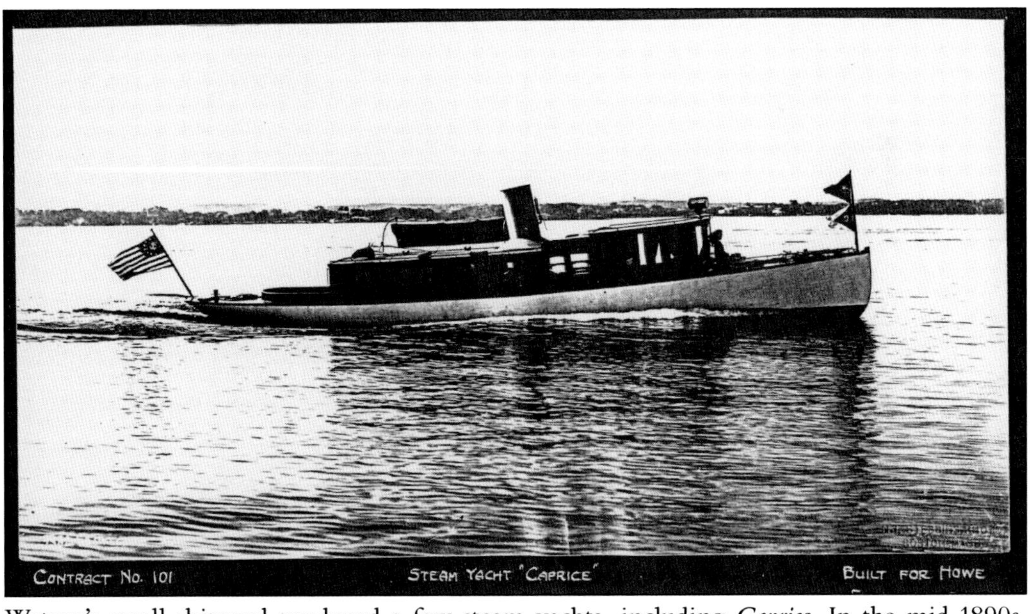

Watson's small shipyard produced a few steam yachts, including *Caprice*. In the mid-1890s, hard times had fallen upon the region. In order to stay in business, the company branched out by building hulls of small vessels, printing presses, and shoe machinery. The hard times finally ended when the US Navy needed to upgrade its fleet of warships. (Courtesy of the Braintree Historical Society.)

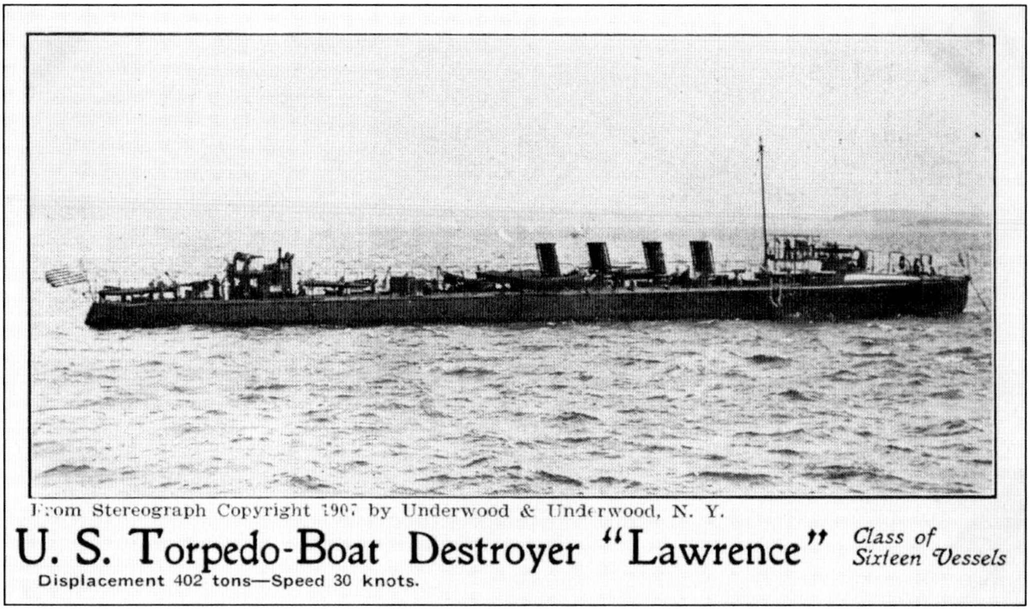

The $562,000 contract for USS *Lawrence* and USS *Macdonough* allowed the company to increase capacity and employ many more men. The ships were more complex and powerful than anything the shipyard had ever built. In 1907, Dr. Miles's Restorative Nervine issued a series of 16 postcards featuring US Navy ships, including USS *Lawrence* (DD-8). *Lawrence* was launched from the East Braintree shipyard in November 1900.

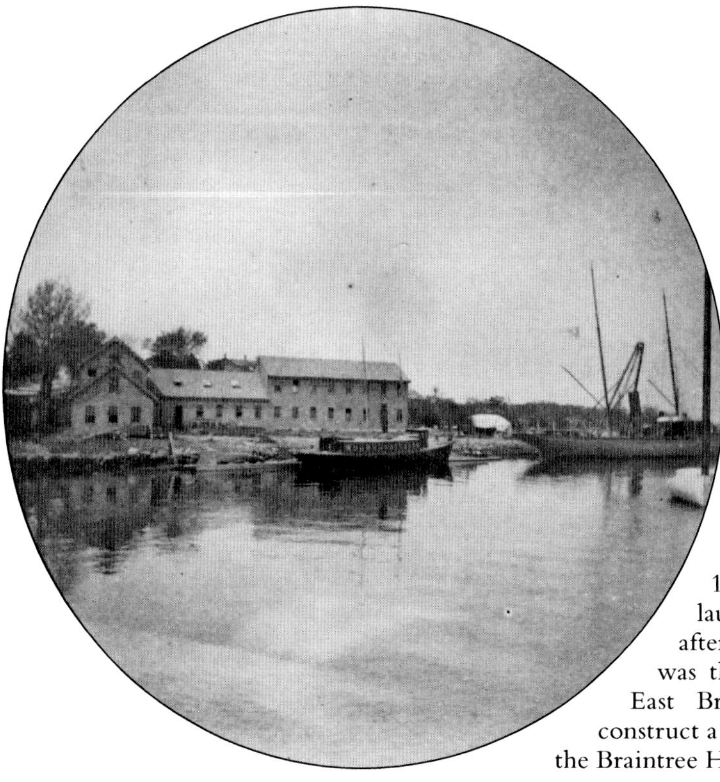

Watson and Wellington had a growing business in East Braintree. The Fore River Engine Company occupied several buildings and had outgrown the present facility. In December 1900, USS *Macdonough* was launched less than seven weeks after USS *Lawrence*. *Macdonough* was the last ship launched from East Braintree. It was time to construct a new shipyard. (Courtesy of the Braintree Historical Society.)

Two

The Fore River Shipyard
The Early Years

When 100 acres of waterfront land came up for sale, Watson's knowledge of geology helped him make the decision to expand the shipyard at Quincy Point, about two miles to the north. He knew from geological study that the land was firm enough to bear any weight put on it, easily excavated, without any ledge, and of sufficient depth to float the largest vessels. The land at Quincy Point was undeveloped, with no structures to interfere with Watson's vision of the new shipyard. Wellington oversaw the construction of the shipyard, which took over four years to complete, with two dozen large structures, railroad tracks, building slips, and more.

Watson and Wellington laid out the configuration of the buildings and placed the structures in such a way that they could be doubled in size and still leave room for vehicles and material to move freely. That was fortuitous planning because in 1902 the machine shop was so overloaded with work that it became necessary to double its length less than two years after its original construction. The buildings were lined up efficiently with the possibility of combining allied departments if the structures were expanded. Ideally, material never touched the ground nor retraced its steps. Raw material entered the shipyard near the forge shop. It progressed steadily from one department to another, being formed and finished, always moving forward in the direction of its final destination, the ship.

From humble beginnings, Watson's small marine engine business grew to become the largest private employer along the South Shore. Views of the new Fore River Shipyard were captured on postcards. They provided insight into what was going on at Quincy Point and allowed the community to share in the success of the shipyard.

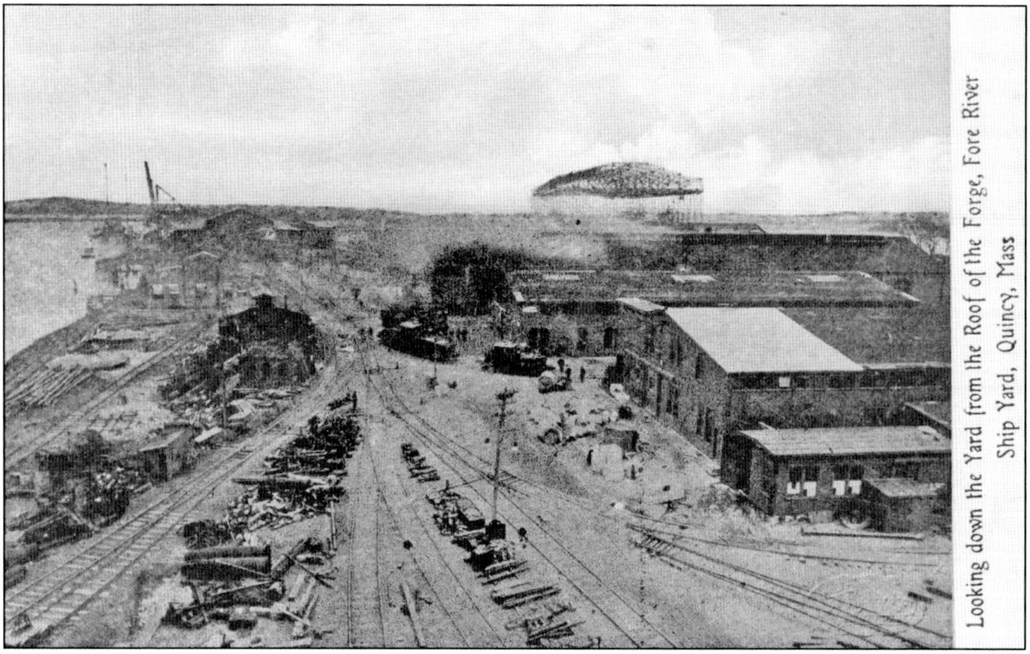

This early view of the shipyard, taken from the roof of the forge shop, shows how quickly the new 100 acres in Quincy Point were developed. By the height of the shipyard construction in 1902, there were over 20 large buildings and 1,000 employees representing 34 cities and towns. There were now 11 ships under construction.

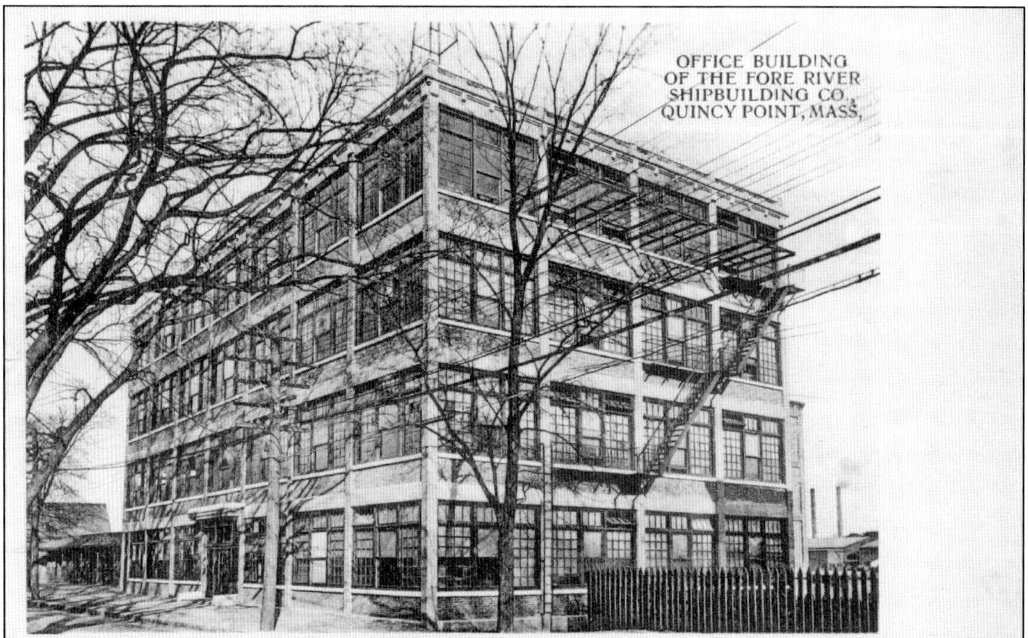

Many of the early postcards were printed in Germany, as was this one of the main office building on East Howard Street. Druggist George W. Gragg of Quincy Point, Massachusetts, published it. The sender of the postcard was an employee at the shipyard who punched the time clock in this building before heading to his desk, which was a quarter mile away.

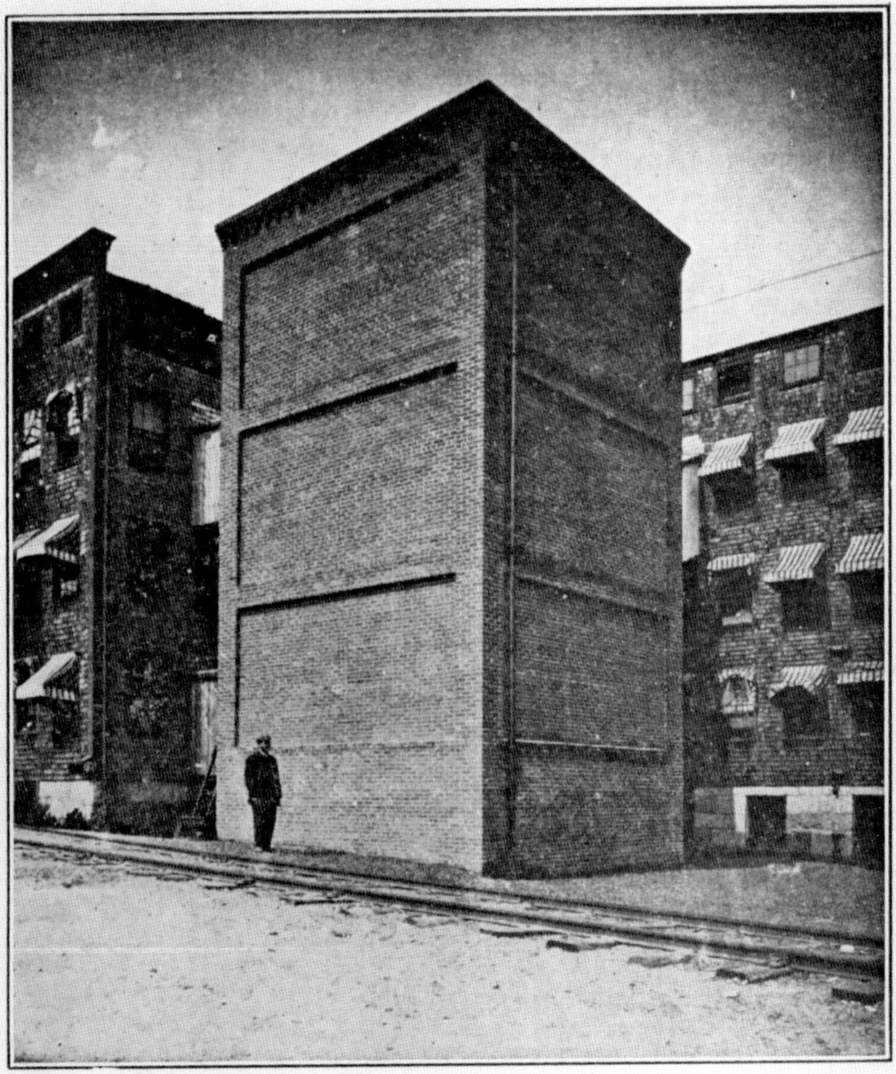

Fireproof Vault Building for Fore River Ship-Building Co., Quincy, Mass.

FRANCIS W. WILSON

ARCHITECT & ENGINEER

BOARD OF TRADE BUILDING, BOSTON, MASS.

Francis W. Wilson, architect and engineer, advertised his services with this postcard of the "Fireproof Vault Building" that was constructed at the Fore River Shipyard. It was a massive concrete structure that was conveniently located behind the main office building on East Howard Street. Irreplaceable documents and valuables were stored inside. To show the importance of the vault, a security guard stood watch; the guard was dwarfed by the size of the building. Wilson also provided engineering services for the main office building with his patented system of combination concrete and mill construction. It was the first building in the United States to use the "Wilson System" of construction.

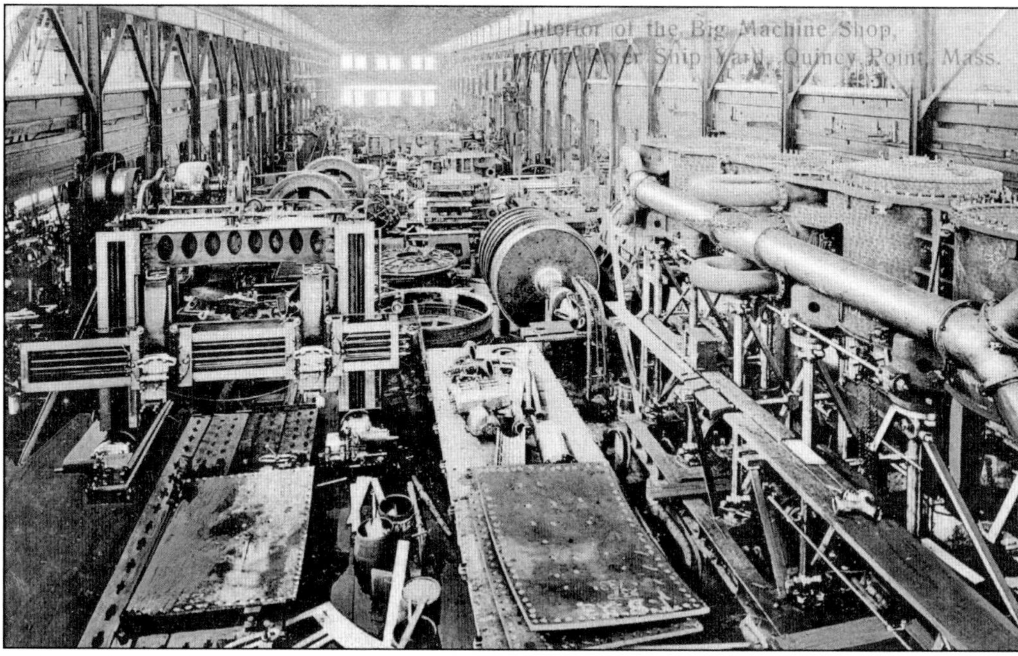

In 1900, the machine shop was built at the East Braintree yard and floated down the Fore River to its new home in Quincy. It was in the machine shop that forgings were shaped, planed, and smoothed into crankshafts, cylinders, and propellers. The machine shop cost the company $350,000 to build and contained 1.75 acres of floor space.

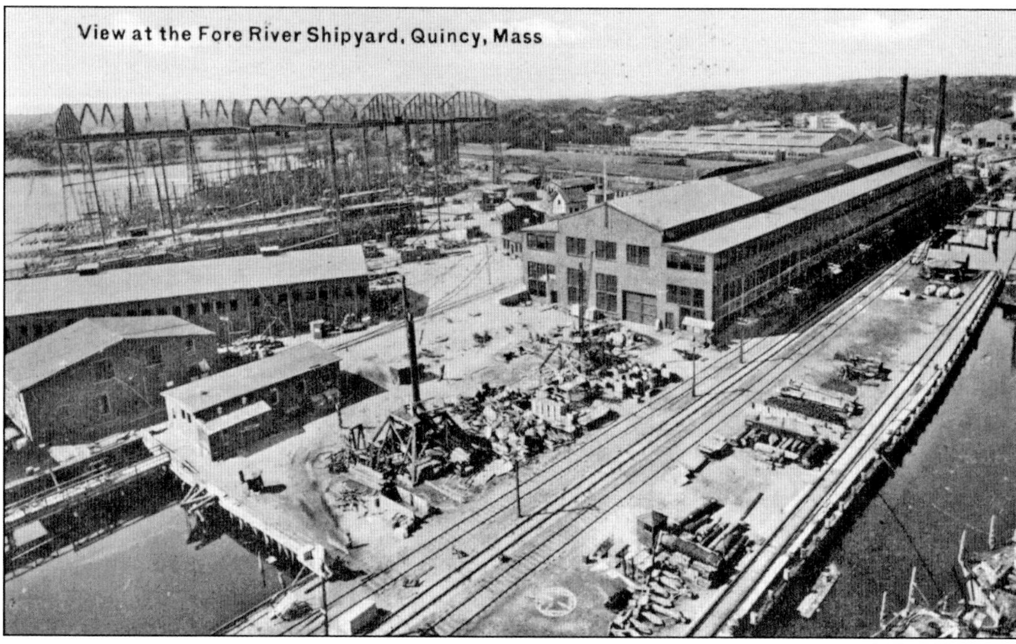

This view of the shipyard was taken from the top of the 75-ton gantry crane, which was located at the outfitting pier. The large building at the right was the machine shop. There were two major additions to the original machine shop before World War I. The structure had hundreds of windows, giving the interior so much light it was like working outdoors.

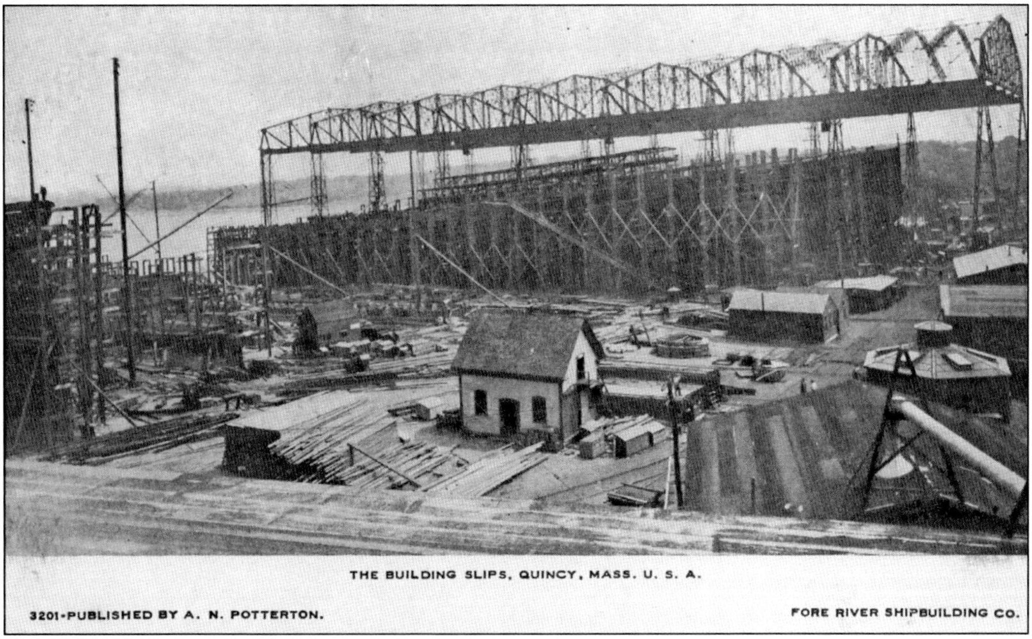

Between the machine shop and the building slips stood the lumberyard. Even though the largest component of a ship was steel, the shipyard still required large amounts of lumber for the interiors of the ships. From the lumberyard, the wood would be sent to the carpenters and cabinetmakers in the joiner shop.

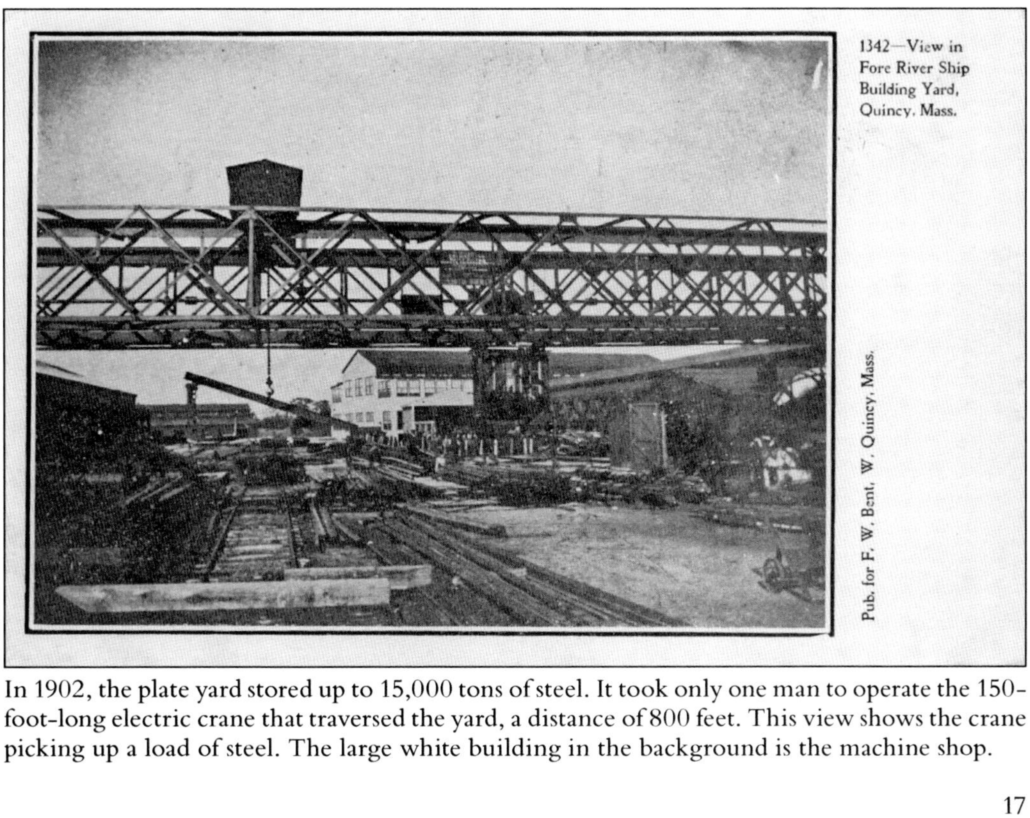

In 1902, the plate yard stored up to 15,000 tons of steel. It took only one man to operate the 150-foot-long electric crane that traversed the yard, a distance of 800 feet. This view shows the crane picking up a load of steel. The large white building in the background is the machine shop.

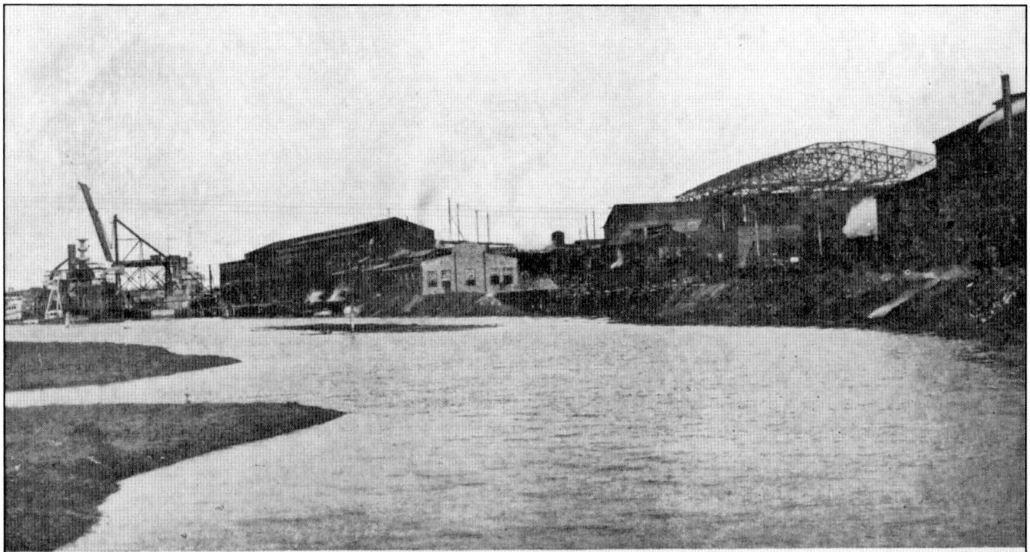

THE POWER HOUSE, MACHINE SHOP & 75 TON DOCK CRANE, QUINCY, MASS. U. S. A.

3200- PUBLISHED BY A. N. POTTERTON. FORE RIVER SHIPBUILDING CO.

The powerhouse provided all the electricity for the shipyard. It was a state-of-the-art power plant with six steam boilers and a capacity of 1,200 horsepower. Every machine had its own motor, and so, the delivery of electricity was efficient and economical. All of the cables were concealed underground, and of course, all of the tunnels were built with Quincy granite.

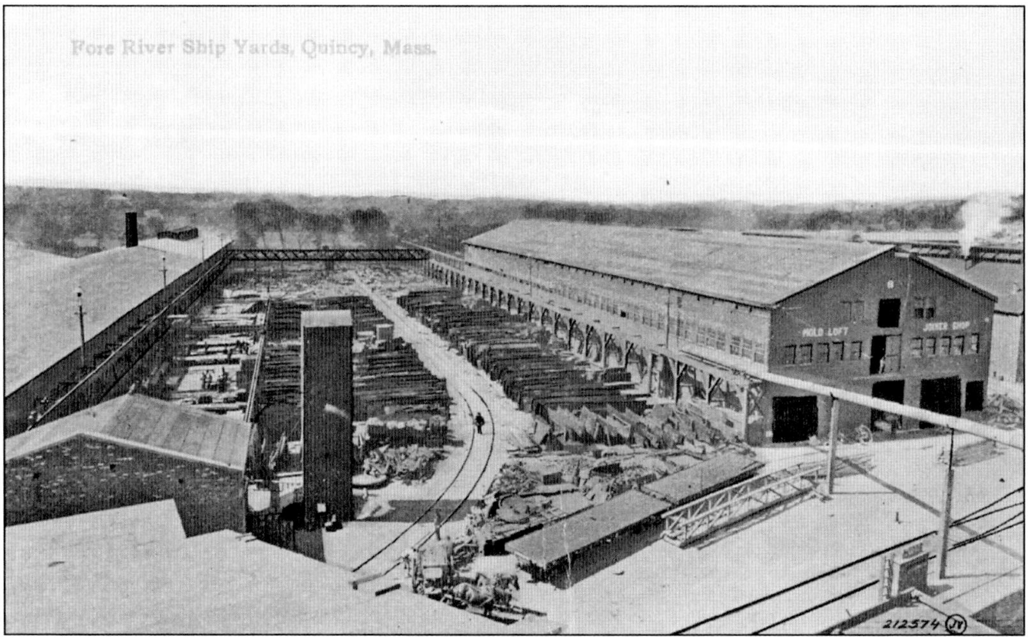

The huge building on the right contained the mold loft and joiner shop. Inside the mold loft, loftsmen worked on the floor making full-size wooden or paper templates of the hull. Afterwards workers cut and trimmed steel plates to match the templates. In the joiner shop, woodworkers built furniture and finished wooden parts of the interiors of ships, such as pilot houses, staterooms, decks, lockers, and ladders.

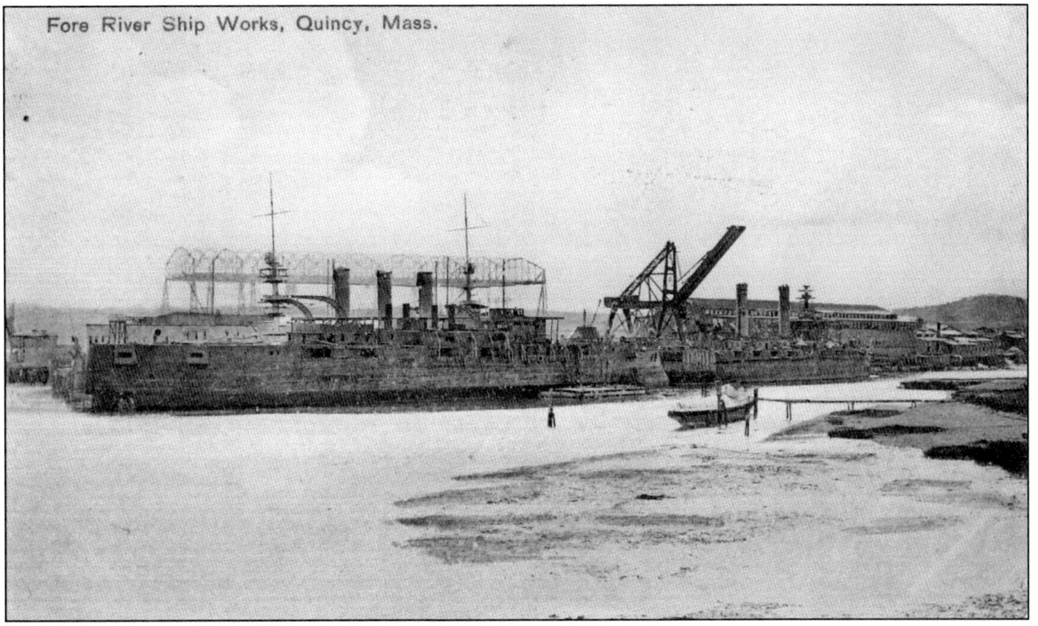

After battleships *New Jersey* and *Rhode Island* were launched, they were docked at the outfitting pier for the final stage of production. When the ships arrived at the pier, they did not have the funnels (smokestacks). The gantry crane would lift the funnels into place at the pier. The battleship to the left was further along, as it had three funnels; the other battleship only had two.

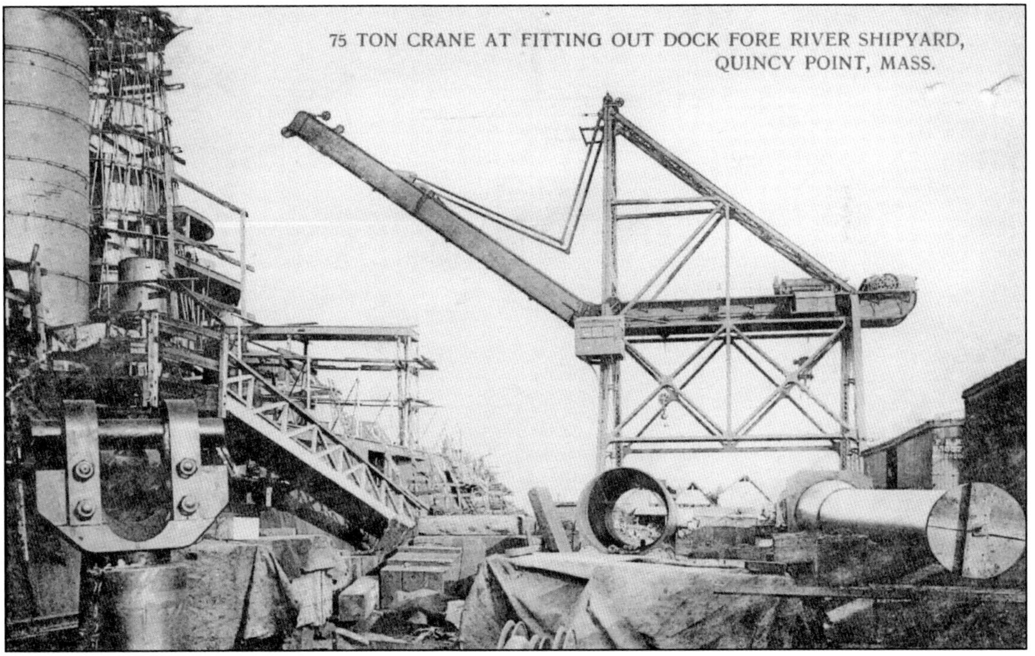

Erected in 1901, the 75-ton gantry crane was the first crane at the shipyard. It would slide along tracks, lifting and delivering equipment and supplies onto the ship. Once alongside the pier, ships still required many months to over a year of work before they went to sea trials and eventually to the customer. The crane operated under all three owners of the shipyard, finally retiring in 1982.

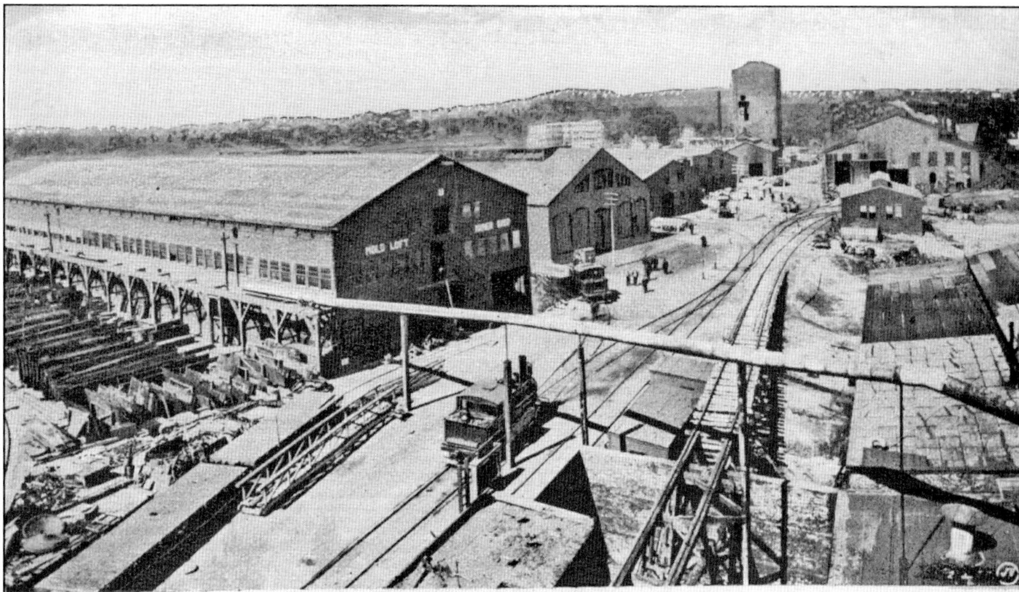

Fore River Ship Yards, Quincy, Mass.

Until 1903, material was brought into the shipyard by trucks and lighters, which were very slow and expensive. The decision was made to build a branch railroad that would connect to the main line of the New York, New Haven & Hartford Railroad. With much difficulty, Watson was finally able to secure all the land necessary for the three miles of track, and the Fore River Railroad was born.

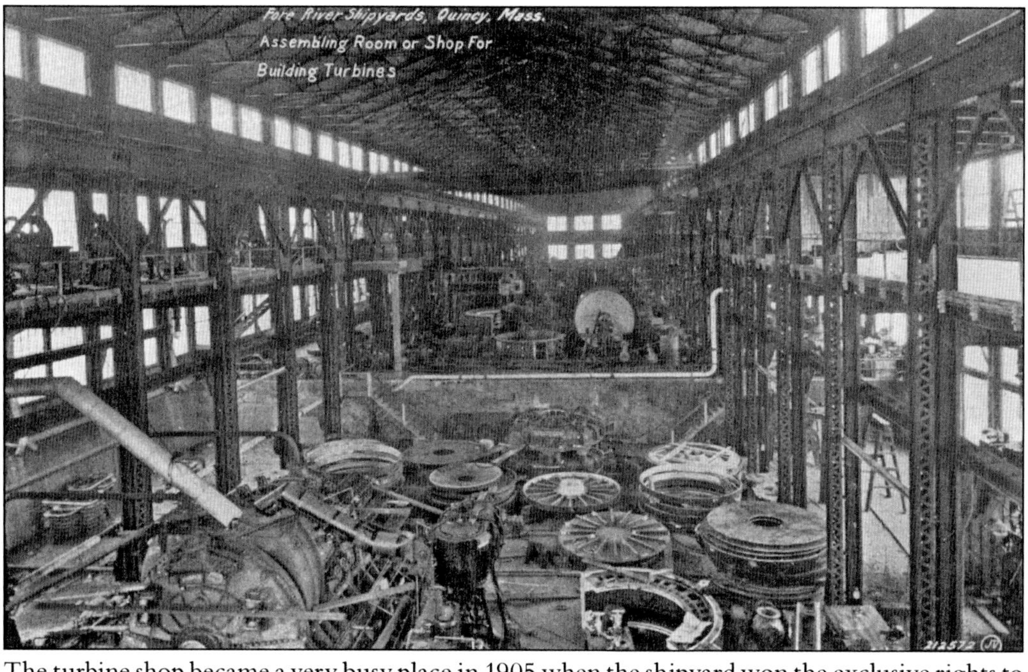

The turbine shop became a very busy place in 1905 when the shipyard won the exclusive rights to manufacture the Curtis turbine. The new turbine was used in USS *Salem* (CS-3) and SS *Creole*. When the turbines failed to meet expectations, the shipyard was sued by the owners of *Creole* for breach of contract and forced to replace the Curtis turbines with reciprocating engines.

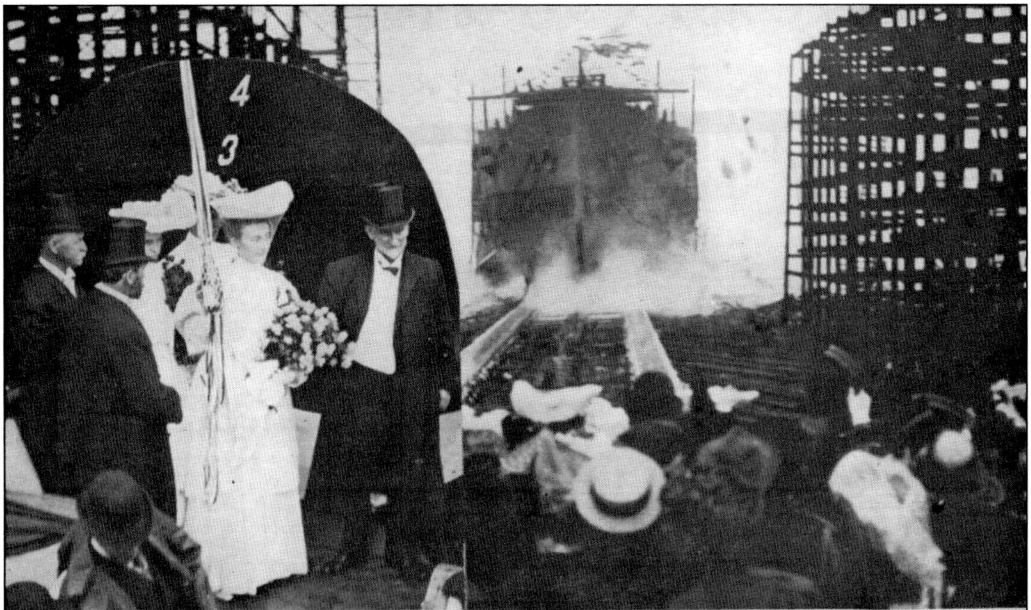

Gov. Douglas, Miss Bell, Gov. Bell Launching Battleship Vermont.

All of the construction to build out the shipyard never interfered with production schedules and ship launchings. When USS *Vermont* was launched in 1905, Governor Douglas of Massachusetts and Governor Bell of Vermont headlined the festivities with Governor Bell's daughter sponsoring the ship. Launchings at the shipyard were a great source of local pride with many dignitaries and the press in attendance.

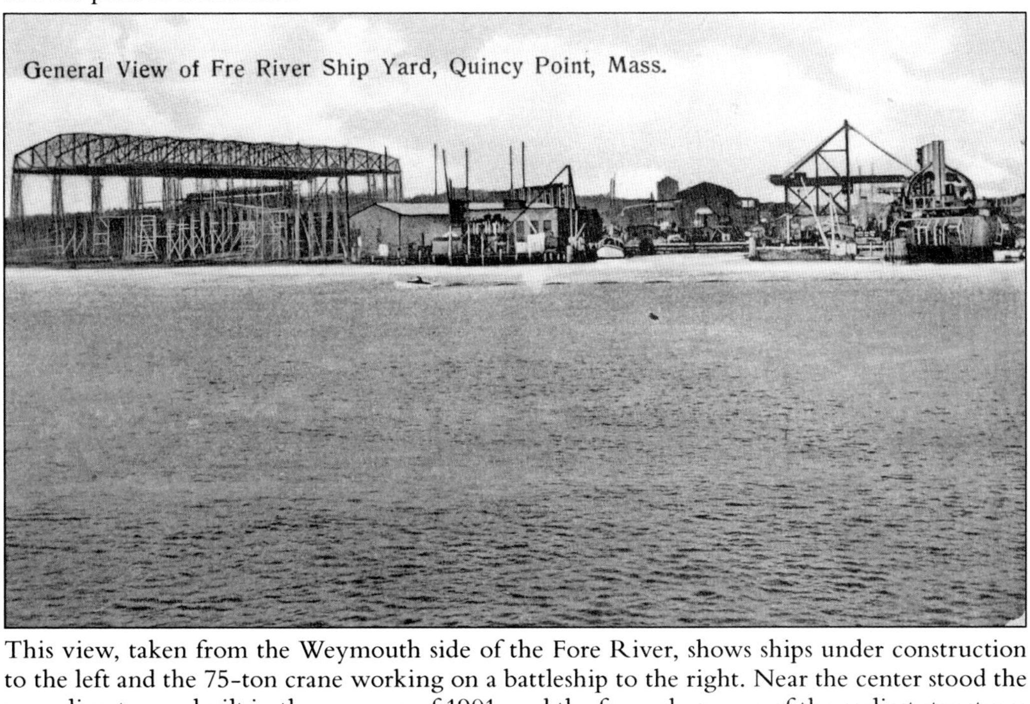

This view, taken from the Weymouth side of the Fore River, shows ships under construction to the left and the 75-ton crane working on a battleship to the right. Near the center stood the annealing tower, built in the summer of 1901, and the forge shop, one of the earliest structures in the shipyard and the largest forge in the country at the time of construction.

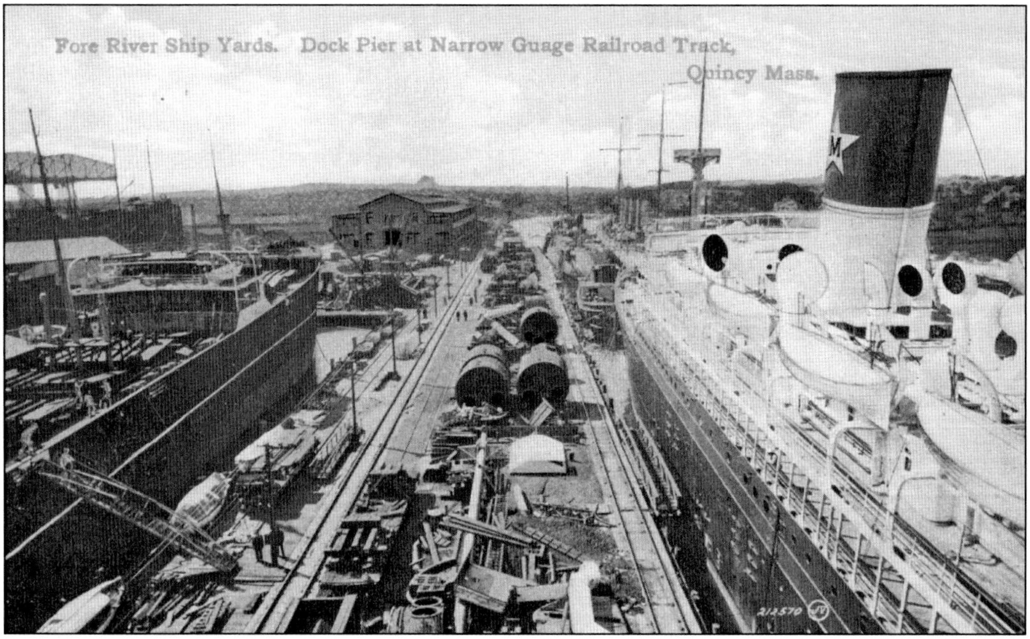

At any given time, several ships were under construction on both sides of the pier. Shown here on the right was a cruise ship near completion. Its smokestack featured a five-pointed star logo with an "M" in the middle. The ship was SS *Creole*, built for the Morgan Line in 1907. Valentine and Sons published this postcard in 1908.

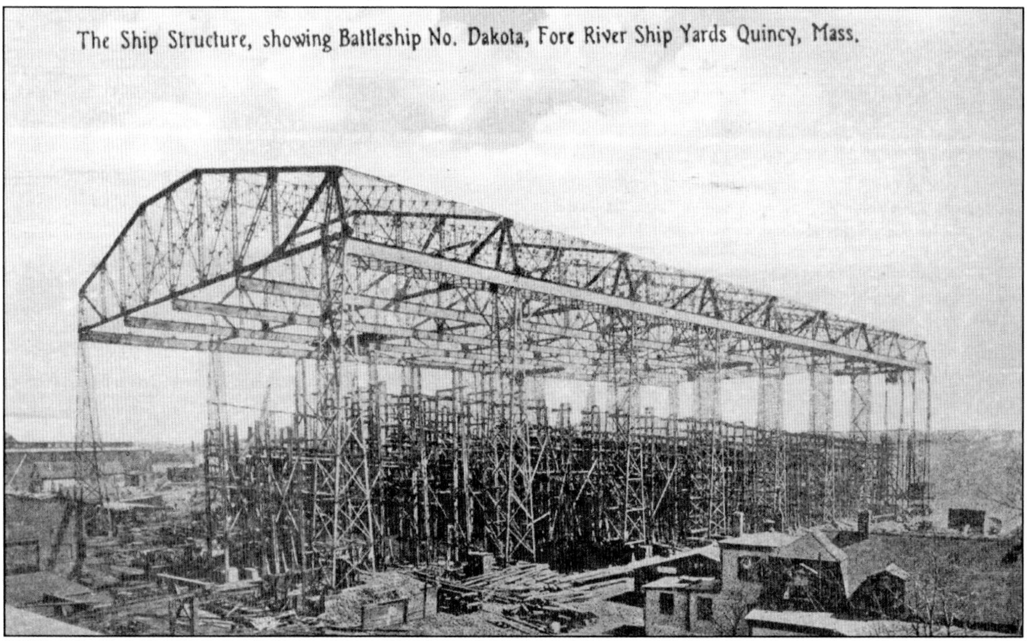

When ready to leave the building slip, USS *North Dakota* would have glided down the ways directly into the water. Ships were launched stern first because the shape of the stern provided more resistance when entering the water, therefore more buoyancy, which helped stabilize the ship. People on the Weymouth side of the river were warned to stay away from the water during ship launchings because of the drowning hazard.

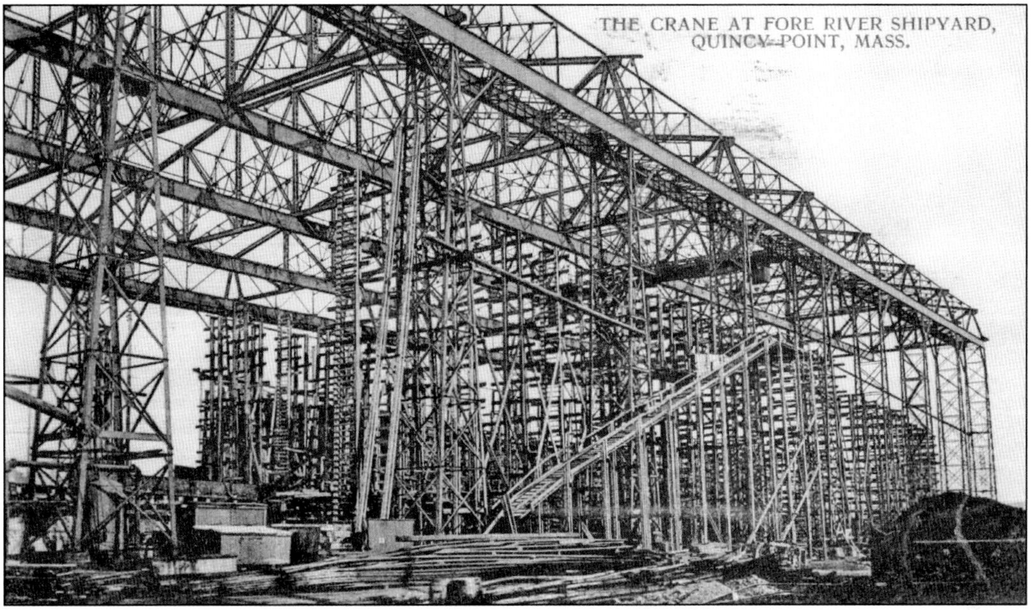

The ship house with its steel girders towered over the other buildings at the shipyard. The structure, large enough to hold up to four battleships at once, was a recognizable landmark. Eight electric cranes hovered over the ships with the operators perched 100 feet from the ground. The first two battleships built at the shipyard spent over two years in the ship house before they were ready to be launched.

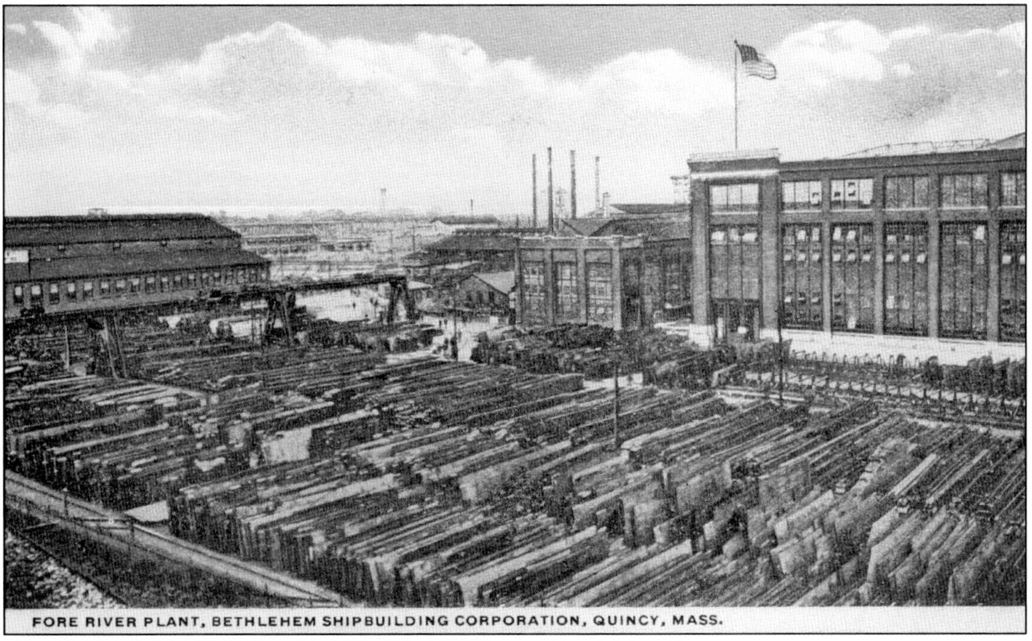

After Bethlehem Steel purchased the Fore River Shipyard in 1913, their shipbuilding division was incorporated as Bethlehem Shipbuilding Corporation with its headquarters in Quincy. It was a natural fit for a shipbuilder to partner with a steel company. The constant source of low-cost steel gave the shipyard a leg up on the competition. In this World War I–era view, the yard was bulging with steel.

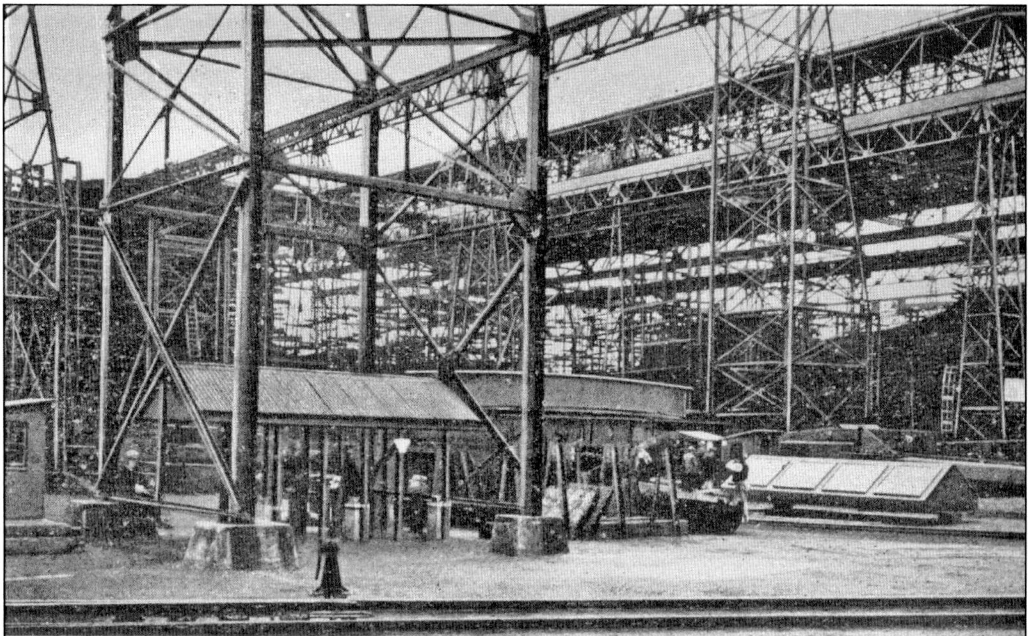

FORE RIVER PLANT, BETHLEHEM SHIPBUILDING CORPORATION, QUINCY, MASS.

Bethlehem Steel came into the shipbuilding business prepared to spend money to upgrade the plant and equipment. A major addition was the construction of a 1,000-foot-long concrete-and-steel building slip at a cost of around $500,000. The slip was 130 feet wide and contained a 50-ton crane and three 7.5-ton cranes. The cranes hovered over 120 feet above the concrete foundation.

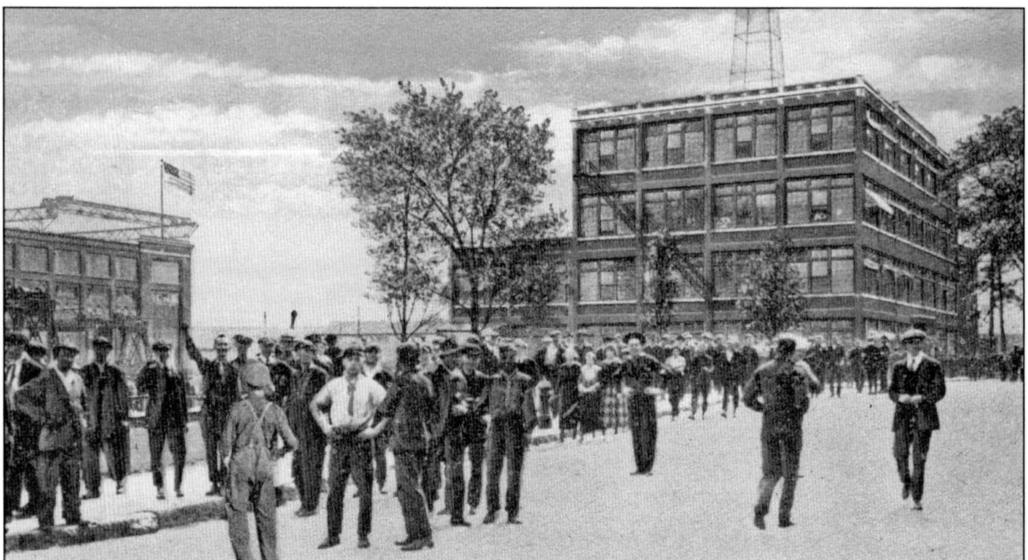

FORE RIVER OFFICE, BETHLEHEM SHIPBUILDING CORPORATION, QUINCY, MASS.

During World War I, there would be many workers on East Howard Street for a shift change. Most of the employees were men, although, there were three women near the center of this postcard, most likely office workers. By contrast, during World War II with so many men at war, "Rosie the Riveter" was a common sight at the shipyard.

Three

The First Ships
1900 to 1907

Quincy's population grew from 16,723 in 1890 to 32,642 in 1910, almost doubling in 20 years. Between the shipyard and the granite industry, these were boom times for Quincy.

In order to win the contract for battleships *New Jersey* and *Rhode Island*, the Navy Department demanded that Watson and Wellington dissolve their partnership and form a stock corporation. In February 1901, the name of the company was changed to the Fore River Ship and Engine Company, and Watson was named president. Incorporating did not change the demands for cash to support the expansion, so Watson was forced to sell more and more of his telephone stock to keep the business afloat.

The demands for cash came to a head in 1902, when the company needed to sell $1.25 million in bonds at six-percent interest. The agreement with the bondholders gave them the right to name a majority of the board of directors, and Watson had to agree to resign as president of the company should the board want to put in their own man. There was also a suspension of dividends on the common stock, which cost Watson most of his income since all of his property had been turned into Fore River stock.

By October 1903, the company was forced to reorganize, and Adm. Francis T. Bowles replaced Watson as president. Less than a year later, Watson resigned as chairman of the board, which marked his final exit from the shipbuilding business. He had started the business in a kindergarten building 20 years before with only one helper, and by the time Watson left, he had created a business employing 4,000 with a multimillion-dollar payroll.

From 1900 to 1907, there was a diverse mix of customers, as management sought to reduce its dependency on the US Navy. The shipyard also worked on schooners, freighters, steamers, and colliers for commercial customers.

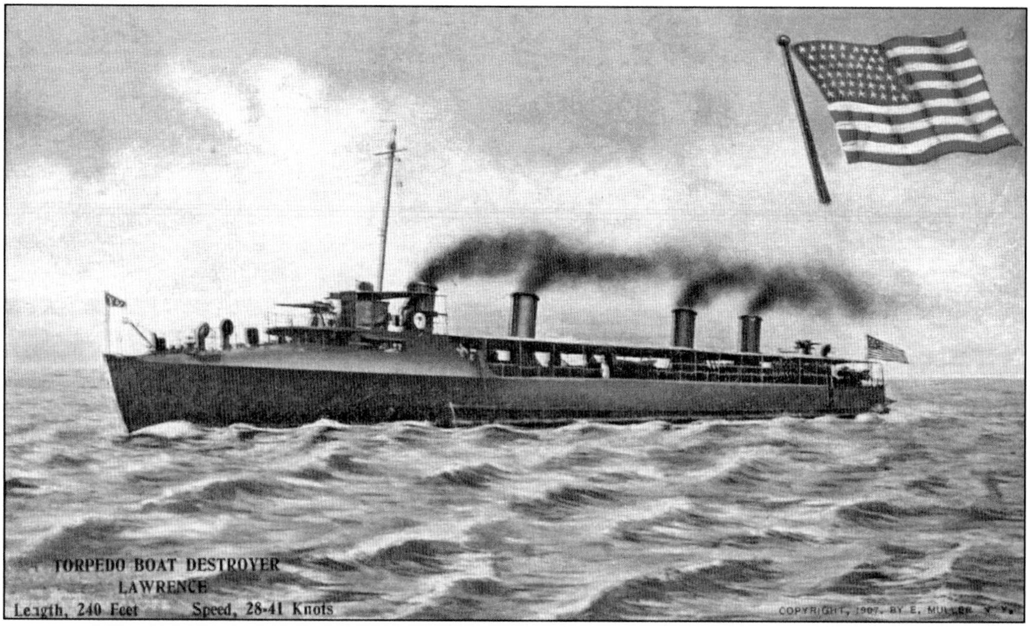

Commissioned in April 1903, USS *Lawrence* (DD-8) was named for US Navy captain James Lawrence, who uttered the heroic words, "Don't give up the ship," during the War of 1812. A torpedo boat destroyer, she served along the Pacific coast during the Mexican revolution and guarded the approaches to the Panama Canal during World War I. She was decommissioned in 1919 and scrapped in 1920.

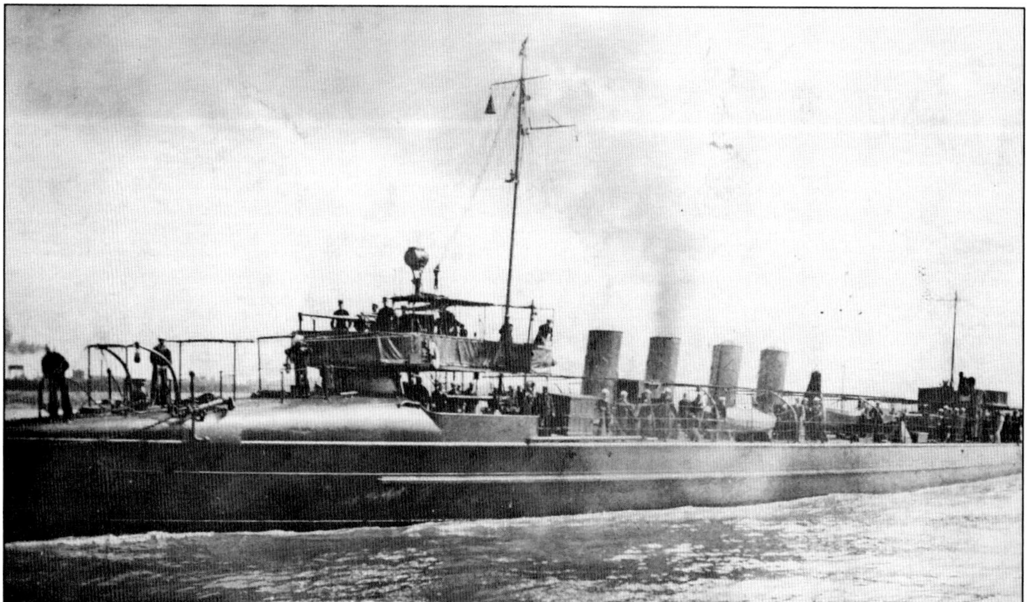

Commissioned in September 1903, USS *Macdonough* (DD-9) spent seven months training midshipmen at the US Naval Academy. In 1909, she steamed up the Mississippi River for the St. Louis centennial celebration. During World War I, *Macdonough* was used as an escort and patrol ship off the coast of France. She returned to the United States in 1919 and was sold for scrap in 1920.

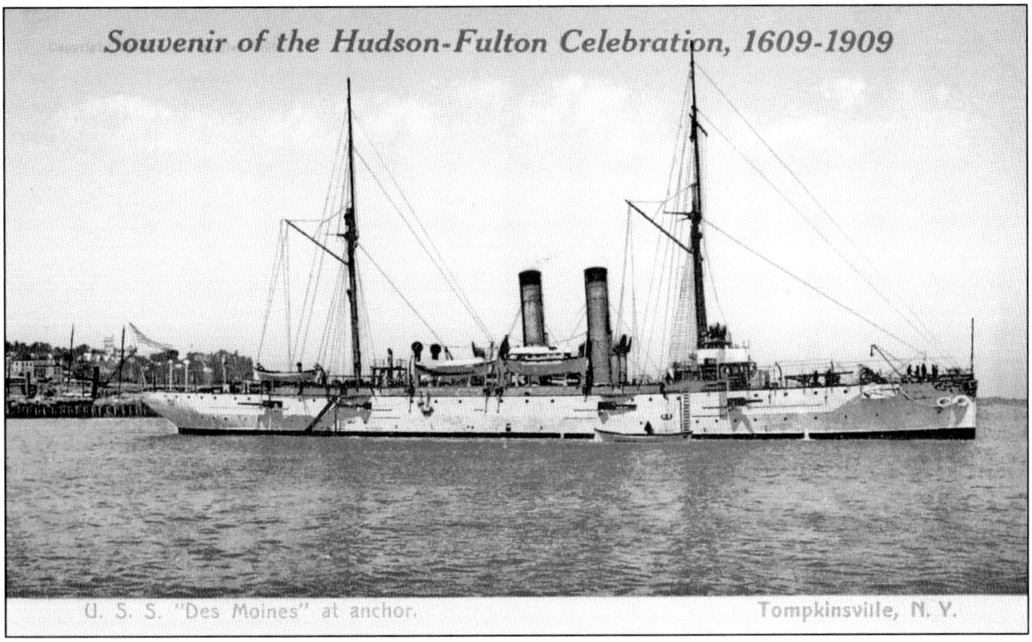

Cruiser USS *Des Moines* (C-15) was launched in September 1902 and commissioned in March 1904. This postcard commemorates the Hudson-Fulton Celebration of 1909 in which *Des Moines* participated with the Great White Fleet. It was a huge spectacle of military might with a naval parade representing over 35 nations, the largest international fleet ever assembled.

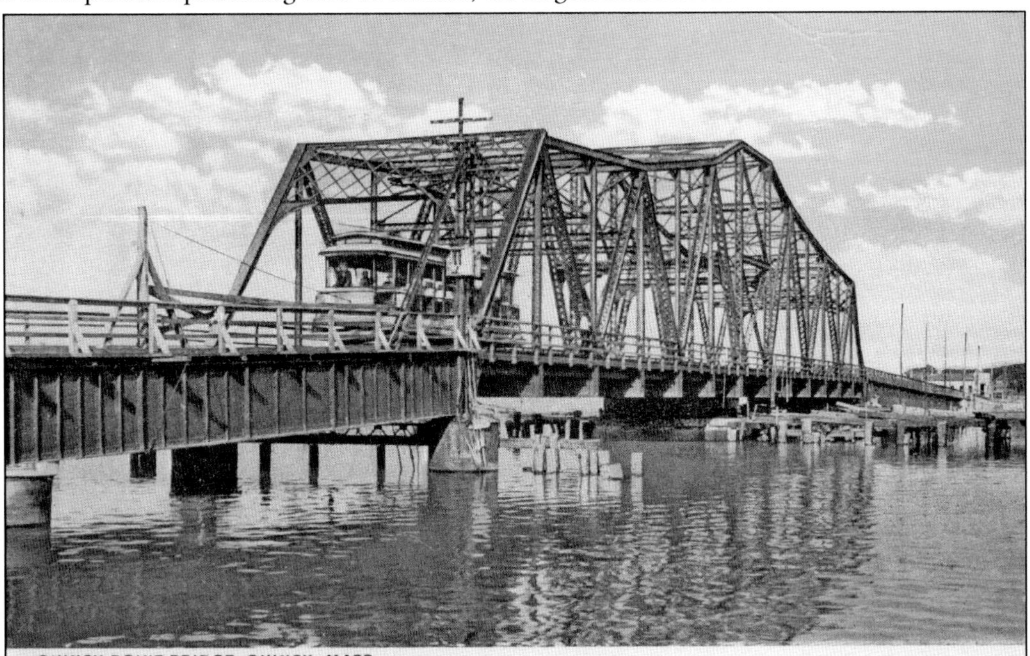

When Watson won the contract to build USS *Des Moines* (C-15), he knew she would not fit through the old wooden bridge spanning the Fore River so he prevailed upon the county to build a new bridge before the ship was finished. He then won the contract to build the bridge as well. The new iron swing bridge was floated downstream and into place in 1902.

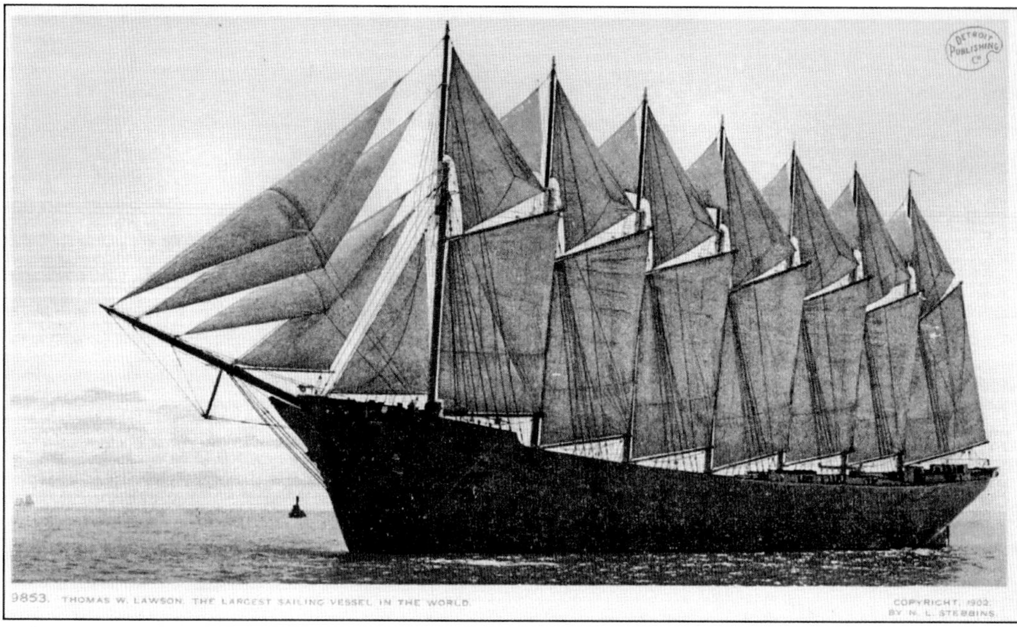

What a magnificent sight *Thomas W. Lawson* must have been when launched in 1902. Built for the Coastwise Transportation Company, *Lawson* was the only seven-masted schooner to sail the seas. She had a steel hull and was 368 feet at the waterline. *Lawson* was a pure sailing ship with no auxiliary engine. She was deemed sluggish and unwieldy, almost capsizing several times. Refitted to ship oil in 1906, she set sail from the Marcus Hook Refinery on her first transatlantic trip to London on November 19, 1907. She was filled with over two million gallons of light paraffin oil. Although they started out in good weather, soon it turned stormy. By the time the ship reached the Scilly Isles on December 13, she had lost most of her sails in a ferocious gale.

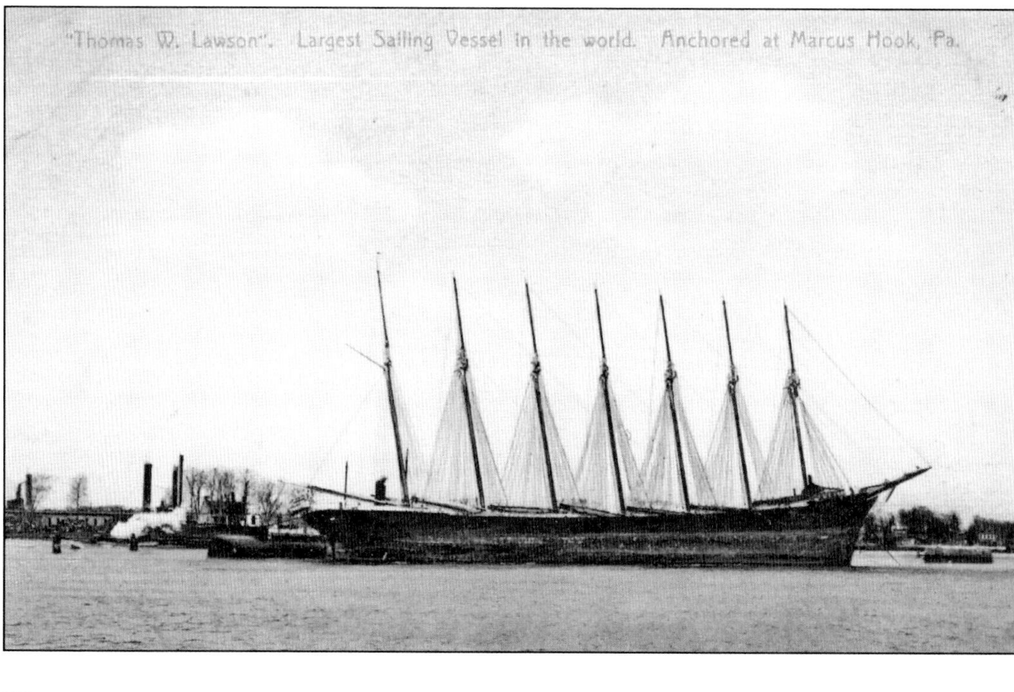

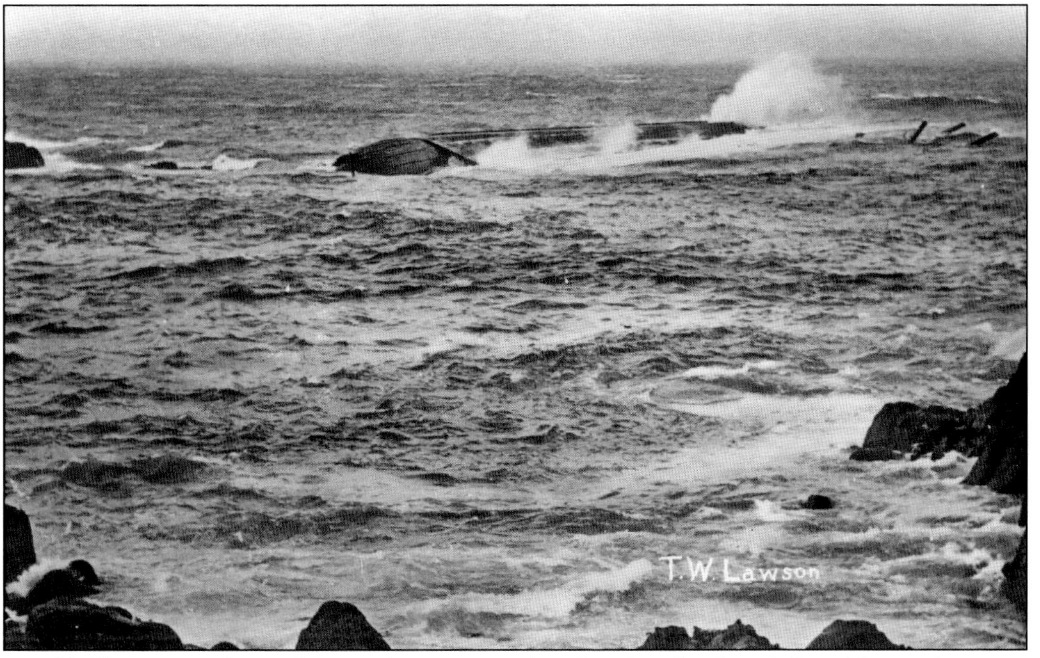

Local lifeboat crews begged *Lawson*'s captain to abandon ship, but he tried to ride out the storm using the ship's anchors. When they snapped, 16 crewmen were lost as well as the local pilot who had come on board. This postcard by Gibson & Sons, Penzance and Scilly Isles, shows *Lawson* on her side, half submerged. *Lawson*'s remains are still underwater, and the museum at St. Mary's has many artifacts.

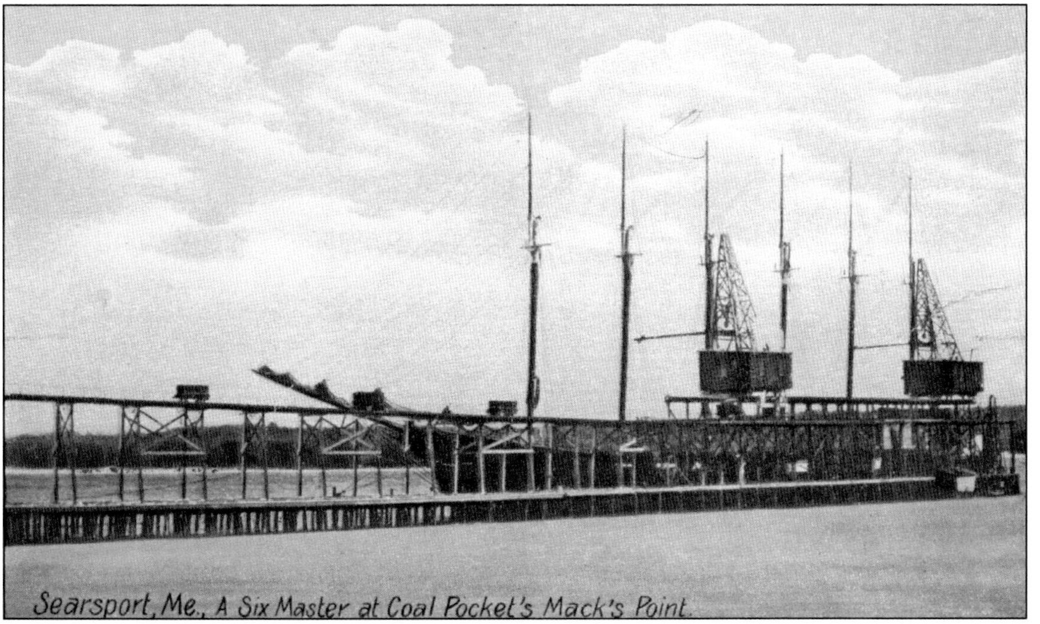

William L. Douglas was one of only 10 six-masted schooners ever built. *Douglas* was named for the shoe magnate and future governor of Massachusetts. Delivered to Coastwise Transportation in 1903, *Douglas* was also the only six-master with a steel hull. She delivered coal to ports up and down the Atlantic coast, including Searsport, Maine.

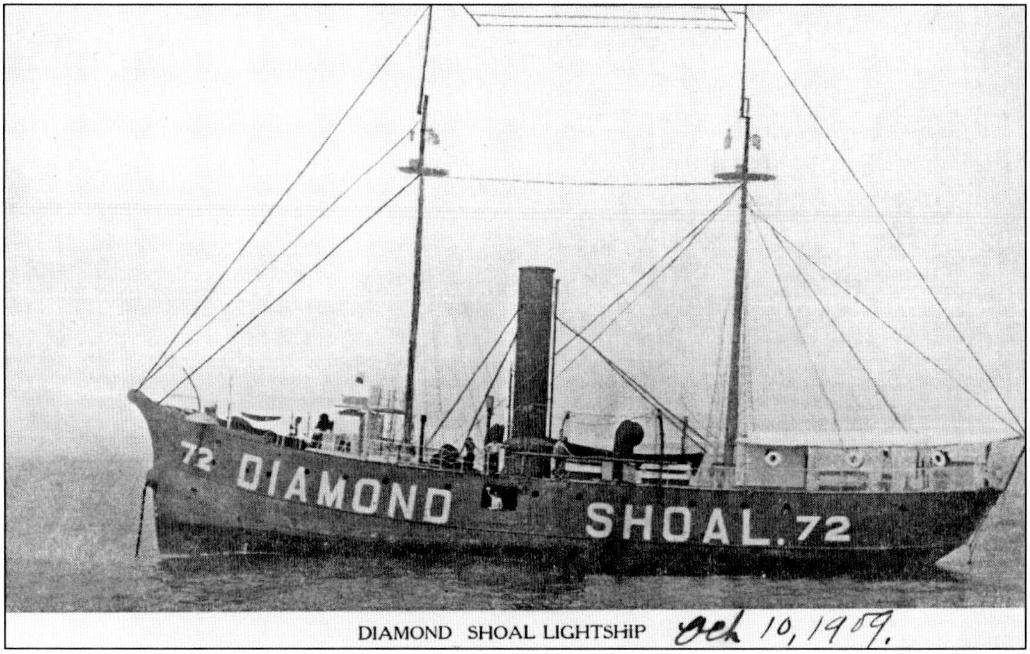

In 1901, the US Lighthouse Service commissioned *Diamond Shoal* (LV-72). This postcard was dated 1909, and at the time, there were 56 lightship stations along the coasts of the United States. In 1919, *Diamond Shoal* was stationed off Cape Hatteras, one of the most dangerous spots along the Atlantic coast. She replaced *Diamond Shoal* (LV-71), which had been sunk by a German U-boat during World War I.

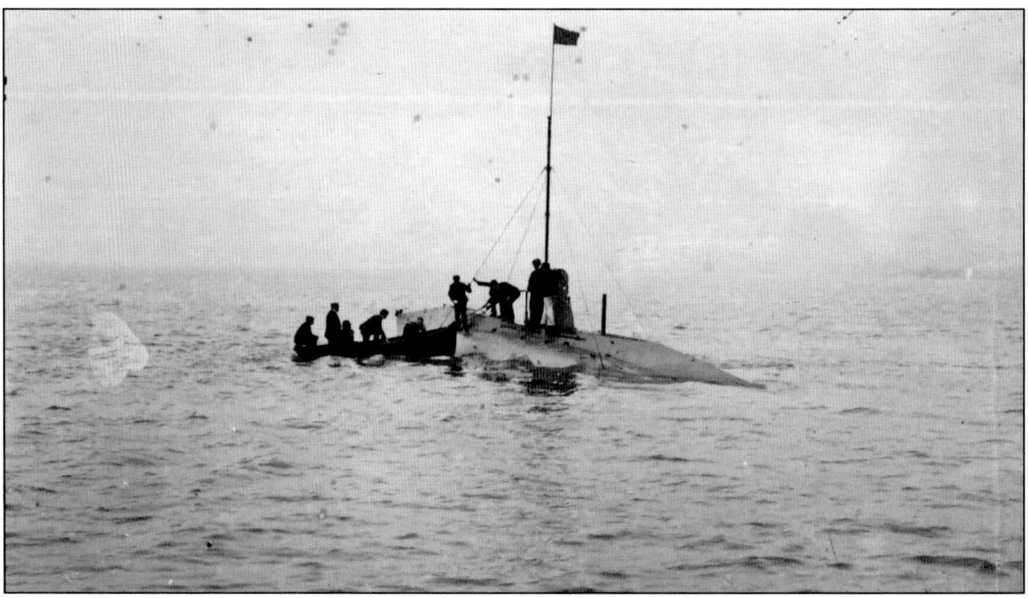

Fore River built five 67-foot Holland-type submarines for the Imperial Japanese Navy at the height of the Russo-Japanese War in 1904. They were shipped in sections to Japan and reassembled at Yokosuka but did not see action, as the war was ending. This early-Japanese real-photo postcard shows the crew of a Japanese submarine receiving supplies from a rowboat. The original five submarines were scrapped in 1921.

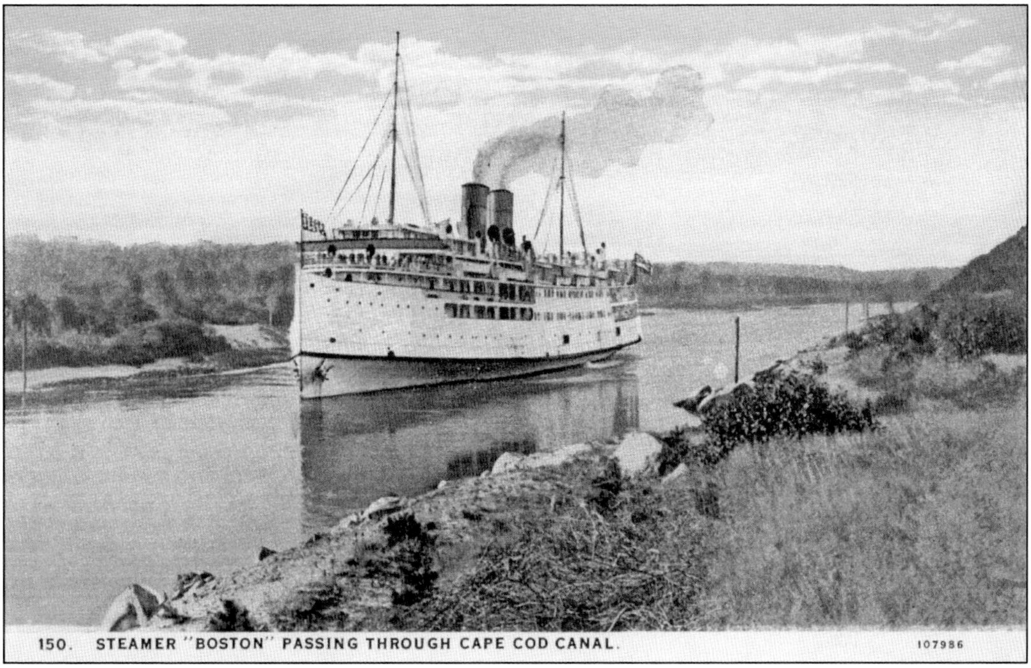

Steamer *Boston* would be the first of many steamships built at the shipyard. She was delivered to the Fall River Line in July 1904. This 1920s view shows *Boston* passing through the Cape Cod Canal, which was completed in 1916. The canal extends from Sandwich to Buzzards Bay and is eight miles long, saving over 60 miles on a trip from New York to Boston.

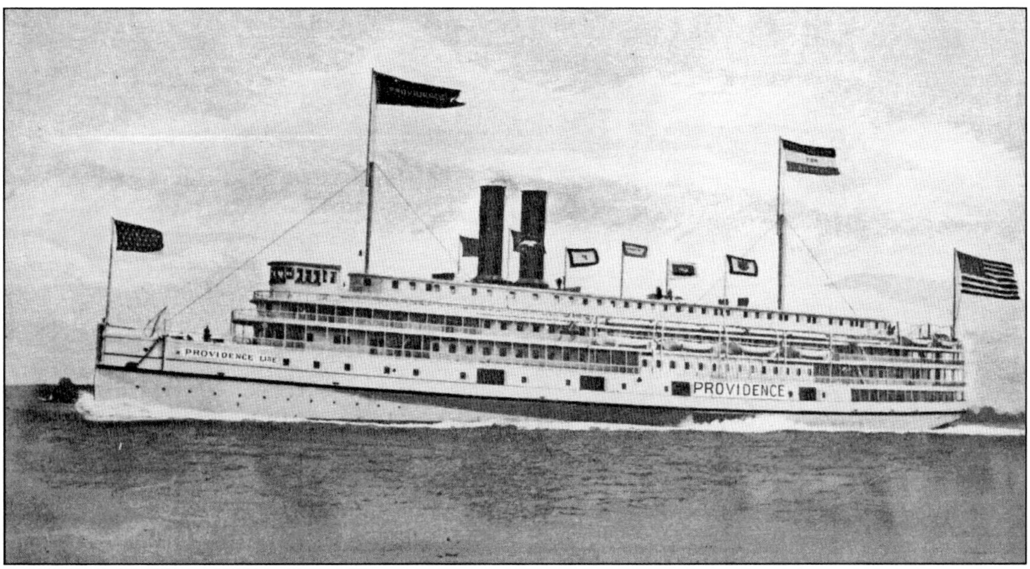

Delivered in March 1905 to the Fall River Line, steamer *Providence* cruised Long Island Sound from New York City to Fall River, Massachusetts. She had a close call on March 13, 1908, when a fire broke out at 4:30 a.m. Fortunately, the steamer *Richard Peck* was nearby. All 400 passengers were transferred without injury, and the fire was successfully extinguished. She served until 1938.

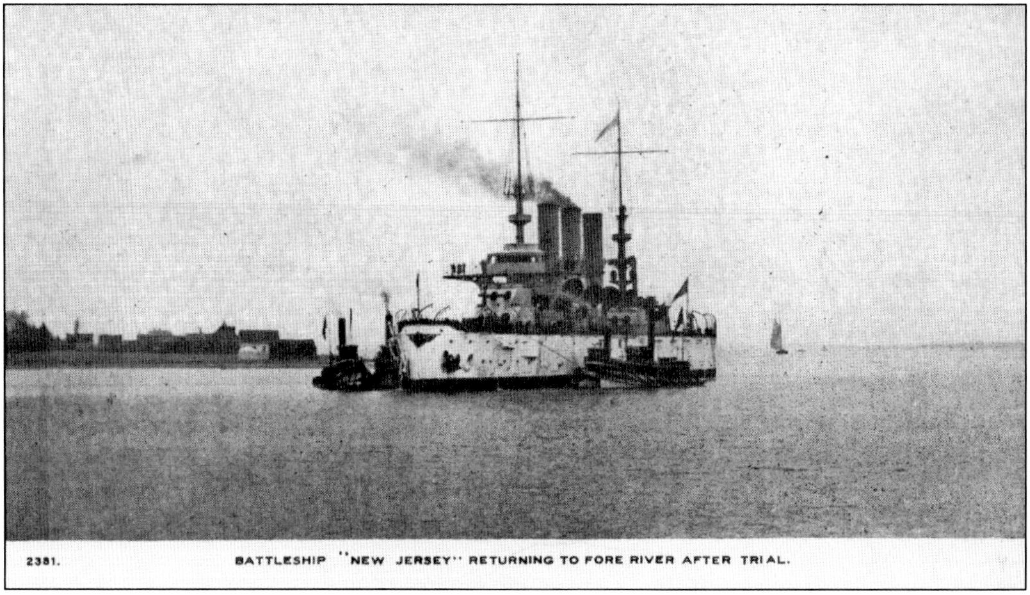

Launched in November 1904, Virginia class battleship USS *New Jersey* (BB-16) was spotted returning from her sea trials. The trial course was off Cape Ann at the northern end of Massachusetts Bay, about 35 miles from the shipyard. For a successful trial, *New Jersey* would have needed to maintain a speed of 19 knots for four hours. Her hull was painted white as a member of the Great White Fleet that circumnavigated the globe, sailing 43,000 miles from December 16, 1907, to February 22, 1909. Built at a cost of $3,405,000, she was 435 feet long with 23,000 horsepower and over twice the tonnage of warships from the Spanish-American War era.

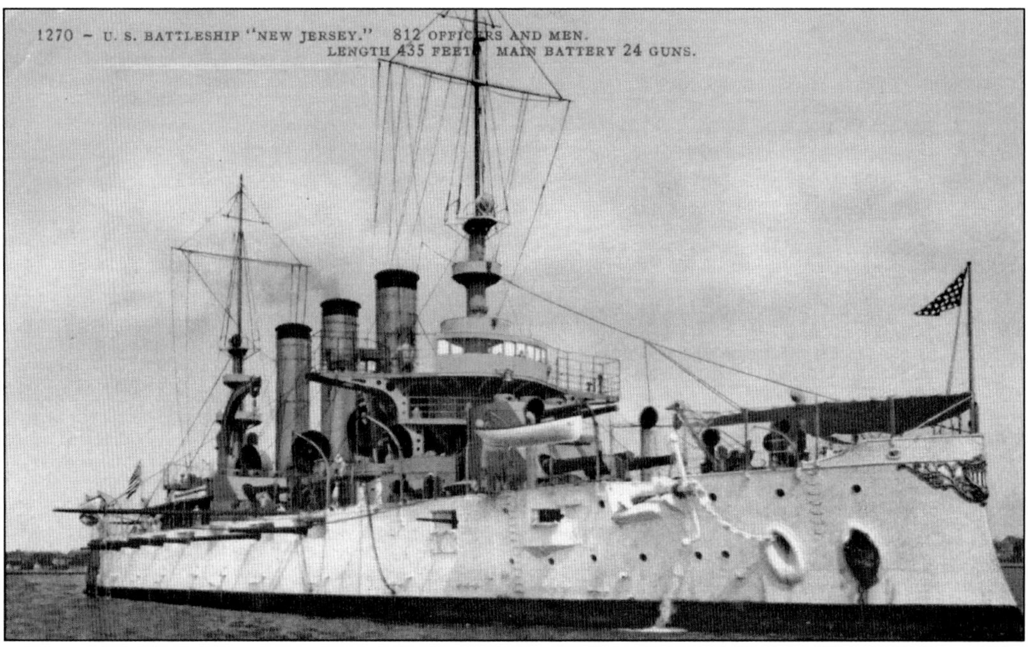

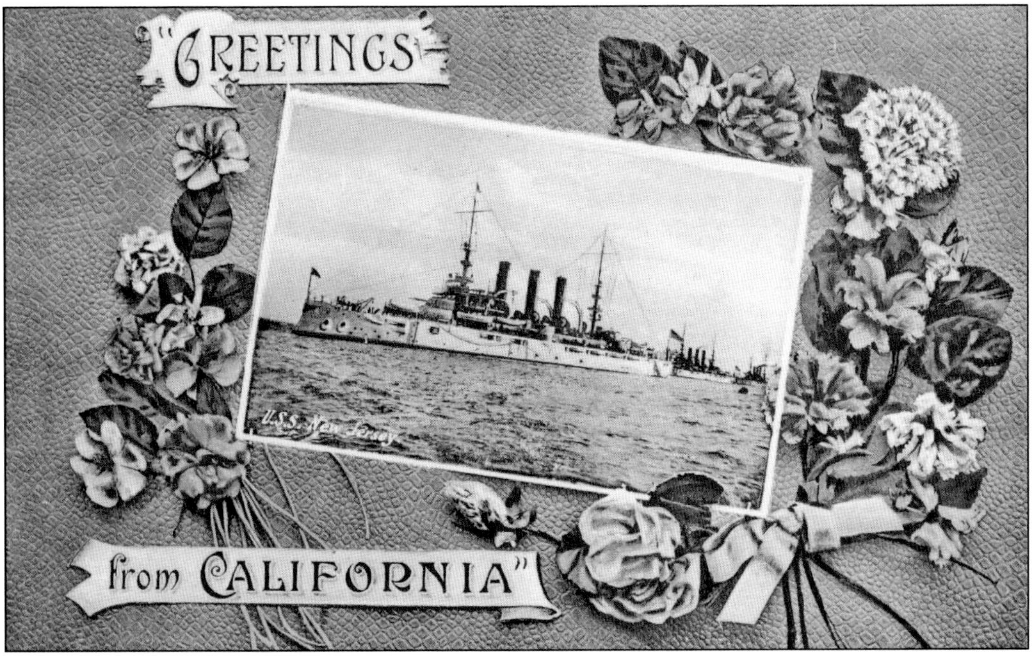

In 1908, the Great White Fleet arrived in California, and publisher Allen Fanjoy was ready to capitalize on the opportunity with his "Greetings from California" postcard series. *New Jersey* made stops in California at Coronado, Los Angeles, Santa Cruz, and San Francisco before heading north to Washington State and west to Hawaii, New Zealand, Australia, and Japan. In 1909, after *New Jersey* returned from the trip around the world, she was repainted grey and outfitted with new cage masts. During World War I, she made four voyages to France to pick up American troops for the trip back home. Decommissioned in 1920, *New Jersey* was sunk by Army Air Service bombers as a target off Cape Hatteras in 1923.

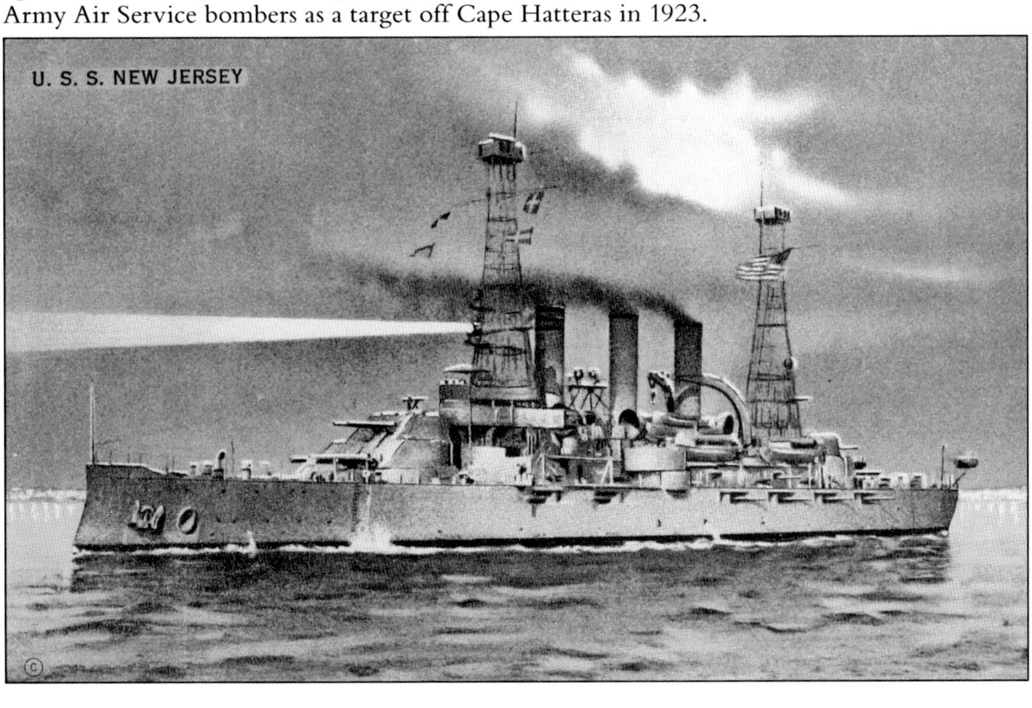

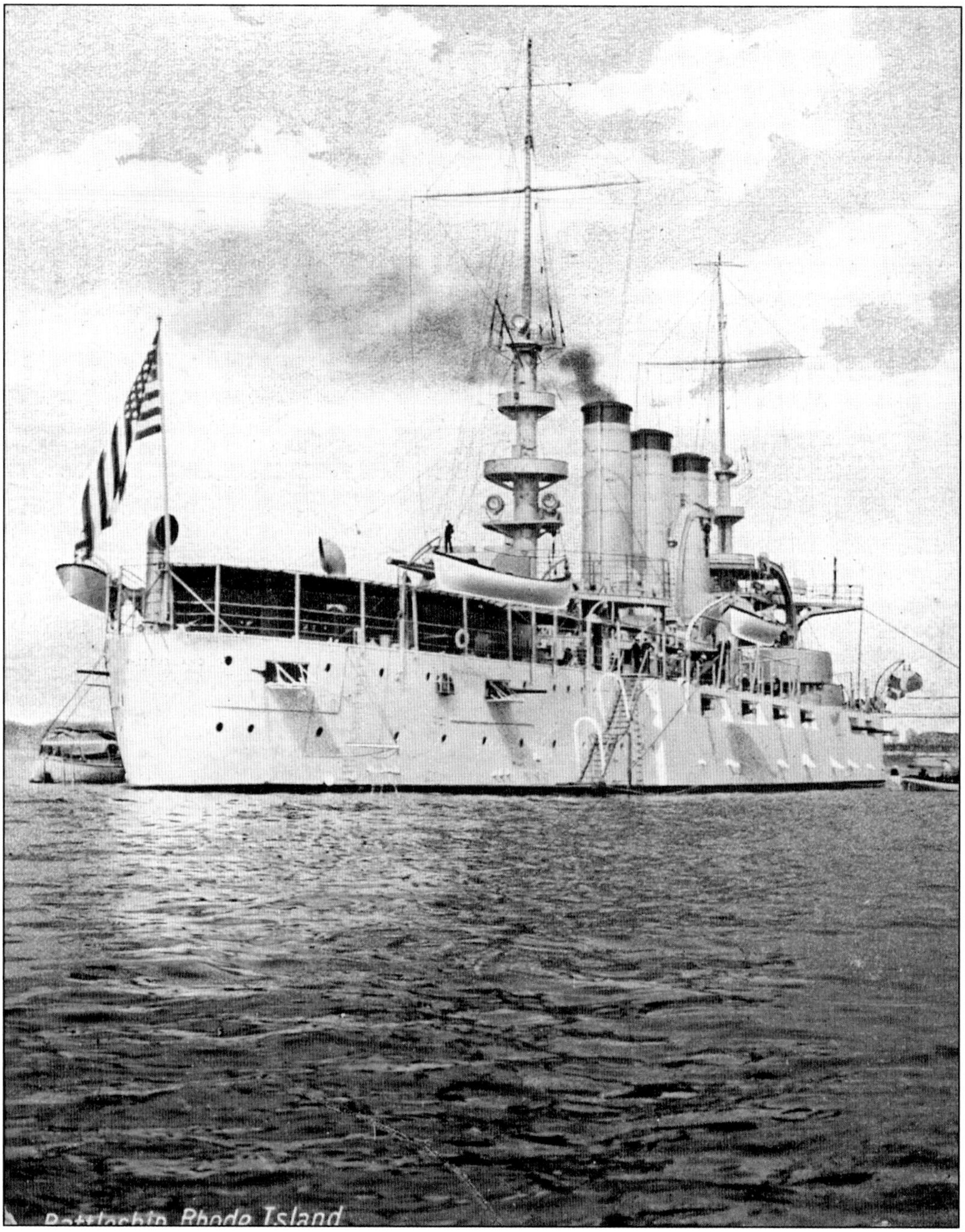

USS *Rhode Island* (BB-17), a Virginia class battleship, was launched in May 1904 and commissioned in February 1906. Like her sister ship USS *New Jersey*, she was a member of the Great White Fleet and assigned to the Atlantic Fleet. In late 1913, *Rhode Island* was sent to Veracruz, Mexico, to protect American citizens and property. She did not see action during World War I, serving stateside where she engaged in exercises and drills and patrolled for U-boats. After the war, *Rhode Island* made several trips to France, bringing home over 5,000 troops. She was sold for scrap in 1923, but the ship's bell was saved and can be seen at the Rhode Island State House in Providence.

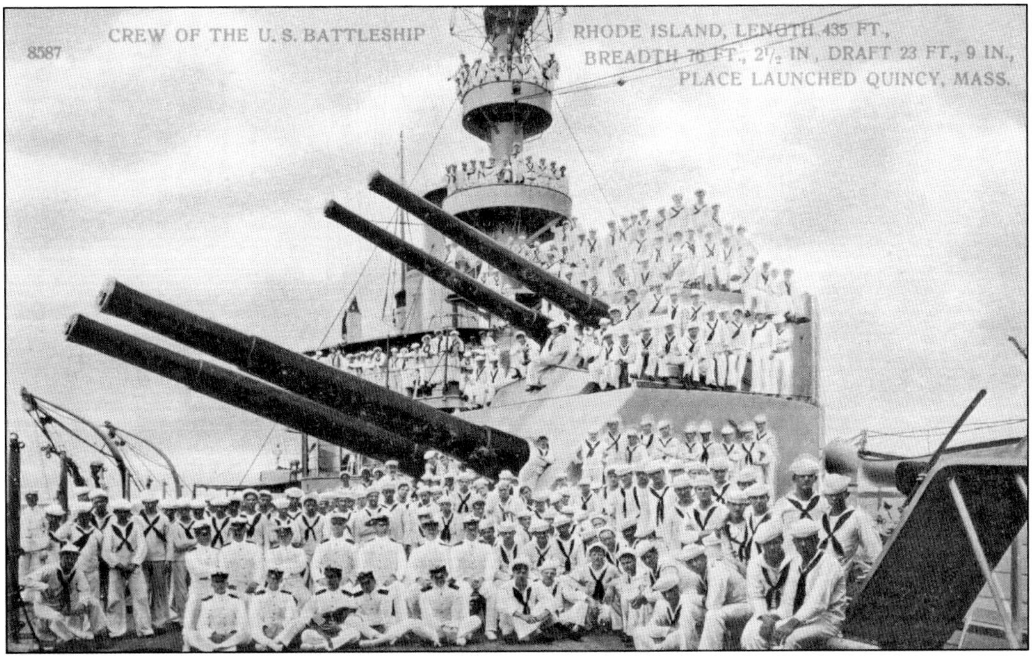

Rhode Island carried a complement of 40 officers and 772 men. In this A.C. Bosselman postcard, the crew posed for the photograph in their dress whites. The men were perched on top of the gun turrets and observation towers, hoping to be in the photograph. The *Rhode Island's* 12-inch guns are also in view.

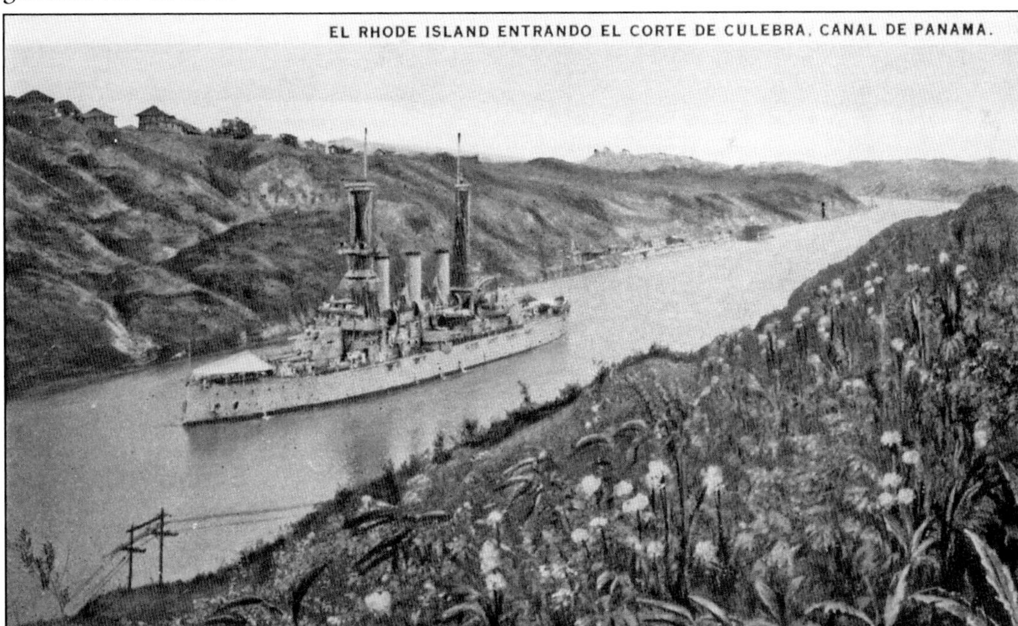

In the summer of 1919, *Rhode Island* passed Culebra Cut, Panama Canal, on her way to Mare Island Navy Yard, just north of San Francisco. She was designated the flagship of Battleship Squadron One, Pacific Fleet, based at Mare Island until June 1920, when she was decommissioned and placed in reserve status.

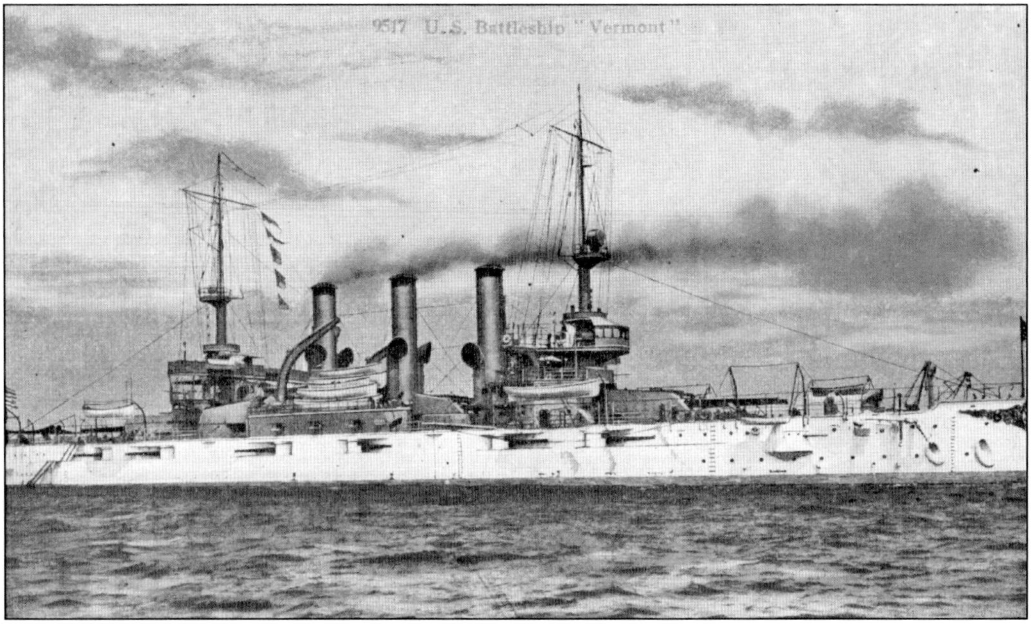

The contract to build battleship USS *Vermont* (BB-20) would be the last one Watson worked on before his departure from the company. *Vermont* was a member of the Great White Fleet, a participant in the Haiti occupation in 1916, and a training ship during World War I. Like many of the battleships built in the first decade of the 20th century, she was decommissioned in 1920.

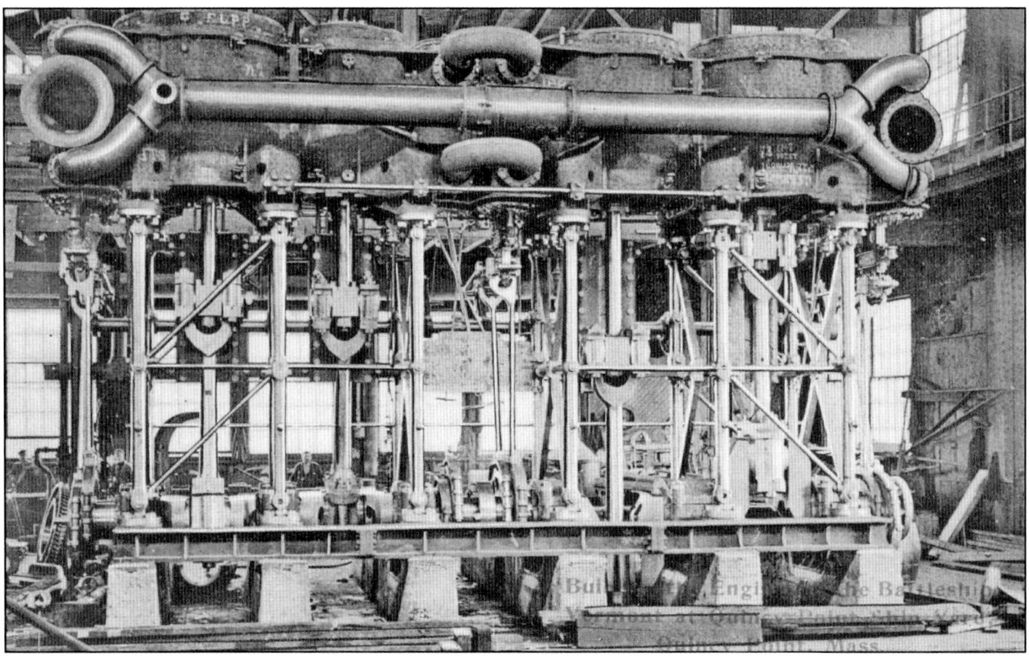

Battleship *Vermont* had two triple-expansion, four-cylinder, reciprocating engines. Each engine was located in a watertight compartment, giving *Vermont* 16,500 horsepower. Coal was the source of power, and *Vermont* would stop for coal every two weeks. Replenishing the ship with coal was a very dirty job, taking several days to complete, and it was all done by hand.

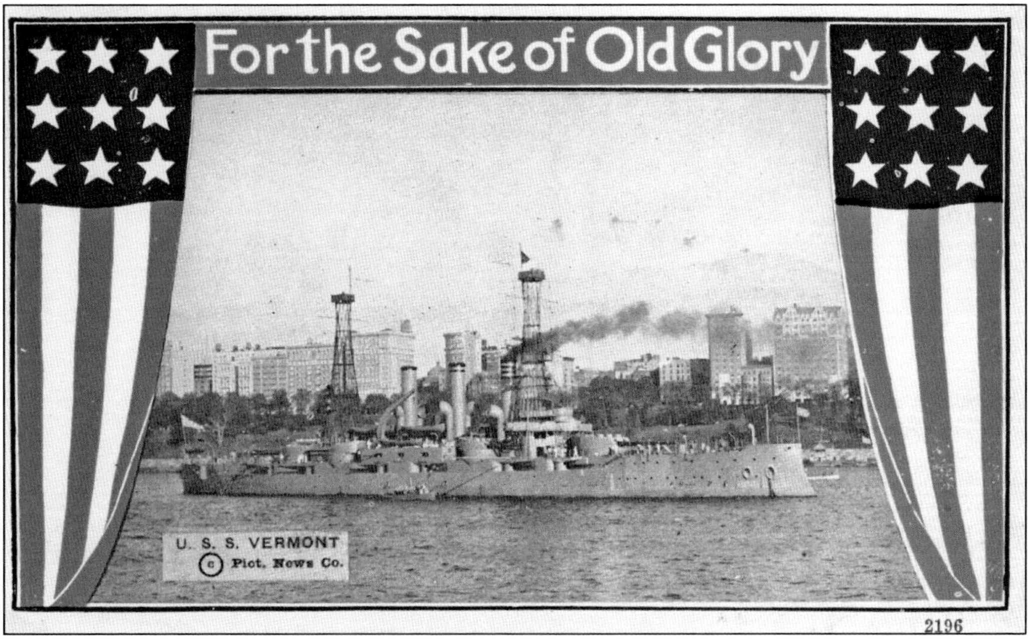

The loss of USS *Maine* in Havana Harbor during the Spanish-American War was still fresh in the minds of Americans when publishers created patriotic flag-draped postcards. During the Mexican Revolution in 1914, *Vermont* was part of the fleet sent to Veracruz to block a shipment of arms. A battalion of 320 men went ashore, and a Marine from *Vermont* was killed in the battle.

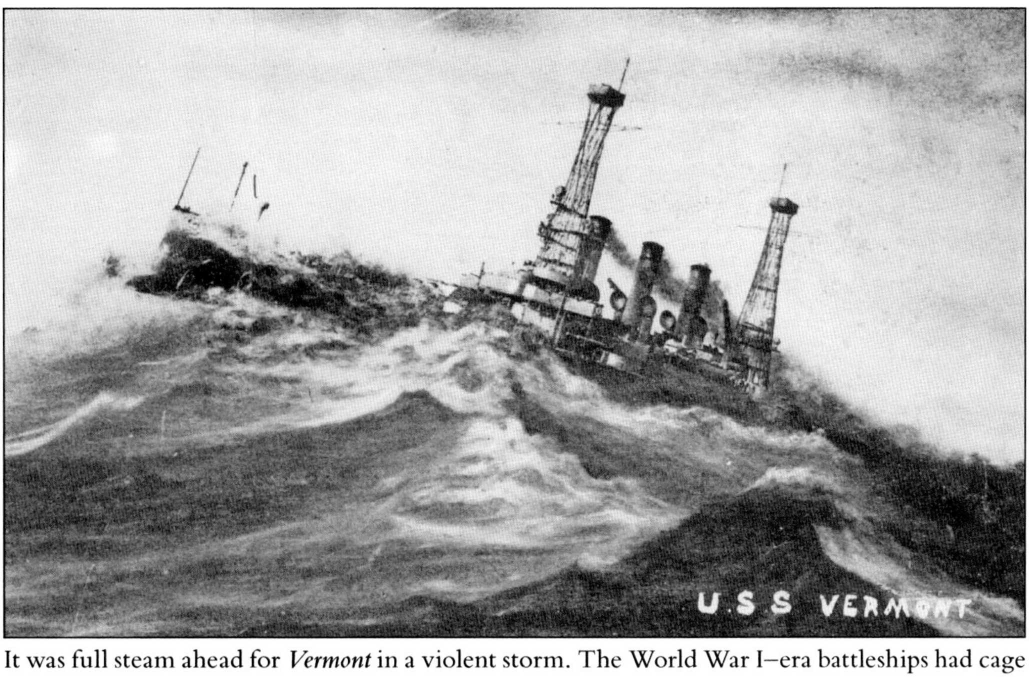

It was full steam ahead for *Vermont* in a violent storm. The World War I–era battleships had cage masts to protect the observation posts from enemy shells and to absorb the recoil shock when firing their 12-inch guns. However, the tall cage masts proved unreliable and unstable in heavy weather and were replaced on battleships at the start of World War II.

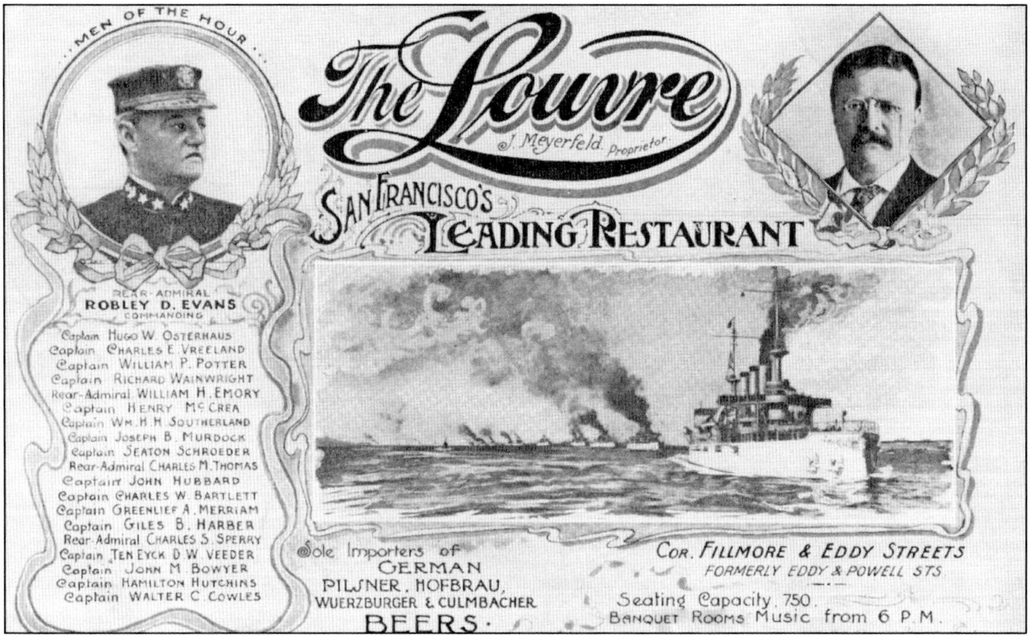

When the Great White Fleet sailed into San Francisco in May 1908, the Louvre Restaurant was ready with a commemorative postcard. In addition to inset photographs of Pres. Theodore Roosevelt and Rear Adm. Robley D. Evans, there was a list of the captains of the fleet. Three of the 16 battleships were built at Fore River. Listed are Captain Southerland of USS *New Jersey*, Captain Murdock of USS *Rhode Island*, and Captain Potter of USS *Vermont*. The Japanese government also issued a postcard commemorating the visit of the Great White Fleet, postmarked October 18–24, 1908, in Yokohama. The visit established goodwill between the United States and Japan but also displayed the power of an upgraded US Navy.

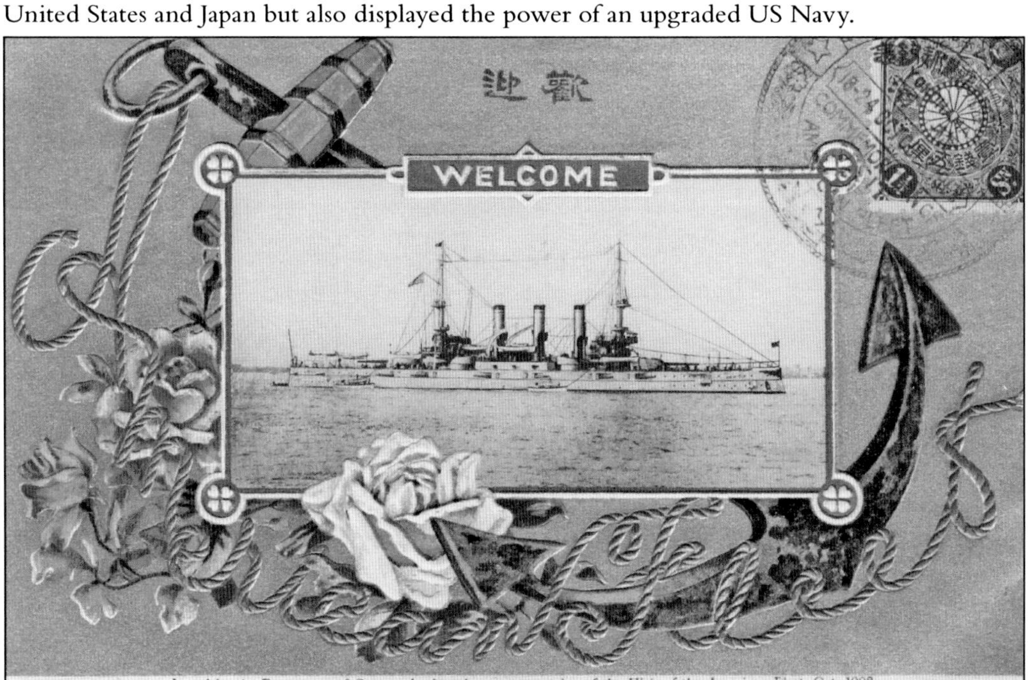

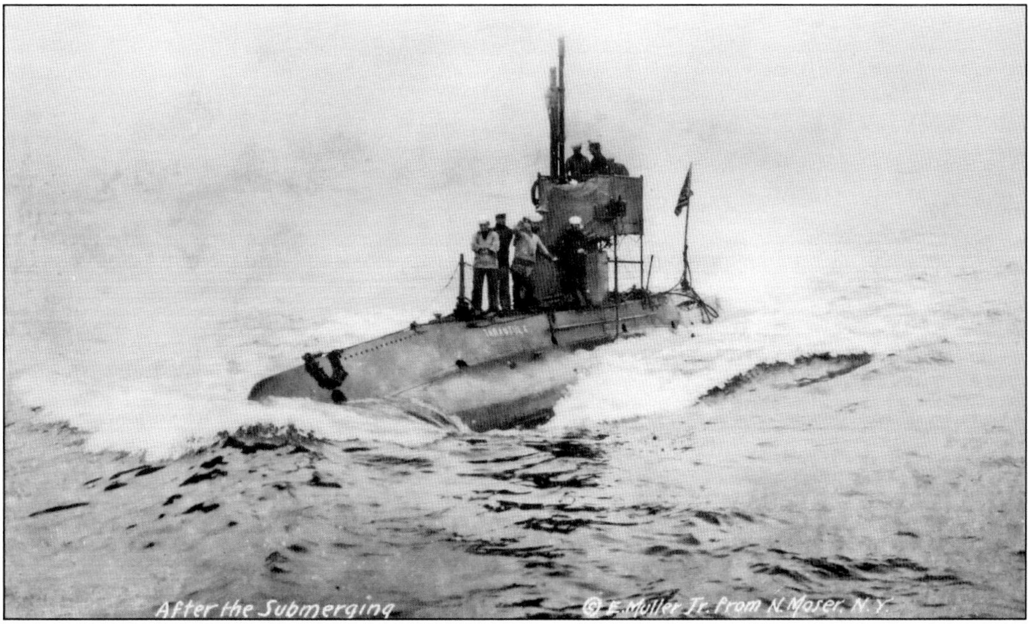

When commissioned in 1907, USS *Tarantula* (*B-3*) (SS-12) carried a crew of one officer and nine enlisted men. In 1904, Pres. Theodore Roosevelt spent nearly one hour submerged in a submarine. After the experience, he signed an executive order giving submariners extra pay, a tradition that stands today. *B-3* served in the Philippines from 1913 to 1920. Decommissioned in 1921, she was sunk as a target in Manila Bay.

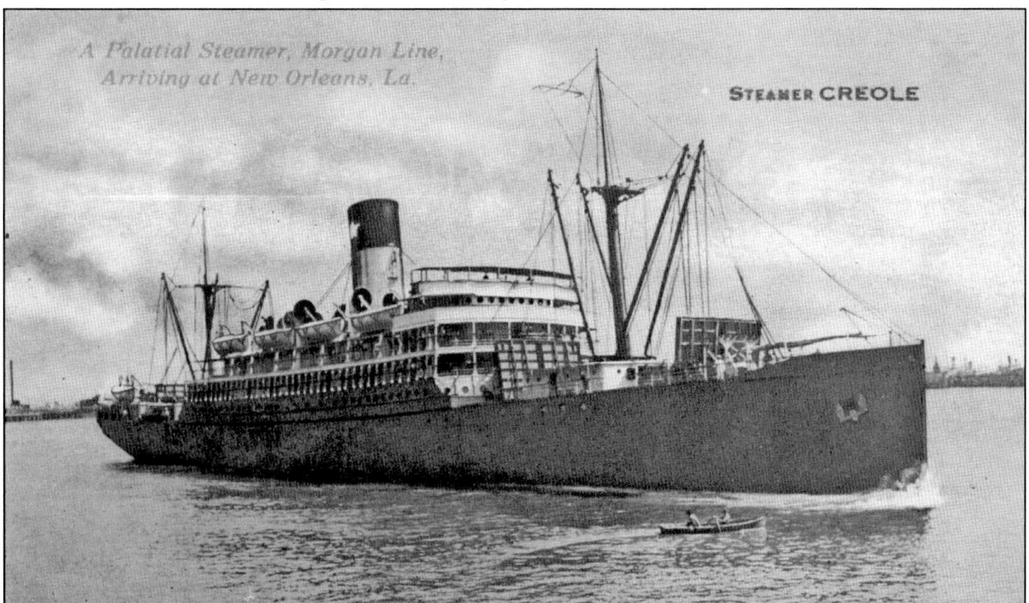

Cruise ship SS *Creole* was delivered in December 1907 to the Morgan Line of the Southern Pacific Company. *Creole* sailed in grand style between New York and New Orleans until the mid-1930s. The luxurious dining room was finished in rich mahogany, featuring ample promenade decks, smoking room, bar, library, barbershop, and a Marconi wireless telegraph.

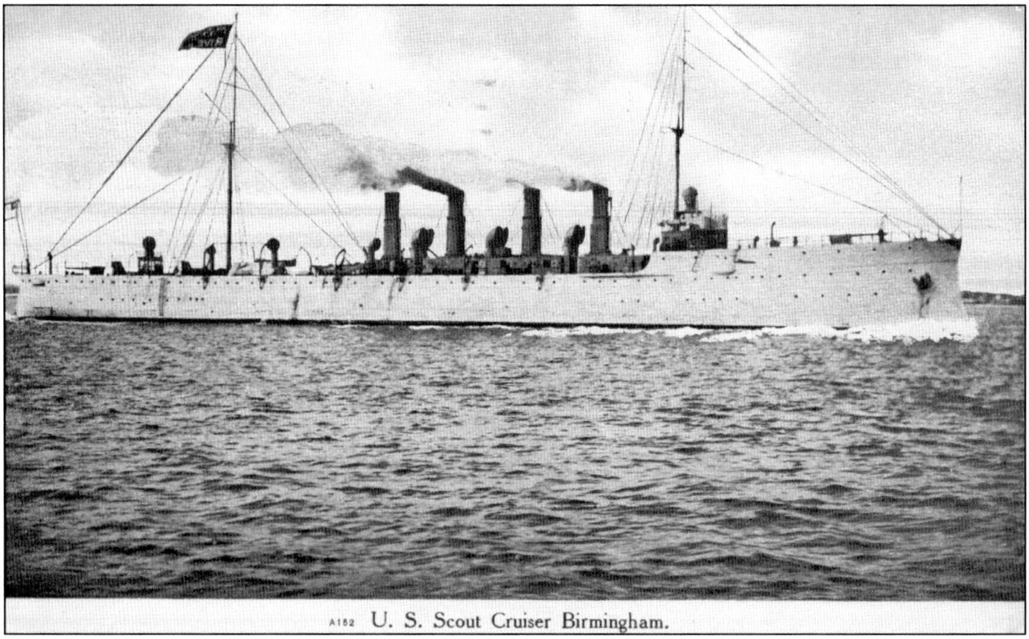

A Chester class scout cruiser, USS *Birmingham* (CS-2) was commissioned in April 1908. Built for speed, the scout cruiser was used for fleet reconnaissance. After America's entrance into World War I, she escorted the first troop convoy to France. After the war, she was based in San Diego as flagship of Destroyer Squadrons, Pacific Fleet. *Birmingham* made history on November 14, 1910, when Eugene B. Ely took off from the deck of the ship in a primitive Curtiss biplane. A temporary platform was built to facilitate the flight. Ely almost drove the plane into the water before becoming airborne, successfully flying two miles to shore. Ely made a handsome living performing but was tragically killed in 1911 at an air show in Georgia. In 1933, he was posthumously awarded the Distinguished Flying Cross.

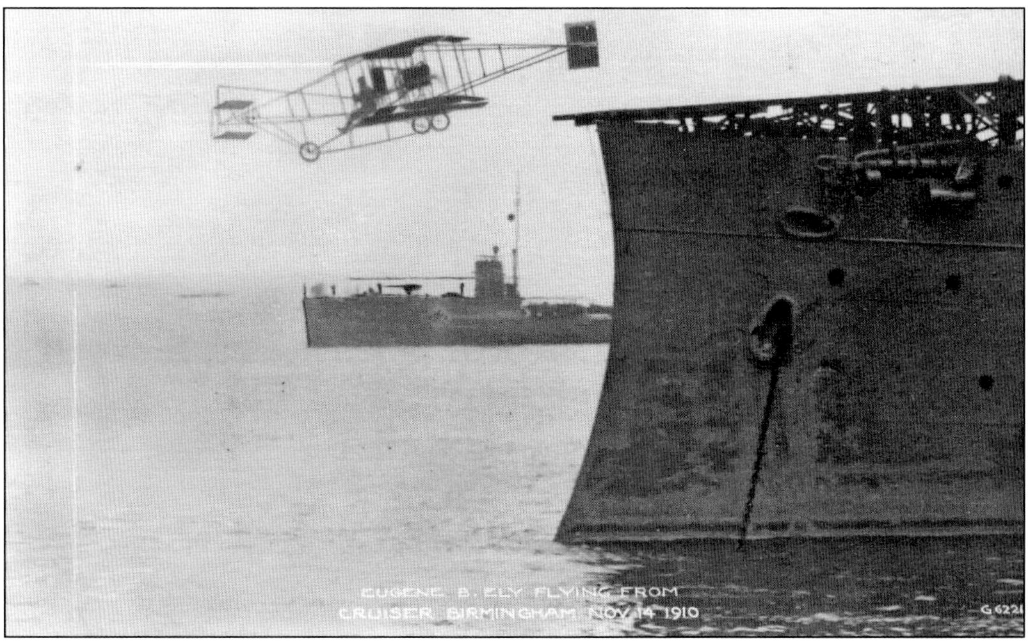

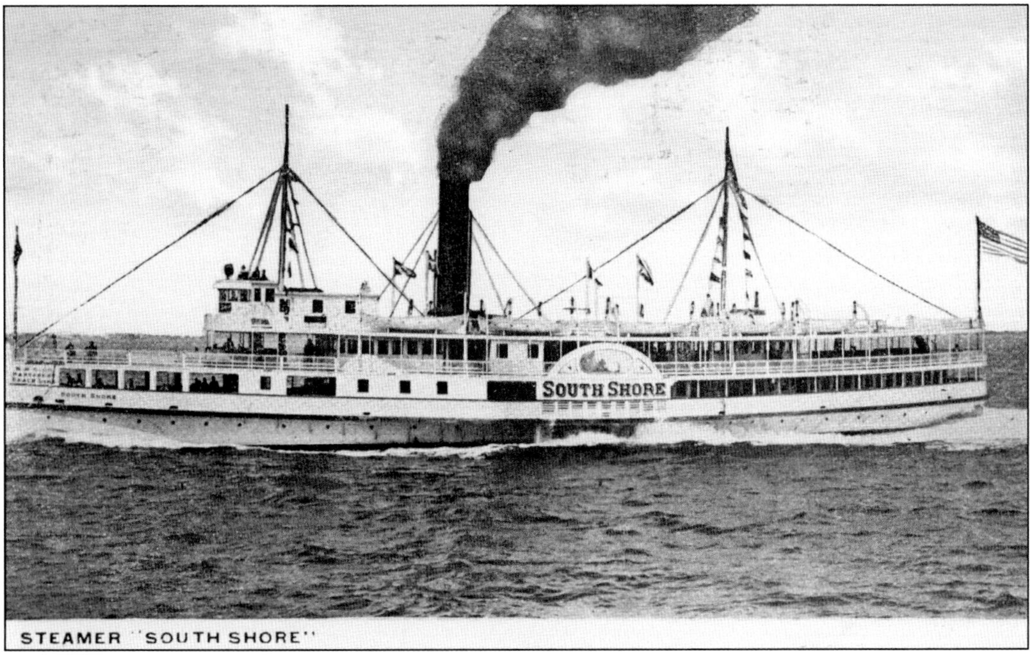

South Shore, a 207-foot passenger steamer was delivered to Nantasket Beach Co. in June 1906. She departed from Rowe's Wharf in Boston, steaming to Plymouth everyday at 10:00 a.m. The ship had staterooms, a dining room, and an orchestra providing entertainment. A chicken and lobster dinner was sold for $1 and a round-trip ticket was also $1. Those were the days!

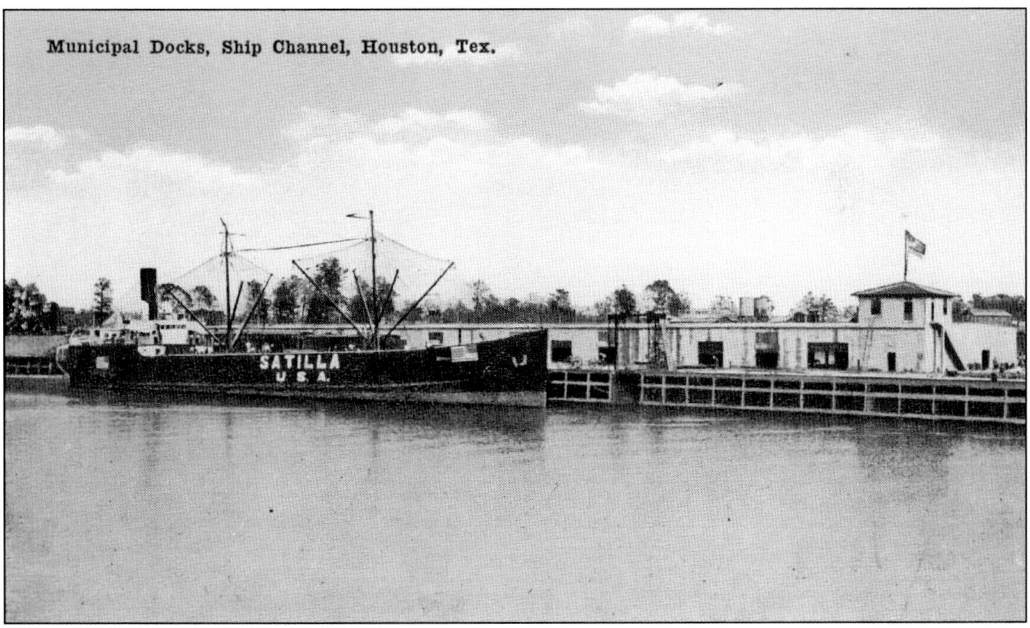

SS *Satilla*, a 313-foot freighter, was built for the Brunswick Steamship Company in 1906. She carried cargo in the Gulf of Mexico and is seen on this postcard at the Municipal Docks in Houston, Texas. In 1916, *Satilla* was sold to a Norwegian company and renamed *Hans Kinck*. On February 7, 1917, while on a voyage from Rotterdam to Newcastle, she was sunk by the German U-boat *UC-39*.

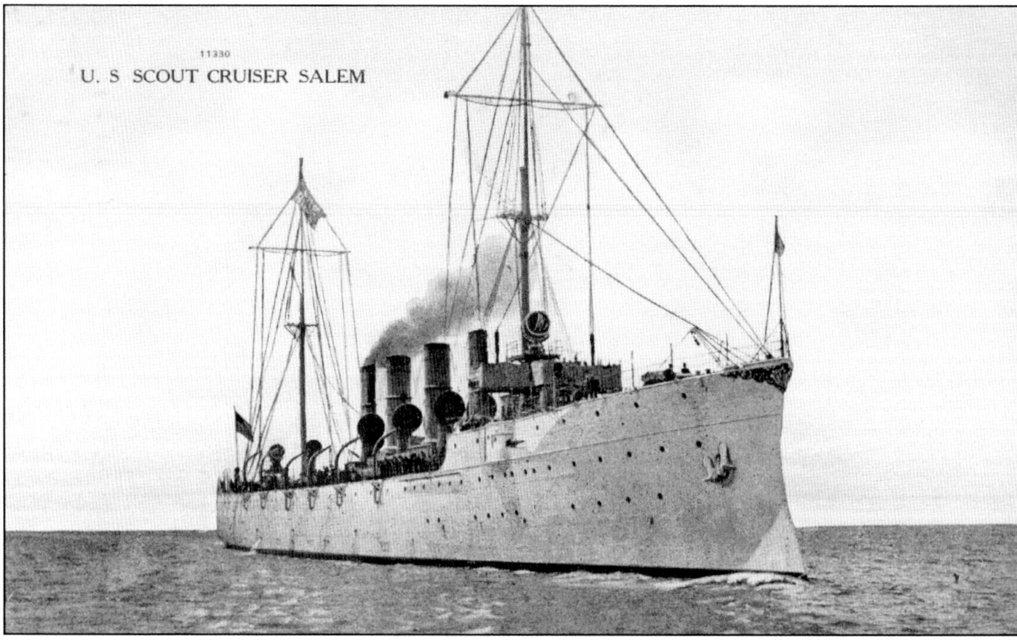

USS *Salem* (CS-3), a Chester class scout cruiser, was launched in July 1907 and was the first of two ships built at Fore River to be named after the city of Salem, Massachusetts. *Salem* provided support at Veracruz during the Mexican Revolution in 1914. During World War I, she was assigned to Key West as the flagship for submarine chasers searching for German U-boats.

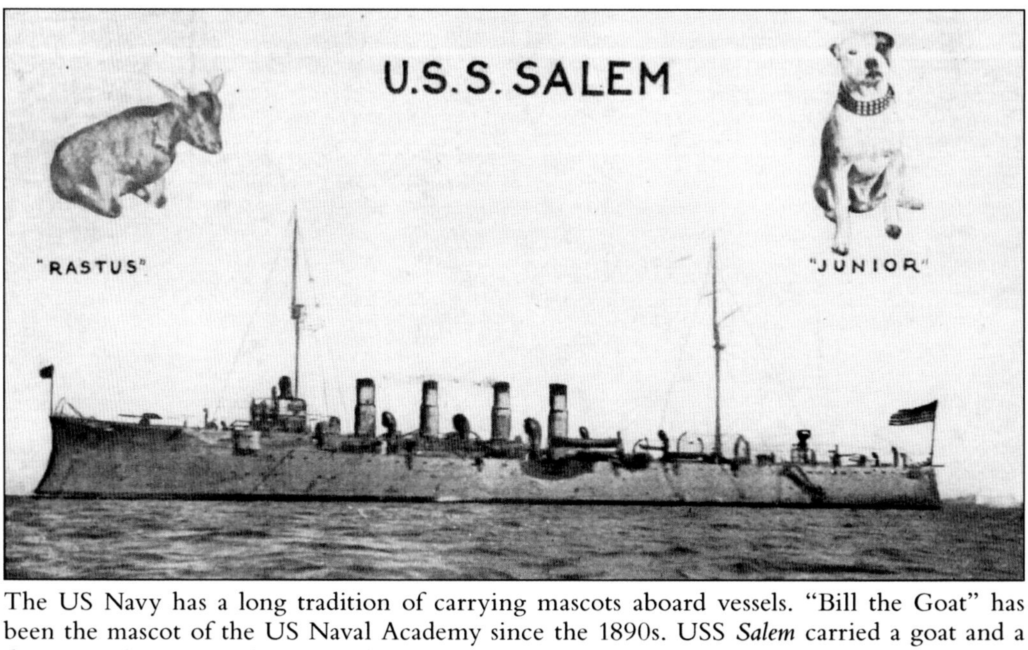

The US Navy has a long tradition of carrying mascots aboard vessels. "Bill the Goat" has been the mascot of the US Naval Academy since the 1890s. USS *Salem* carried a goat and a dog, named Rastus and Junior. They must have been beloved by the crew to be featured on a postcard with their ship.

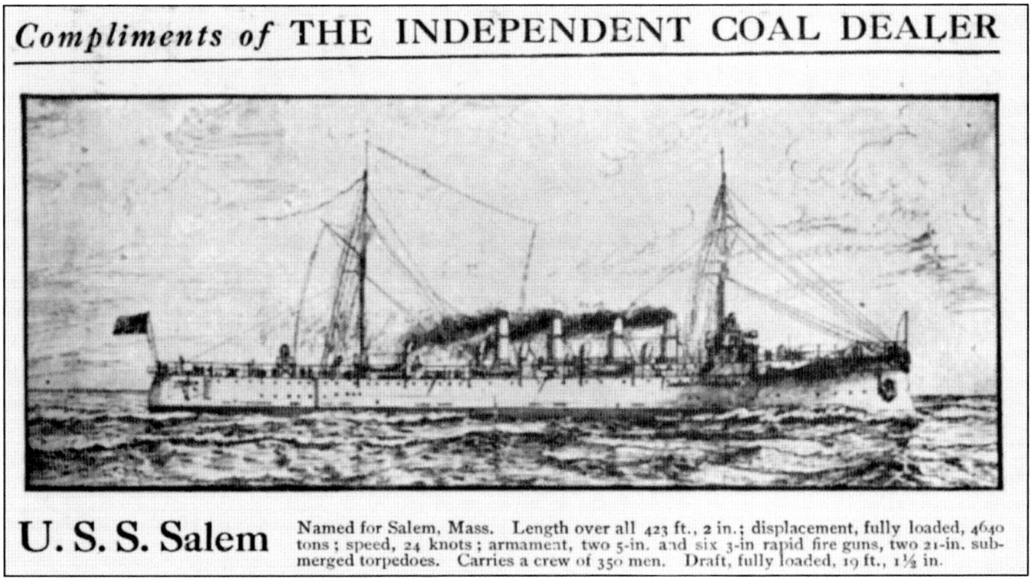

Since the inception of the postcard, merchants have seen unlimited marketing possibilities with its use. When this postcard was created in 1909, it would have cost only a penny to mail. Antique postcards with advertising are highly sought after by collectors. Here, USS *Salem* is used as a tie-in with "The Independent Coal Dealer."

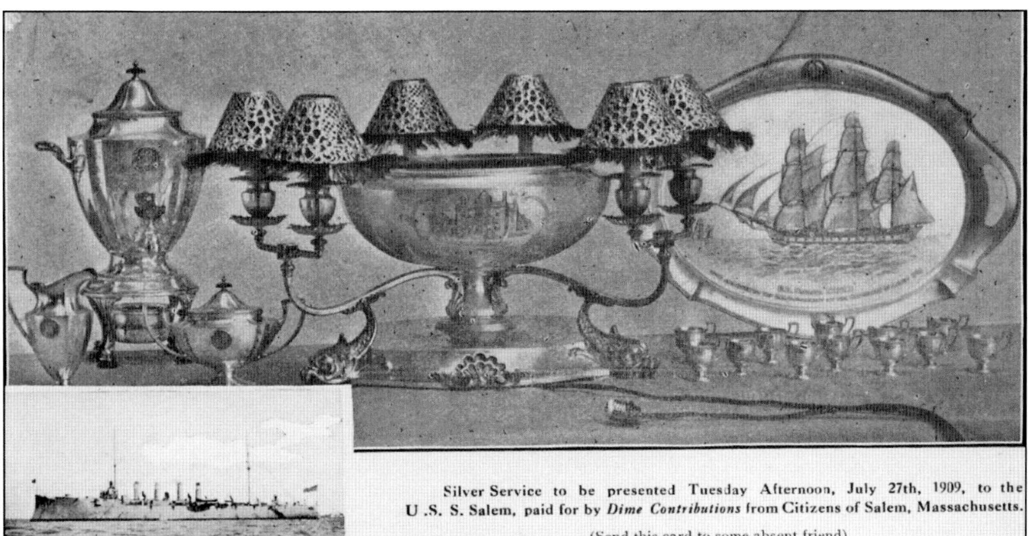

This unusual oversized postcard advertised the presence of USS *Salem* and crew for Salem Old Home Week, July 25–31, 1909. The front featured an inset photograph of *Salem* as well as the silver service paid for by "Dime contributions from Citizens of Salem, Massachusetts." On the back is a "Programme" of the festivities, which included a parade of the ship's crew, athletic events, banquet, and fireworks.

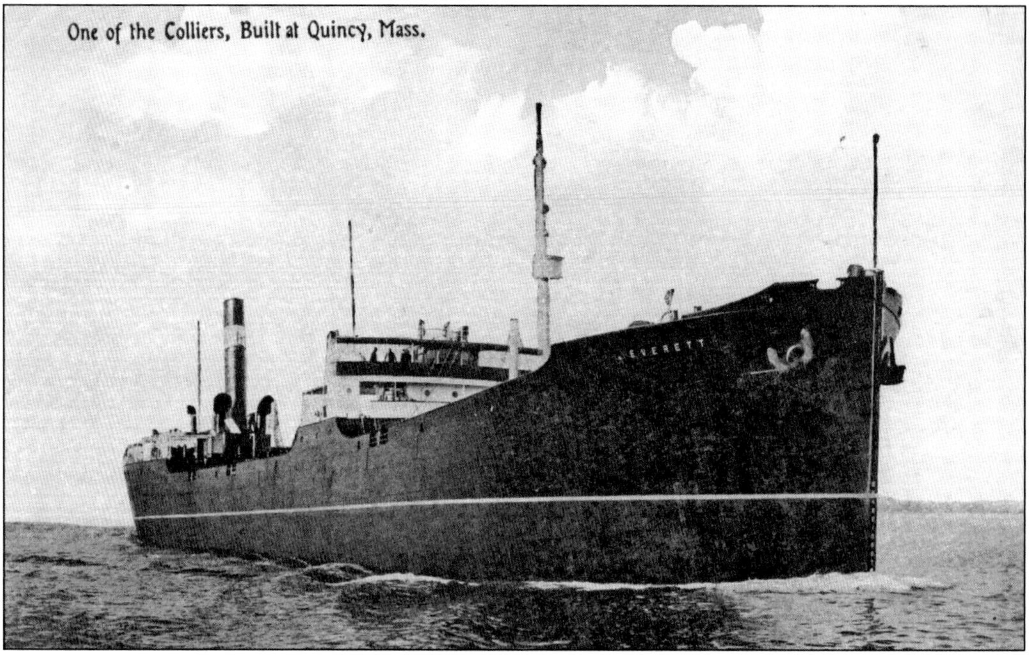

SS *Everett* was the first of three 400-foot colliers built for New England Coal and Coke Company in 1907–1908. Sister ships were *Malden* and *Melrose*, all named after cities near Boston. *Everett* was a single screw steamship capable of steaming 4,000 miles fully loaded at 11 knots. She carried coal until 1948, when she was scrapped.

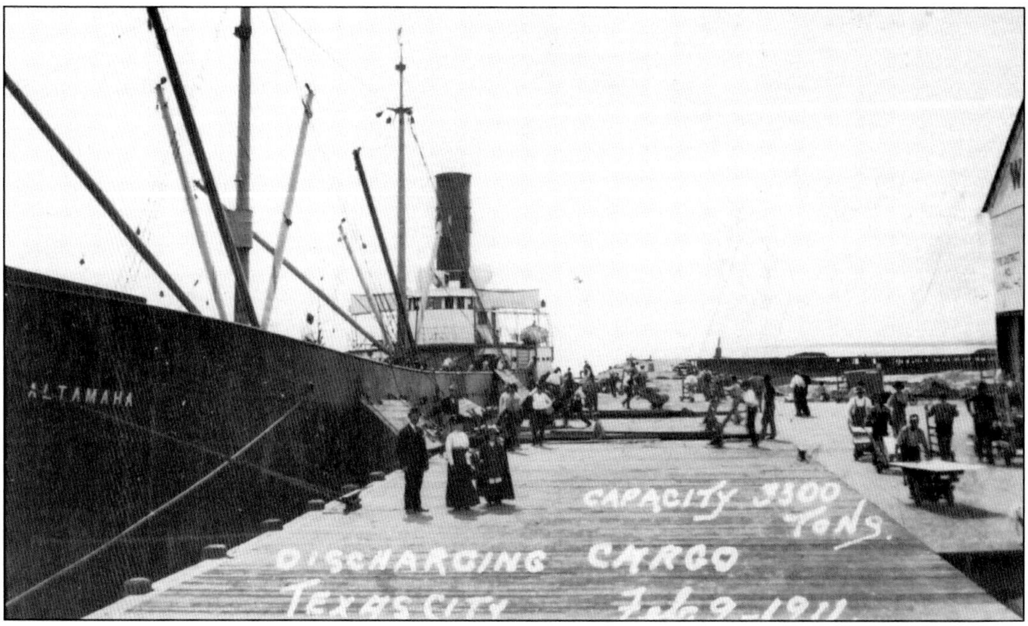

The photograph for this postcard was taken on February 9, 1911, while SS *Altamaha* was discharging cargo at Texas City, Texas. *Altamaha* had a capacity of 3,300 tons, and one can see an active dock with several people working to off-load the cargo. Built for the Brunswick Steamship Company in 1907, *Altamaha* was wrecked in 1923 and cut down to a barge before being abandoned in 1933.

Four

Pre–World War I 1908 to 1916

The work completed at Fore River from 1900 to 1907 proved the shipyard could build many different types of vessels, from warships to commercial ships. That would not change in the next decade, but the ownership of the shipyard would change with the acquisition of the Fore River Shipyard by the Bethlehem Steel Corporation in 1913. The purchase price was $4.8 million, a bargain considering the backlog alone was valued at about $20 million.

Bethlehem Steel Corporation could provide the much-needed cash to keep the shipyard running without interruption. They also had the resources to upgrade the building slips and to add a steel mill and modern hospital. Activities were provided for the employees, including a 32-member band, a glee club, and a baseball team. The team was so competitive that on August 12, 1943, the great Satchel Paige pitched for the Kansas City Monarchs of the Negro League against the Fore River Club at Boston's Fenway Park. Between work and play, the shipyard at Quincy Point could be considered a city unto itself.

In 1910, officials from Argentina came to Quincy to see if the shipyard had the capacity to build two battleships, *Rivadavia* and *Moreno*. This would be the first and only foreign order for battleships in Quincy. The contract stipulated the ships be built in two separate yards to speed up completion. *Moreno* was subcontracted to the New York Shipbuilding Company and *Rivadavia* was built in Quincy. After launching, both ships had engine trouble that needed to be addressed; the ships finally arrived in Argentina in 1915. Despite the long delay, both battleships survived until the mid-1950s.

A record 19 contracts were signed in 1916 as the United States geared up for World War I. Only three contracts were commercial, the rest were signed with the US Navy for destroyers and submarines. There were now 15,000 people employed at the shipyard.

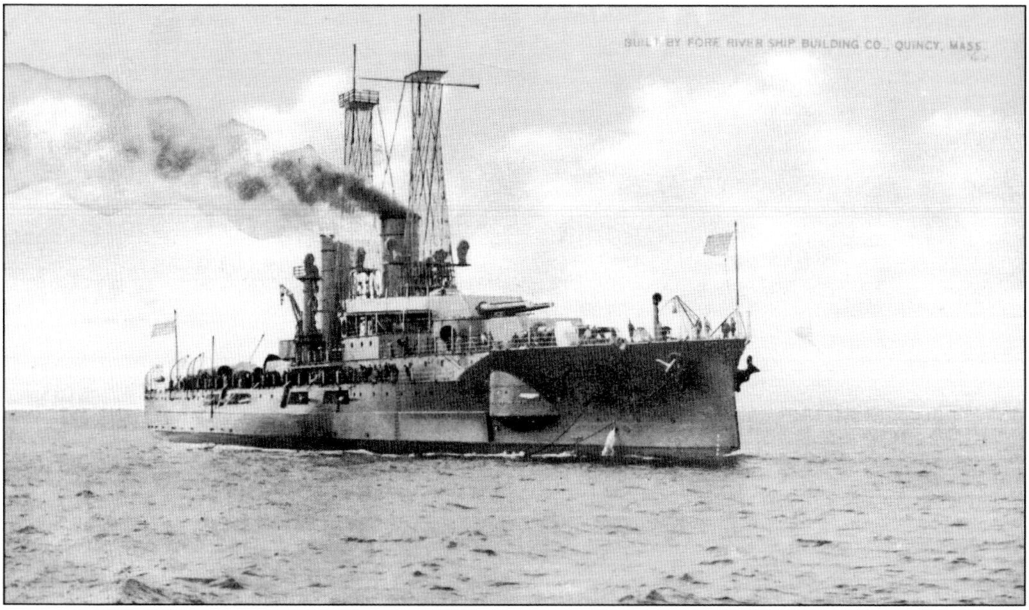

USS *North Dakota* (BB-29) was launched in November 1908 as a Delaware class battleship. In September 1910, only five months after being commissioned, there was an oil pipe explosion and fire at sea that killed three men. Six men received the Medal of Honor for extraordinary heroism during the fire. Later that year, *North Dakota* made her first Atlantic crossing, visiting England and France.

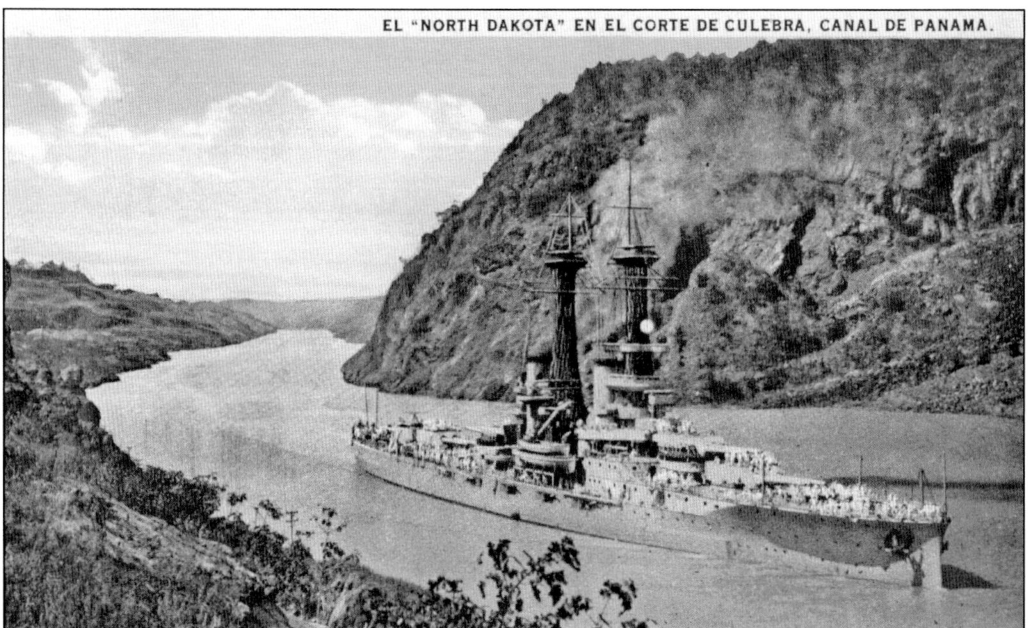

In April 1914, *North Dakota* steamed through the Panama Canal on her way to Veracruz during political unrest in Mexico. *North Dakota* operated in Mexican waters for several months. She did not see action in World War I but was used as a training ship along the Atlantic coast. In 1919, she visited ports in the Mediterranean and toured Scandinavia in 1923.

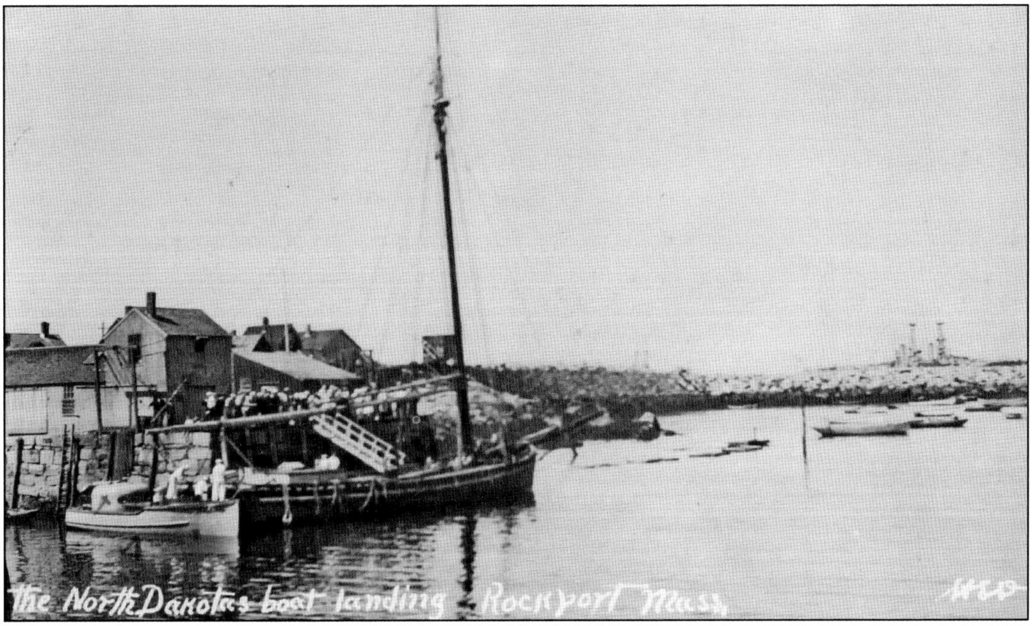

In September 1919, *North Dakota* anchored in Rockport, Massachusetts, where a sailor took this real-photo postcard. It must have been exciting for the locals to see so many sailors enjoying liberty on Bearskin Neck. This view shows *North Dakota* over the breakwater and the captain's gig alongside the dock.

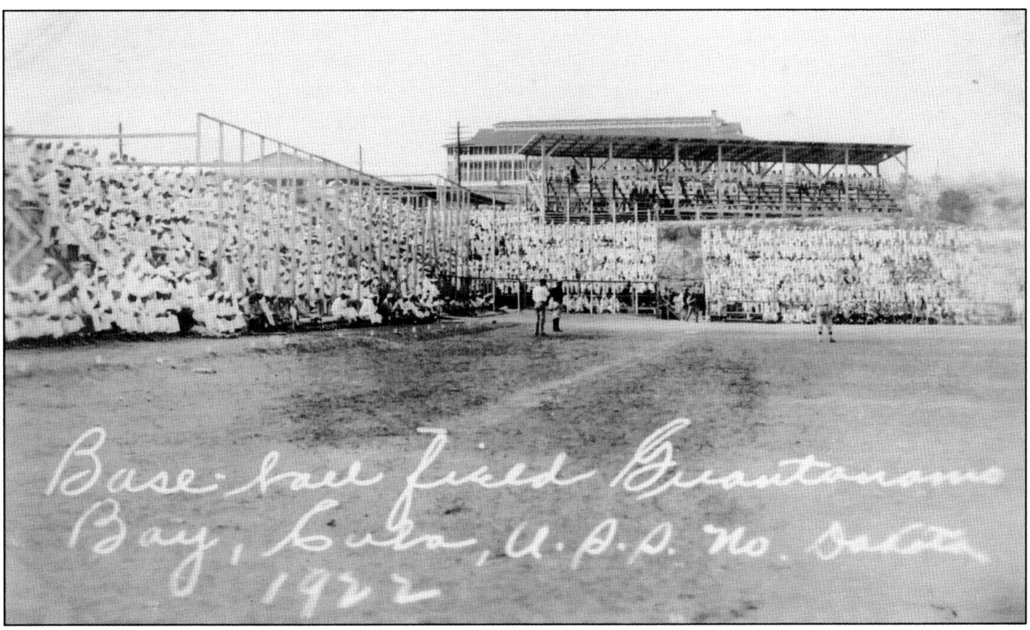

When the US Navy came into Guantanamo Bay, Cuba, there were activities for the men, including baseball games. The competition between *North Dakota* and other ships was fierce, and the crowds were large, as can be seen at this game from 1922. Other sporting events at the base included football, basketball, and rowing. Games helped boost morale and foster camaraderie.

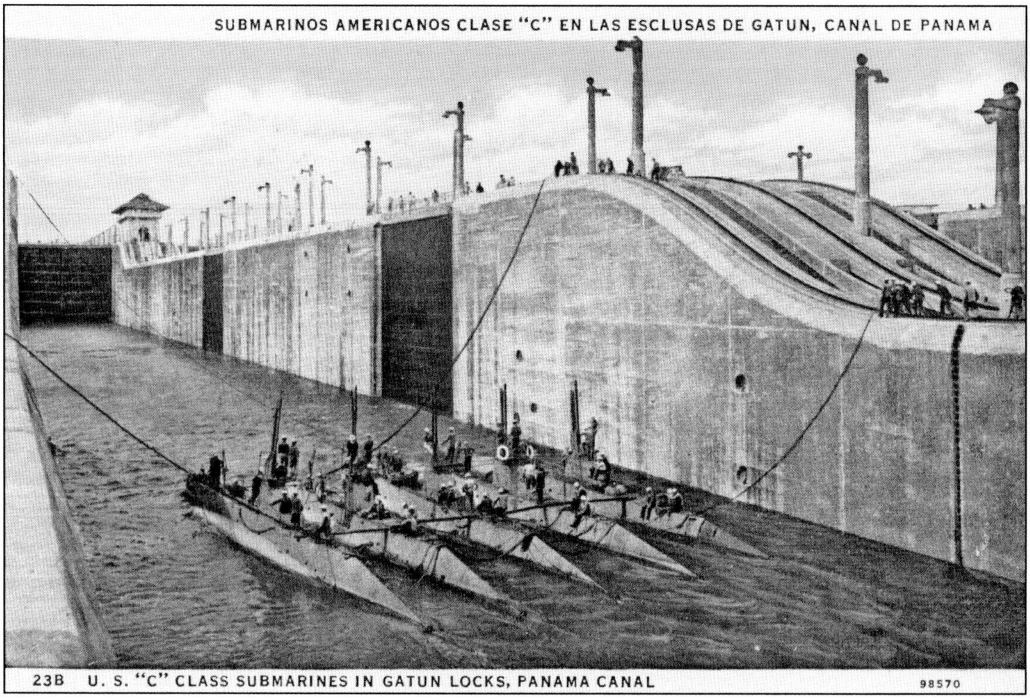

Fore River's five *C* submarines were originally given interesting names of sea life—*Octopus*, *Stingray*, *Tarpon*, *Bonita*, and *Snapper*. In 1911, the US Navy stopped giving names to submarines, so they were redesignated *C-1* through *C-5*. The *C* submarines never ventured across the Atlantic, spending most of World War I in the Canal Zone and on the Atlantic coast of the United States. At only 105 feet in length, *C* submarines were tiny by today's standards. They did not have the space to carry large amounts of food, fuel, replacement torpedoes, or spare parts and therefore required the aid of a "tender" ship to provide supplies and support. USS *Severn* acted as the mother ship as the *C* submarines transited the Gatun Locks.

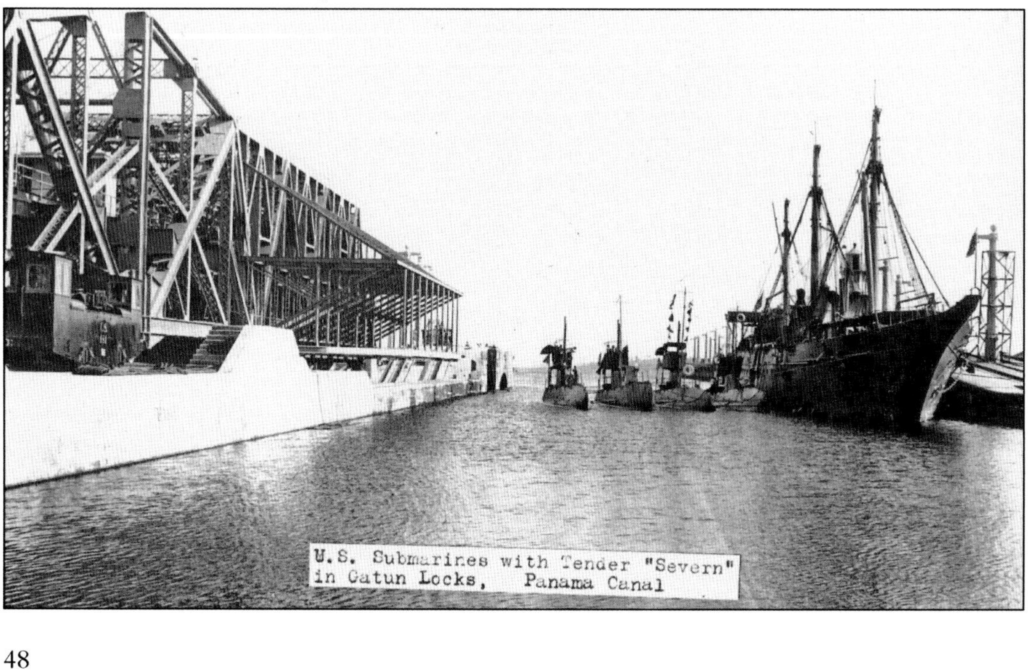

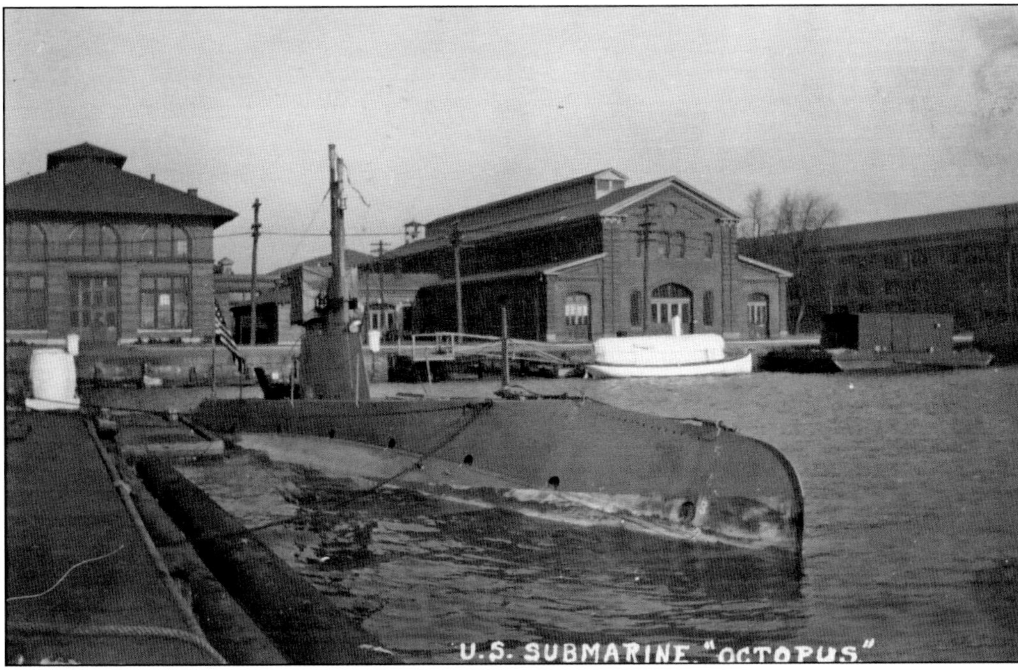

USS *Octopus* (*C-1*) (SS-9) was the first of five *C* submarines built at the shipyard. The contract with the US Navy for the *C* submarines was awarded to Electric Boat Company, which did not have a shipyard, so all their submarines were built in Quincy. *Octopus* was commissioned in June 1908; she was manned by a crew of one officer and 14 enlisted men and based in Newport, Rhode Island. She had one 18-inch torpedo tube and carried five torpedoes. *C-1* served as a training vessel for three years, then in 1913 operated out of Guantanamo Bay, Cuba. During World War I, *C-1* patrolled Panamanian waters. After the war's end, she was decommissioned in the Canal Zone in 1919 and scrapped a year later.

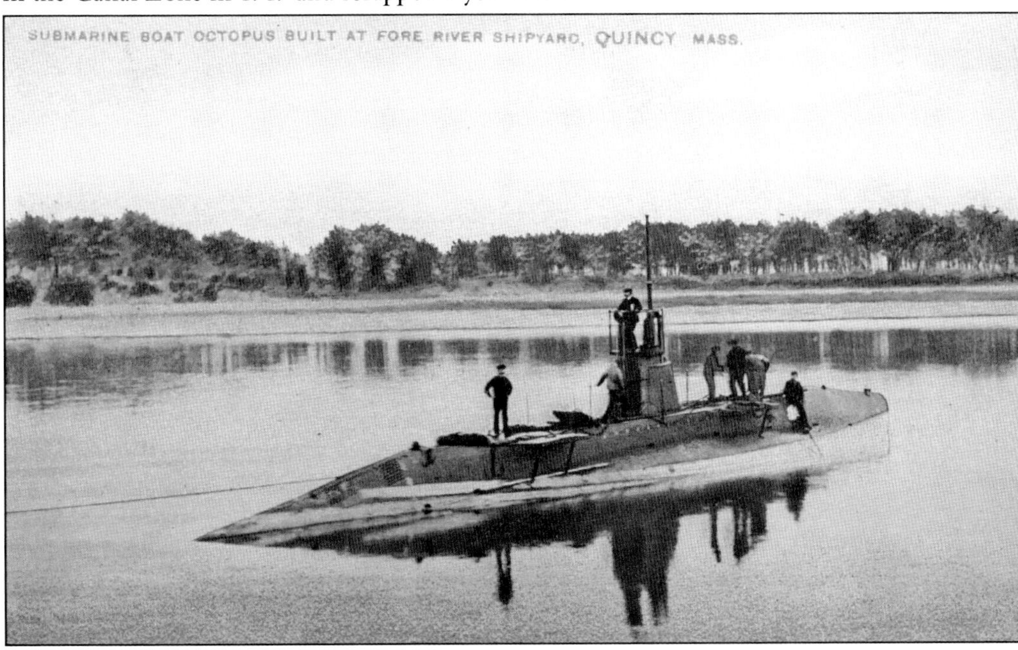

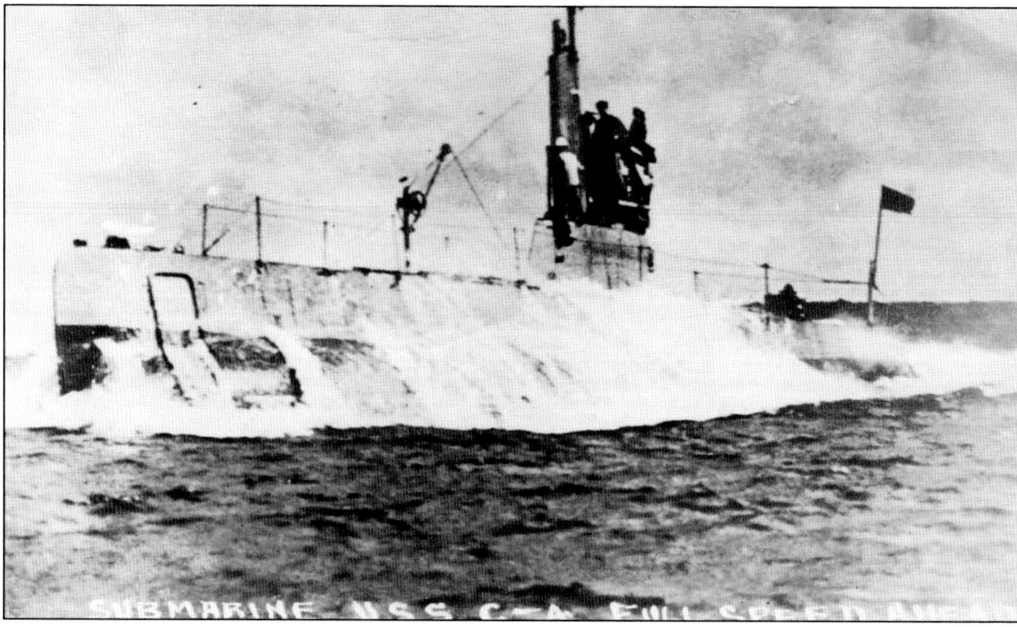

USS *Bonita* (*C-4*) (SS-15) was launched in June 1909 and commissioned that November. The caption says, "Full speed ahead," but for *C-4* that was only 10.5 knots on the surface and 9 knots submerged. By comparison, contemporary battleships had a surface speed of 18 knots and cruisers had 25 knots. During World War I, *C-4* patrolled for U-boats while guarding the entrances to the Panama Canal.

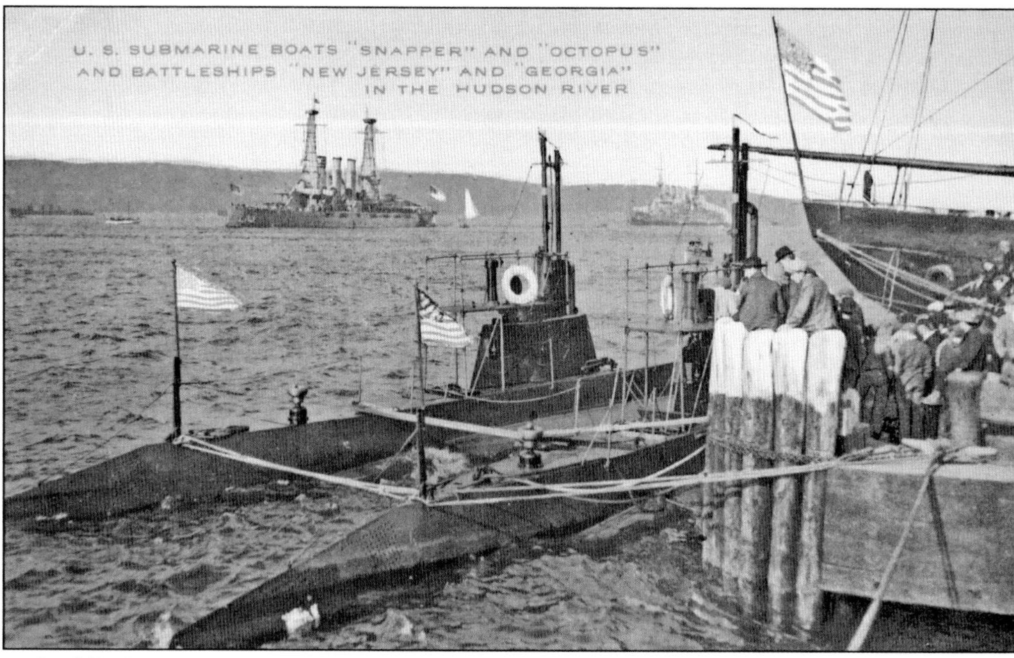

In the fall of 1909, USS *Snapper* (*C-5*) (SS-16) docked on the Hudson River with sister submarine USS *Octopus* (*C-1*). They were sailing with the fleet to the Hudson-Fulton Celebration to participate in the grand naval parade. A young Lt. Chester W. Nimitz was the first commander of *C-5*. Over 30 years later, he would be one of the heroes of World War II as fleet admiral.

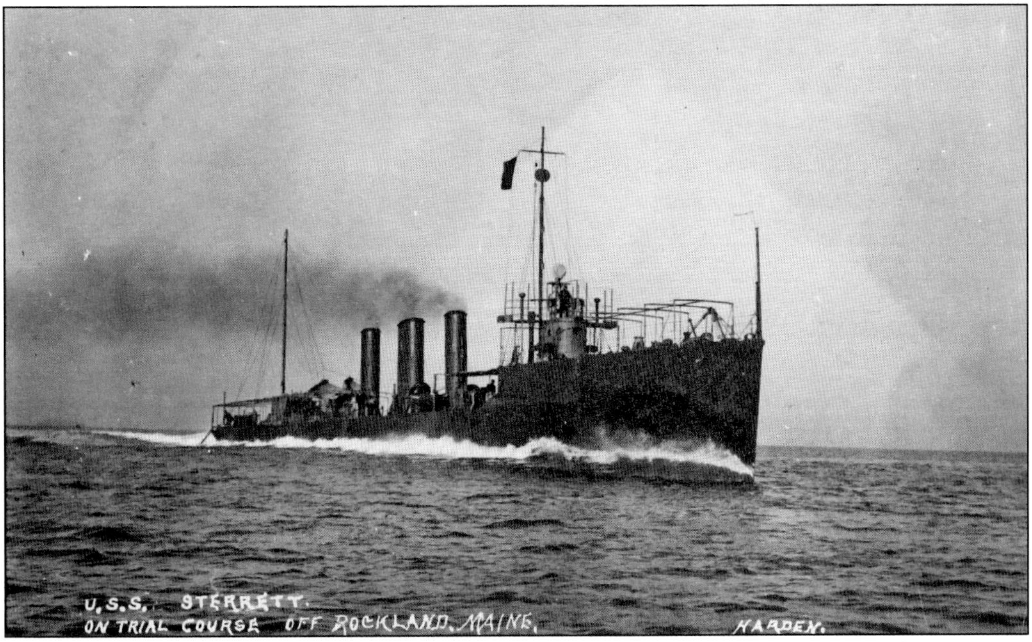

USS *Sterett* (DD-27), a Paulding class destroyer, was launched in May 1910. Before she was commissioned that December, *Sterett* was photographed at the Rockland, Maine, trial course, steaming at a brisk 30 knots. *Sterett* operated out of Queenstown, Ireland, during World War I. After the war, she was deemed obsolete and was decommissioned in 1919.

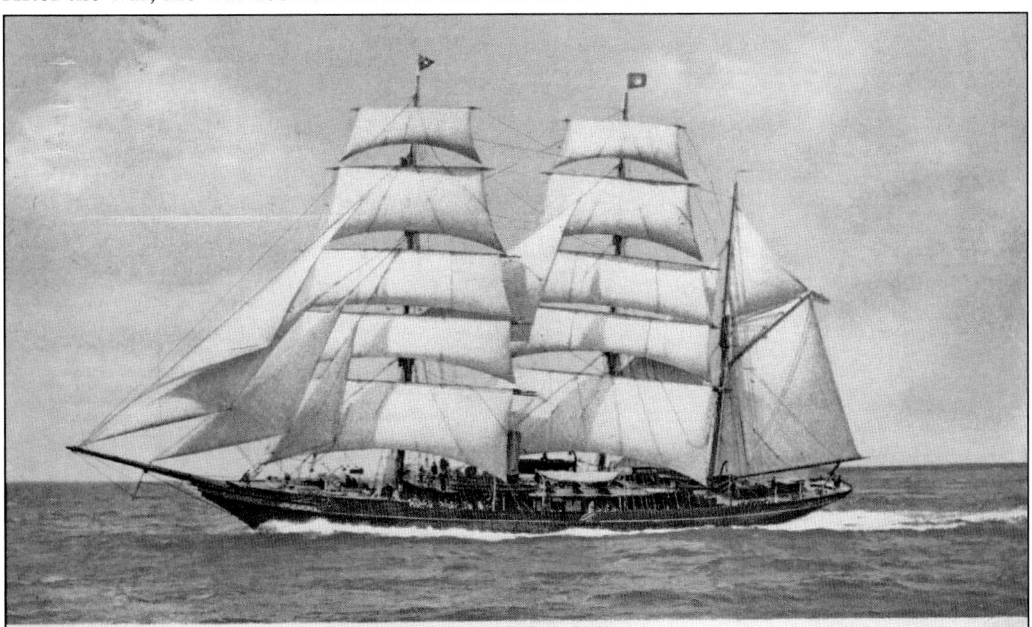

When launched in 1910, *Aloha* flew the most prestigious flag in American sailing, the New York Yacht Club Commodore's flag. She was the club's flagship and was owned by Arthur Curtiss James, railroad magnate, philanthropist, and yachting enthusiast. Six months after launch, James took *Aloha* on a 6,000-mile trip to Europe. His dream was to circumnavigate the globe, which he accomplished in a 259-day journey in 1921–1922.

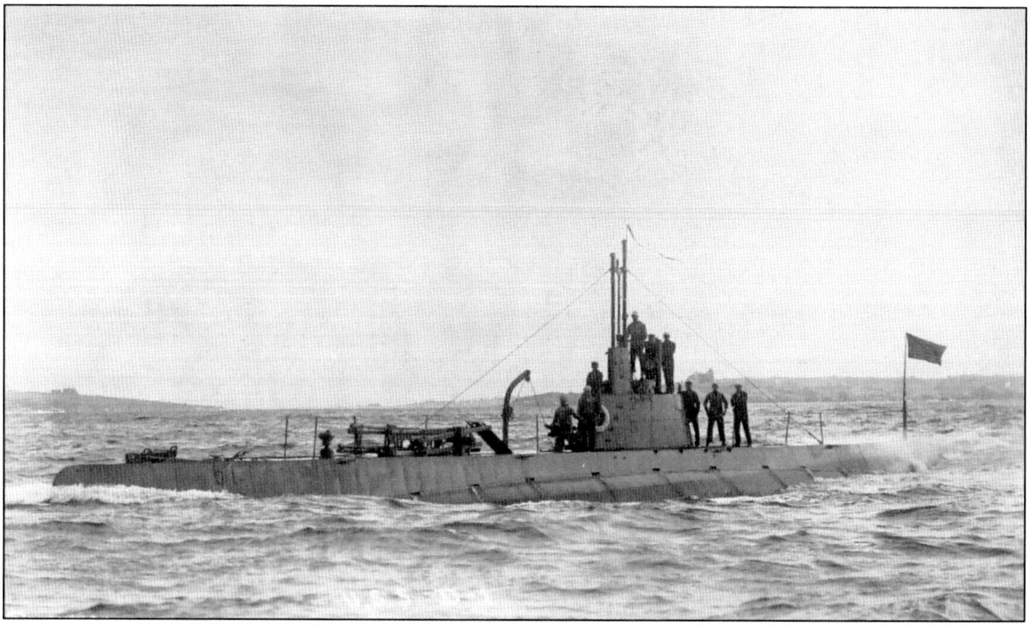

Commissioned in November 1909, USS *Narwhal* (*D-1*) (SS-17) joined the Atlantic Torpedo Fleet, operating from Newport, Rhode Island, to Norfolk, Virginia. In November 1910, Lt. Chester W. Nimitz assumed command of *Narwhal* after leaving USS *Snapper* (*C-5*). He would later command a third Fore River submarine, USS *Skipjack* (*E-1*). In 1920, Nimitz was in charge of the construction of the Pearl Harbor Submarine Base, becoming its first commanding officer.

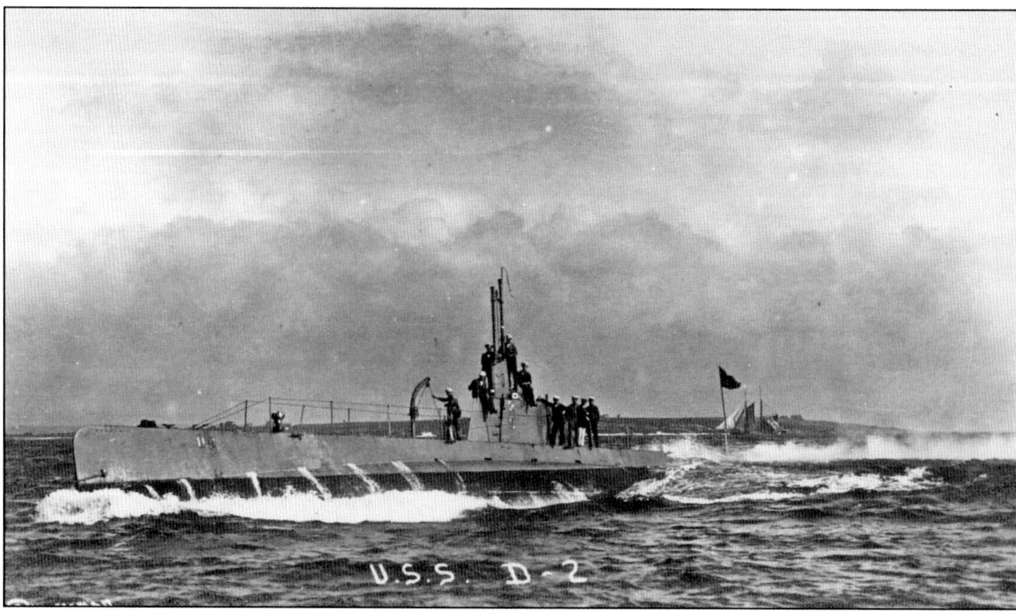

Assigned to Submarine Division Three until 1919, USS *Grayling* (*D-2)* (SS-18) never left the Atlantic coast. During World War I, *D-2* served as a training vessel from her New London, Connecticut, base. The image on this postcard was shot by O.W. Waterman of Hampton, Virginia, a prolific photographer of US Navy ships.

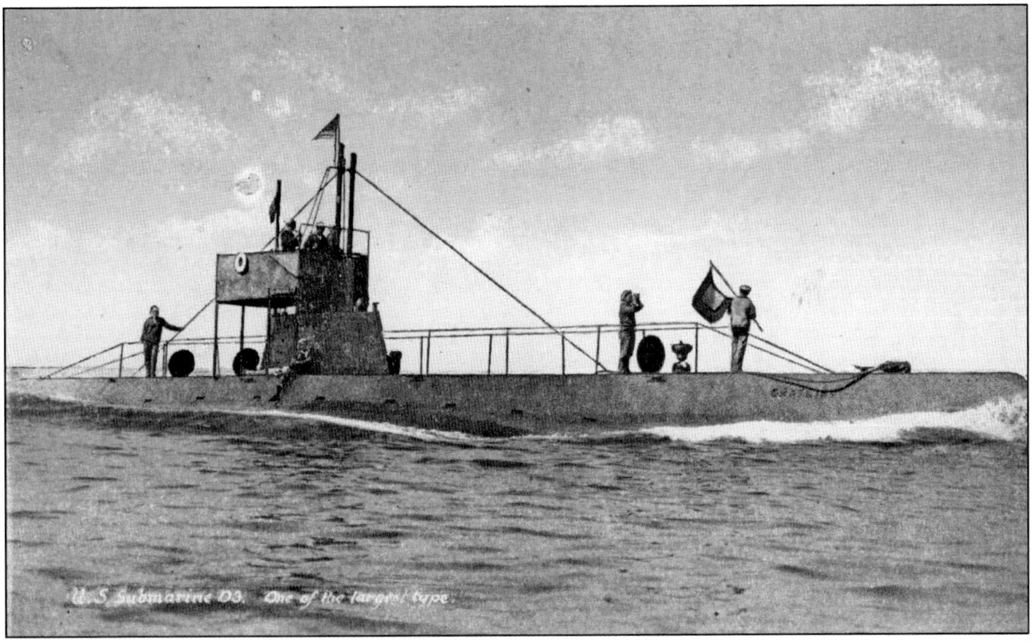

USS *Salmon* (*D-3*) (SS-19) was commissioned in September 1910 as the last of her class and with a major design change from *D-1* and *D-2*. The submarine only had two bulkheads, which resulted in a larger control room mid-ship, but this also created three large compartments that made her vulnerable to sinking should any compartment be flooded. Despite the design flaw, *D-3* served without incident, primarily along the Atlantic coast. The postcard of *D-3* "Coming to the Surface" was authorized by censors during World War I. It was from a photograph by E. Muller Jr., who made a career photographing naval vessels during the war. *D-3* was decommissioned and sold for scrap in 1922.

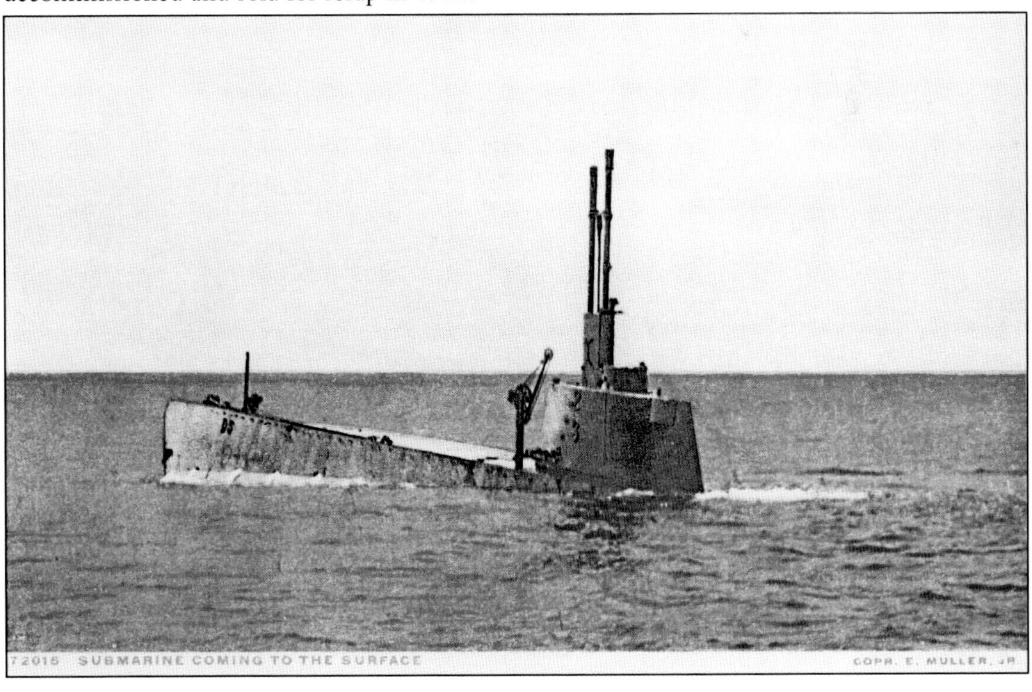

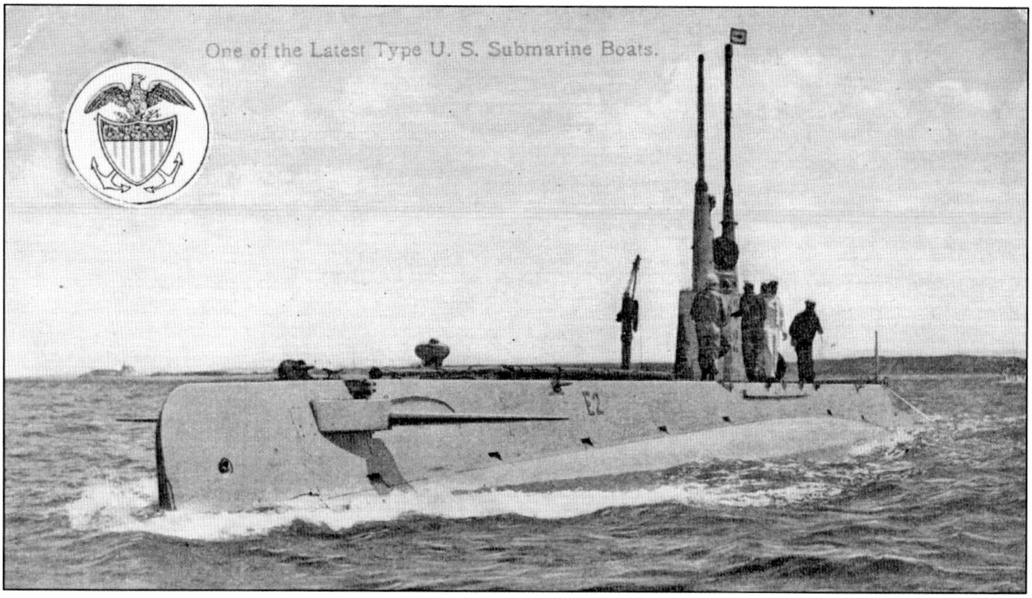

The shipyard launched two *E* submarines in 1911. These were the first submarines with diesel power and radios. In January 1916, there was an explosion and fire onboard USS *Sturgeon* (*E-2*) (SS-25) that killed four men. During World War I, she patrolled the waters off Cape Hatteras for German U-boats, engaging the enemy on one occasion, for which she received a commendation from the chief of naval operations.

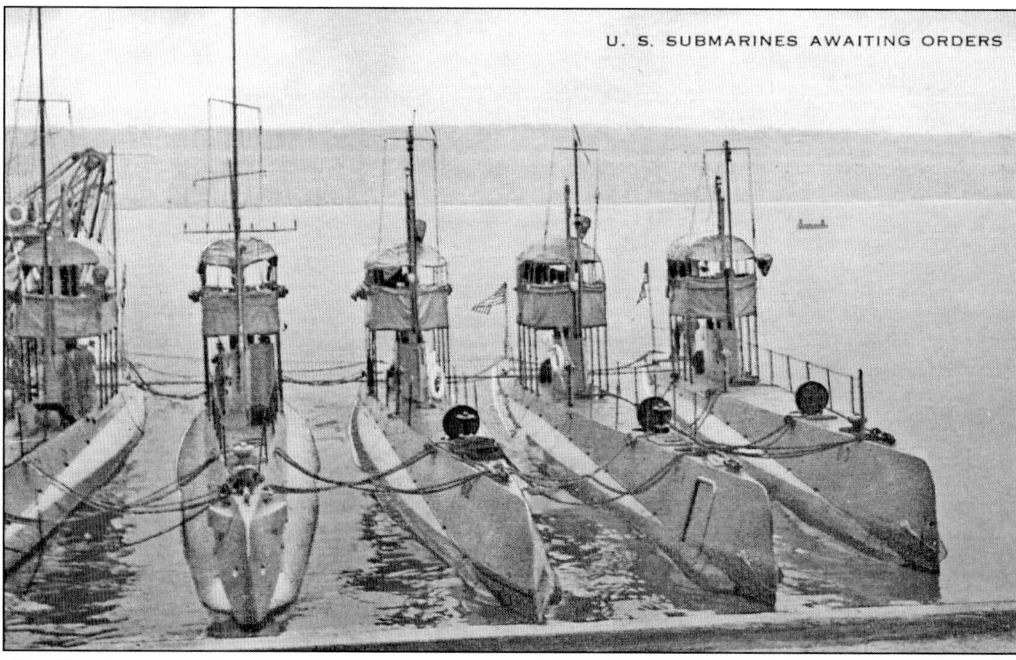

The five Quincy submarines on this postcard are USS *Skipjack* (*E-1*), USS *Sturgeon* (*E-2*), USS *Grayling* (*D-2*), USS *Narwhal* (*D-1*), and USS *Salmon* (*D-3*). In May 1915, they were docked in New York City with the Atlantic Fleet awaiting review by President Wilson. The sight of the submarines generated quite a bit of excitement. Today, one cannot imagine the US Navy exhibiting a new technology so publicly.

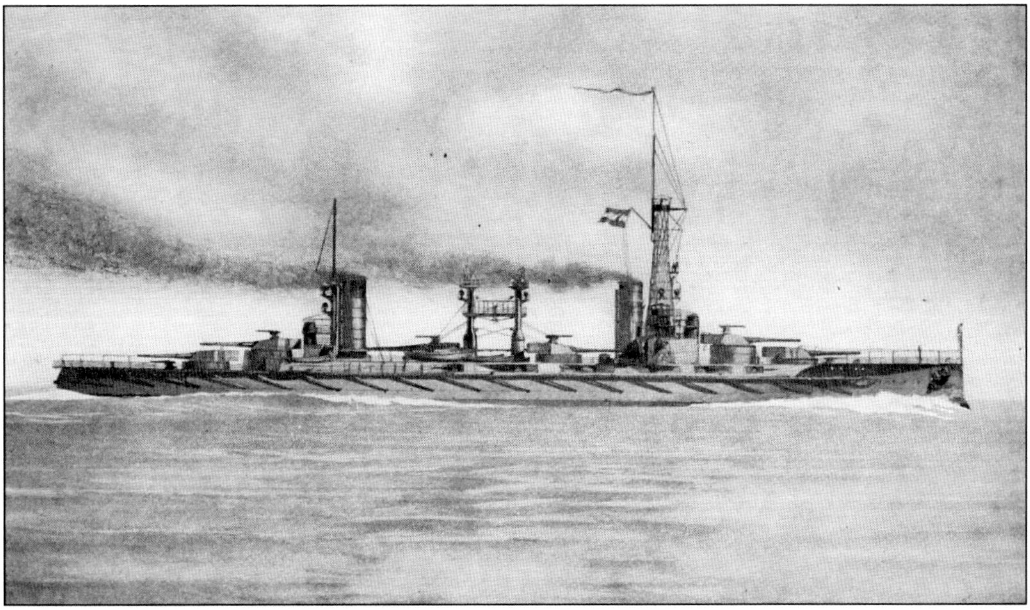

Battleship *Rivadavia* was built for the Argentine navy after a controversial bidding process. In 1908, Argentina sought to purchase new battleships to counter the buildup of the Brazilian navy. After much political wrangling, the contract was finally awarded to Fore River, despite complaints from England, Germany, and Italy, who were favored to win. The Argentine real-photo postcard shows *Rivadavia* arriving in Argentina in February 1915. The arrival of the battleship drew large crowds who were invited onboard to explore the ship. It was during the difficult and lengthy construction of *Rivadavia* that Admiral Bowles, president of the Fore River Ship and Engine Company, recommended that the shipyard be sold to the Bethlehem Steel Corporation.

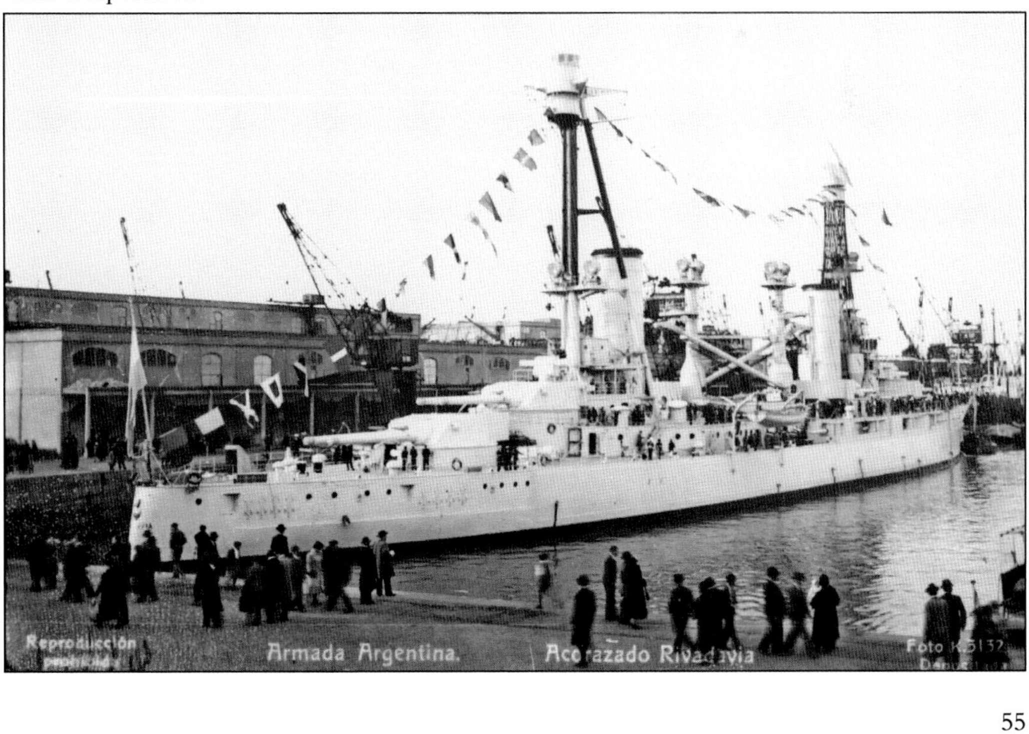

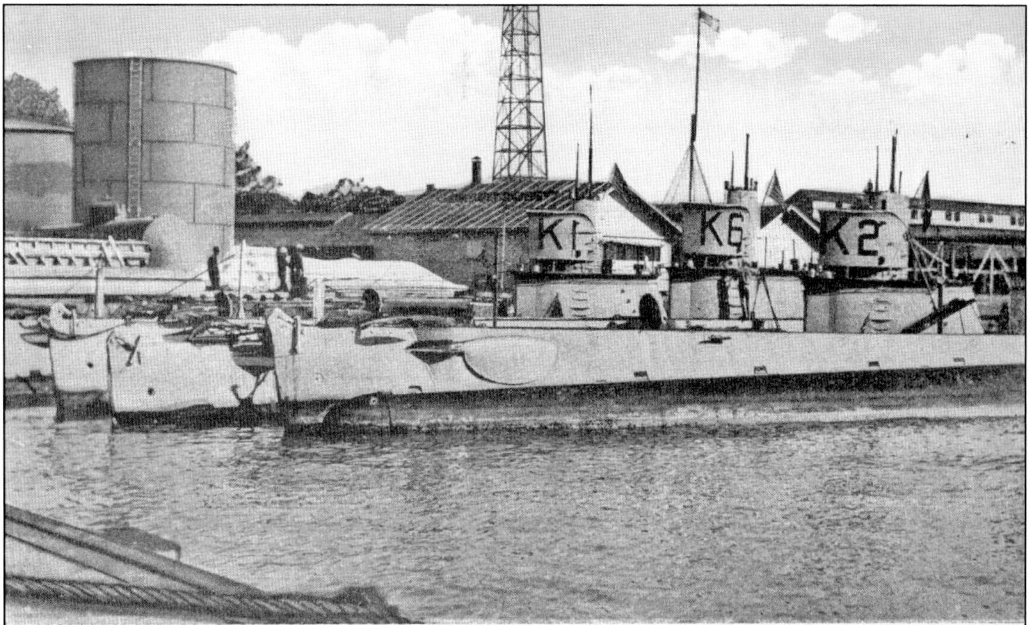

U. S. N. SUB BASE, KEY WEST, FLA.

The three submarines featured on this postcard were all built in Quincy. *K-1* (USS *Haddock*) (SS-32), *K-2* (USS *Cachalot*) (SS-33), and USS *K-6* (SS-37) were commissioned in 1914. The *K* submarines were often stationed at the Key West submarine base while patrolling the Gulf of Mexico. The *K* submarines were the first US submarines to see action during World War I.

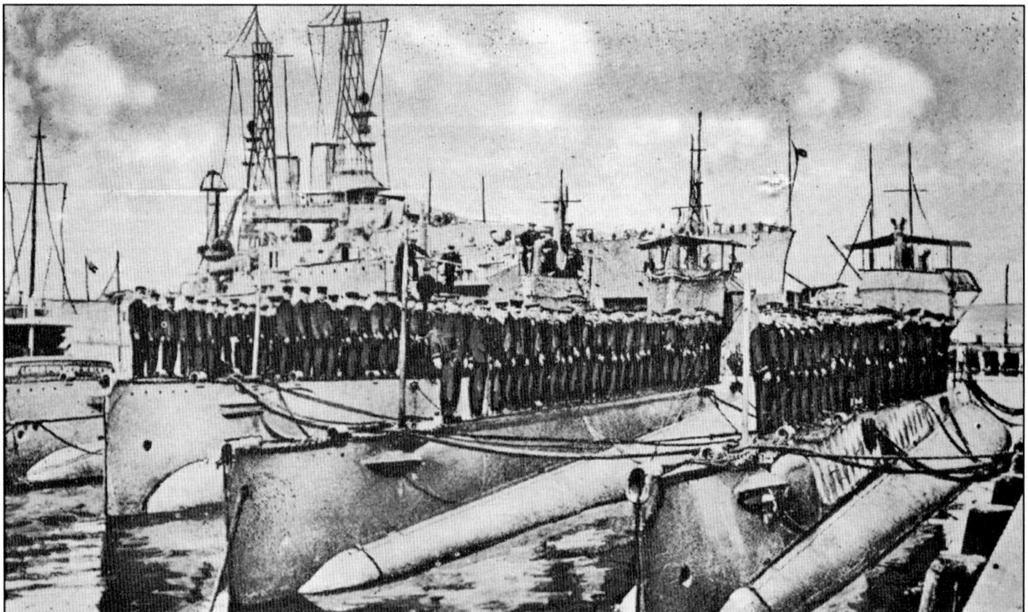

K BOATS AND CREWS.

It was a tight-knit group of men who served aboard World War I–era submarines. The *K* submarines carried two officers and 26 enlisted men in a ship that was 153 feet long and narrower than a football goal post. From left to right, the crews of *K-1*, *K-2*, *K-6*, and *K-5* posed in their dress blues prior to leaving for Europe in 1917.

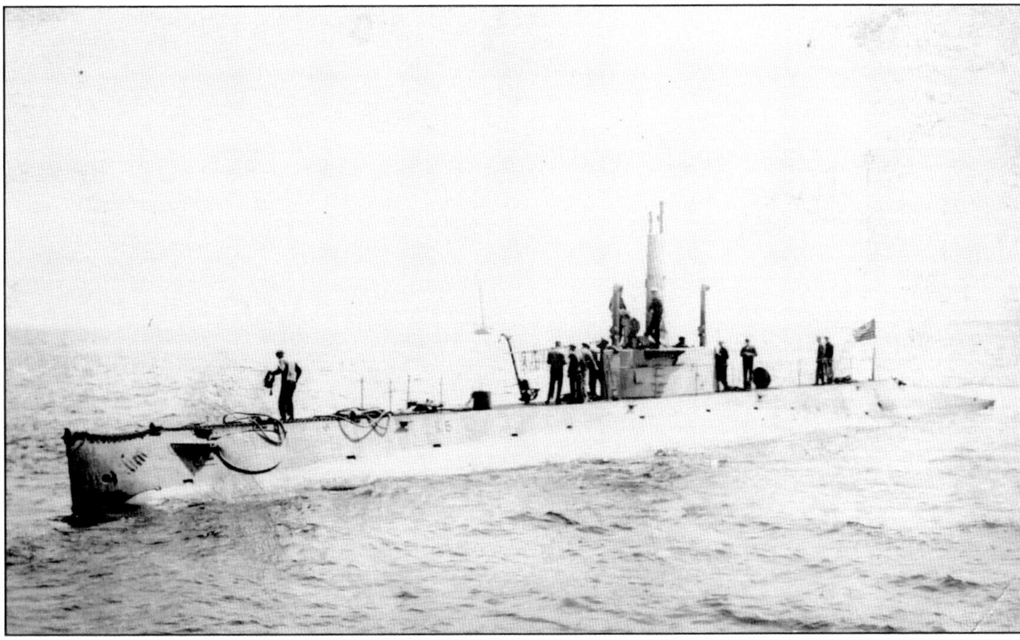

USS *K-5* (SS-36) was the first submarine to cruise the Mississippi River, arriving in St. Louis in June 1919. This view was taken before the United States entered World War I while the *K* submarines still had a "pipe and canvas bridge." The "chariot bridge" became the standard during the war as it allowed for fast diving without disassembly of the bridge. The *K* submarines were decommissioned in 1923.

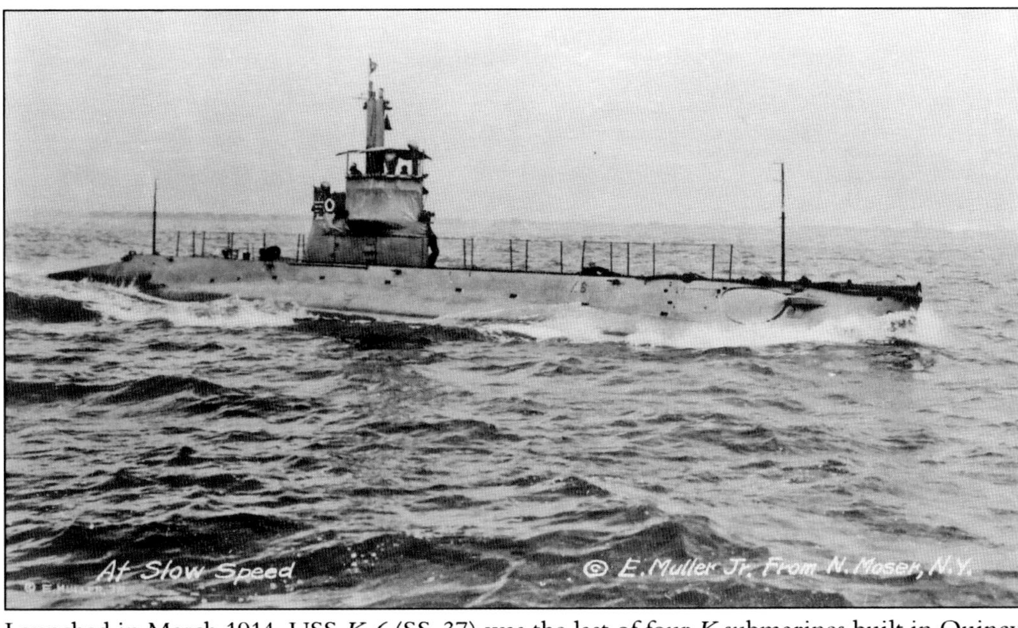

Launched in March 1914, USS *K-6* (SS-37) was the last of four *K* submarines built in Quincy. She spent three years along the Atlantic coast and Gulf of Mexico. During World War I, *K-6* patrolled for U-boats in the Azores. After the war, she operated out of New London, Hampton Roads, and Key West. This postcard, titled "At Slow Speed," is one of many photographs taken by N. Moser.

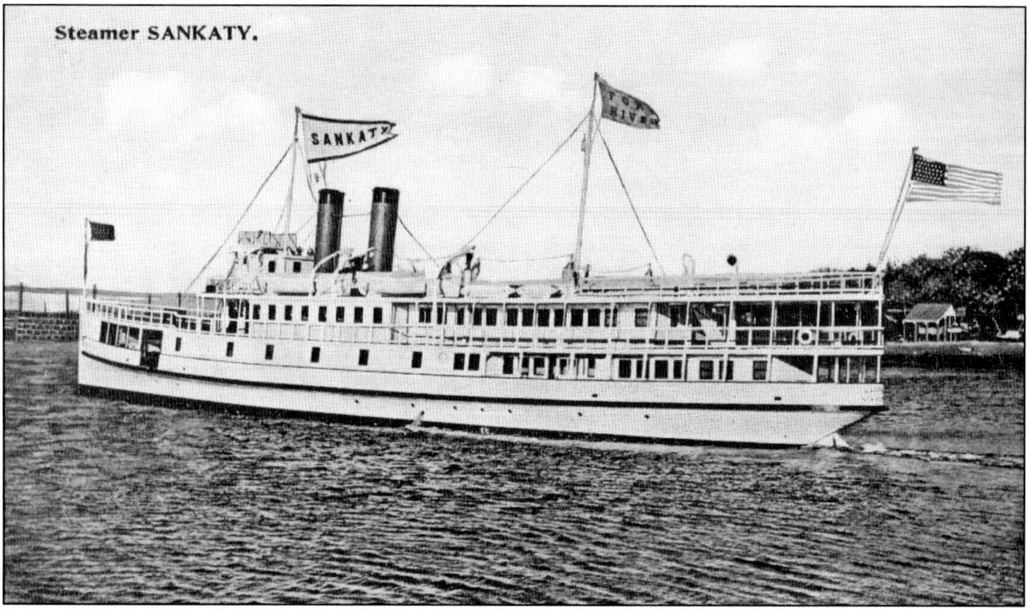

Delivered in 1911 to the New Bedford Steamship Company, steamer *Sankaty* flew the "Fore River" flag. She operated as a passenger ferry between Martha's Vineyard, Nantucket, New Bedford, and Woods Hole. In 1924, she suffered fire damage and was rebuilt, subsequently serving as a car ferry in Rockland, Maine. In 1941, *Sankaty* was purchased by a Canadian ferry but, before going into service, was requisitioned by the Royal Canadian Navy.

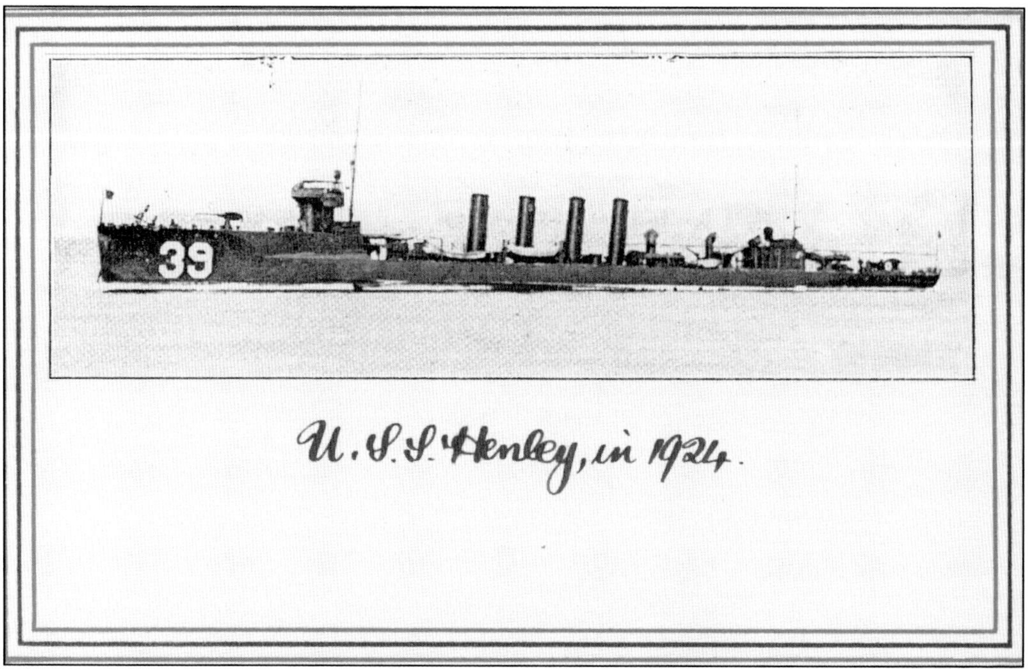

During World War I, destroyer USS *Henley* (DD-39) guarded troop convoys and searched for enemy submarines off New York City. This postcard is dated 1924, the same year *Henley* was transferred to the US Coast Guard to interdict ships that were smuggling liquor. She was returned to the US Navy in 1931 and scrapped in 1934.

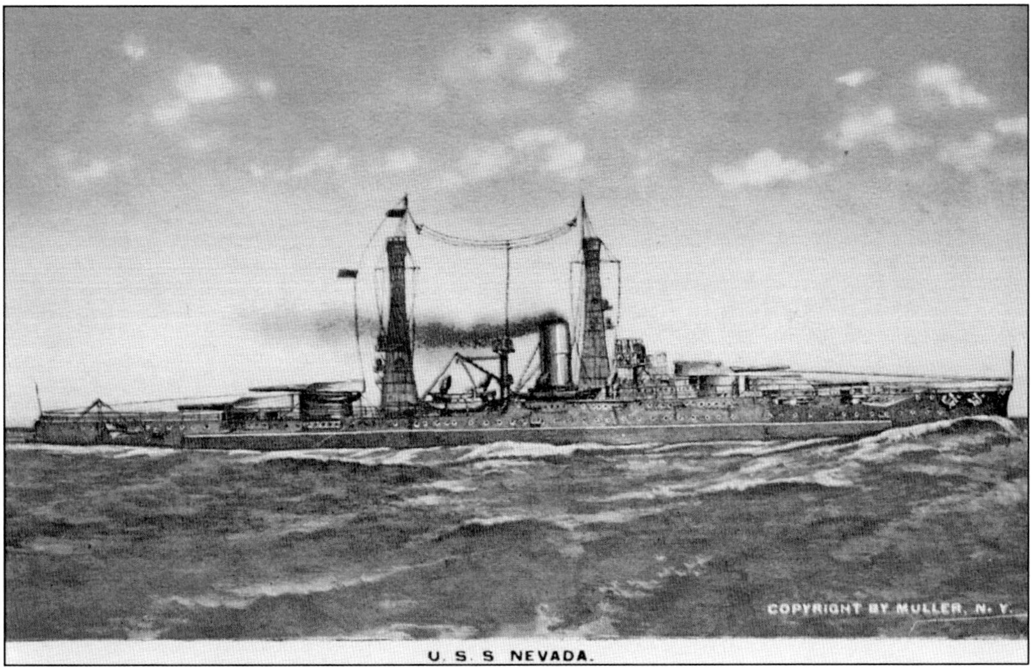

Launched in July 1914, USS *Nevada* (BB-36) was the first Super-Dreadnought, at almost twice the tonnage as USS *Vermont* built just nine years earlier. She was the first battleship to burn oil instead of coal. *Nevada* also used the "all or nothing" armor principle, with the heaviest armor at the waterline and limited armor on deck. She was the only battleship to get underway during the Japanese attack on Pearl Harbor. Though badly damaged, she was repaired and served at Utah Beach during D-Day and later in the Pacific at Iwo Jima. The humorous 1918–1919 Merry Christmas/Happy New Year's postcard must have cheered up people back home. On the back is a printed cartoon of a sailor towing a goat with the exclamation, "We got the Kaiser's goat for Christmas."

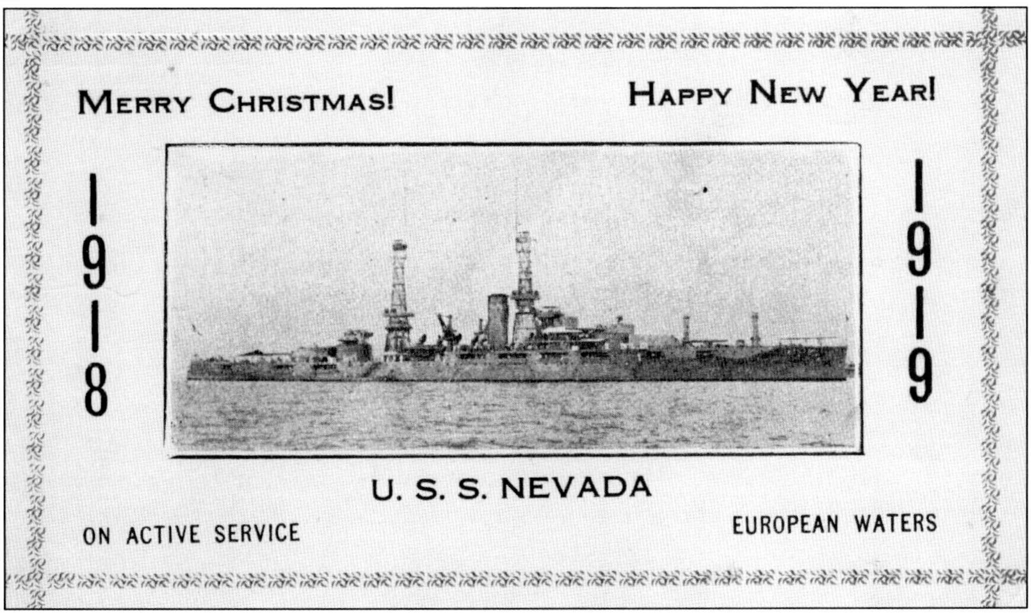

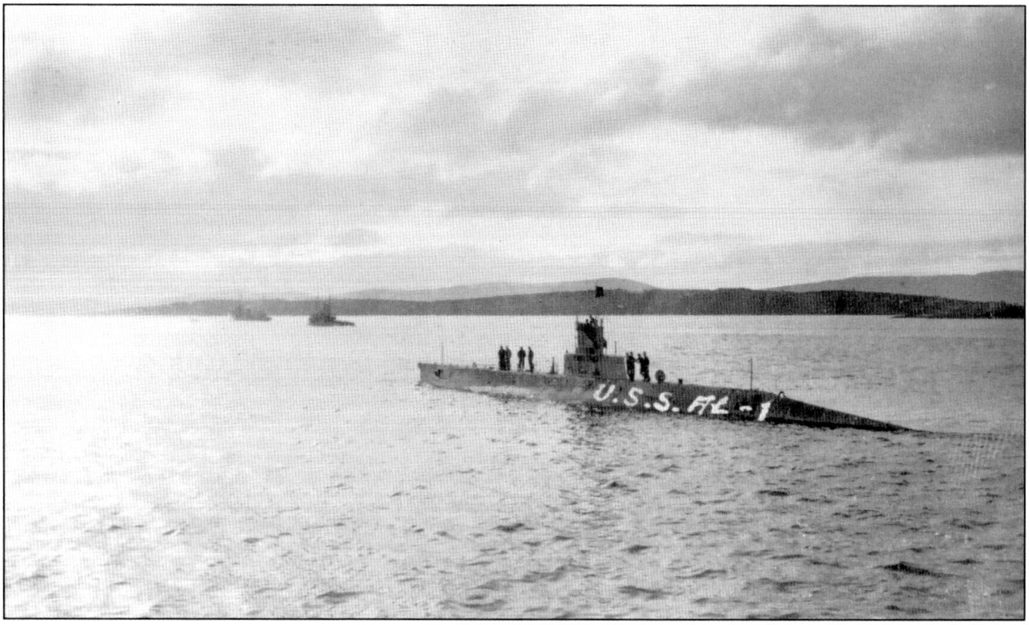

USS *L-1* (SS-40) was the first of eight *L* submarines built at the shipyard, commissioned in April 1916. The letter A (for American) was added in front of *L-1* to differentiate her from the British *L-1* submarine. During World War I, she operated in the Irish Sea, protecting ships from U-boats. After the war, she tested new torpedoes and undersea detection devices, which helped build the next generation of submarines.

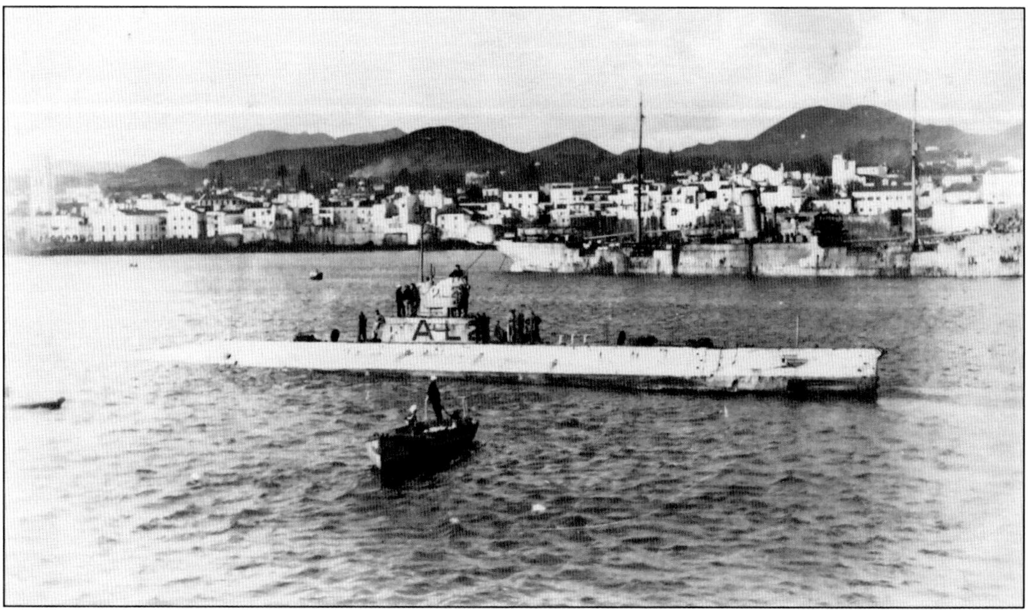

In 1917, USS *L-2* (SS-41) joined other *L* submarines in visiting Havana, Cuba, thought to be the first such visit by American submarines. With the outbreak of World War I, she steamed for Europe, stopping in the Azores where this real-photo postcard was taken. In July 1918, while patrolling off Fastnet Light, Ireland, *L-2* encountered the German submarine *UB-65*. The U-boat was sunk with a loss of 37 men.

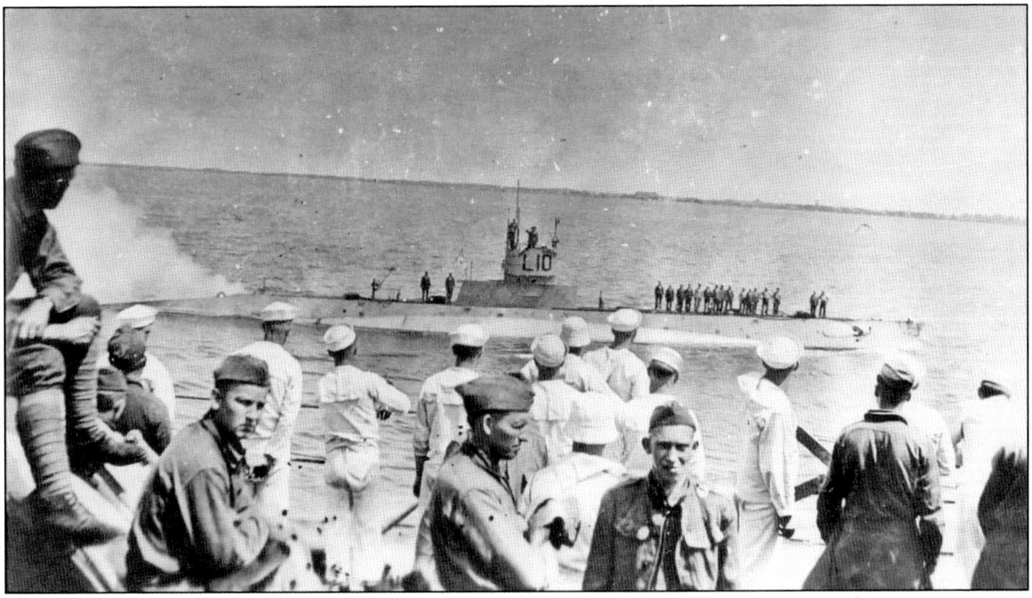

This candid real-photo postcard was taken by a sailor from the deck of a warship returning from Europe after World War I. Many crewmen watched USS *L-10* (SS-50) as she passed by, while the officer atop the bridge of the submarine saluted. Like most early submarines, *L-10* had a short life; she was launched in March 1916, commissioned five months later, and sold for scrap in 1922.

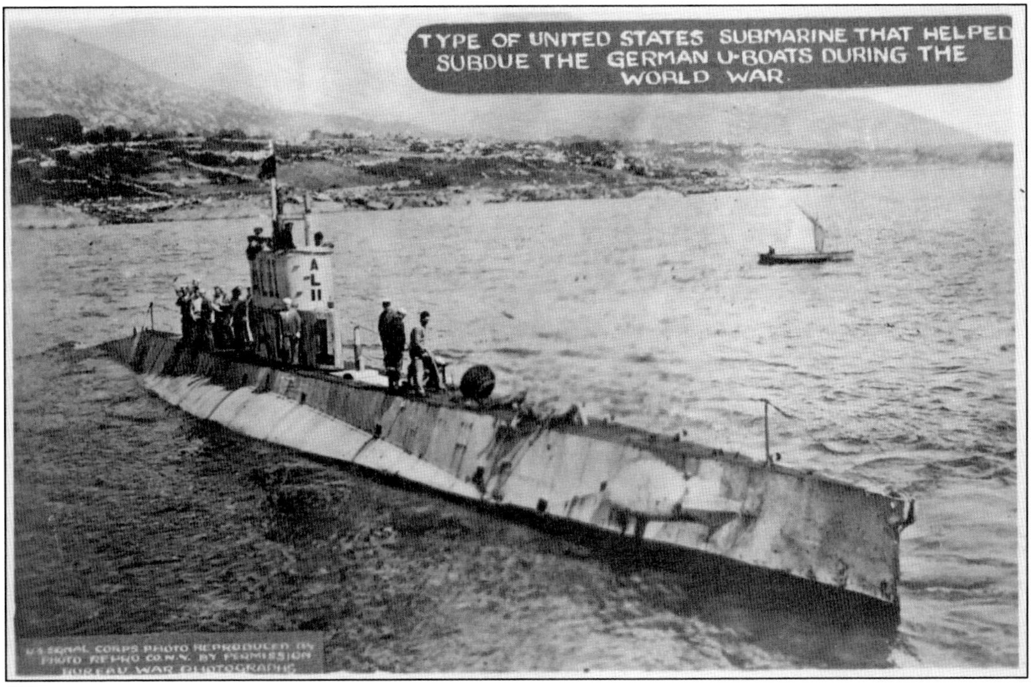

This c. 1920 postcard of submarine USS *L-11* (SS-51) commemorated the Allied victory over German U-boats during World War I. *L-11* sighted U-boats on three occasions, firing her torpedoes in May 1918 with inconclusive results. After the war, *L-11* operated off the Atlantic coast, practicing submarine warfare tactics until being decommissioned in 1923.

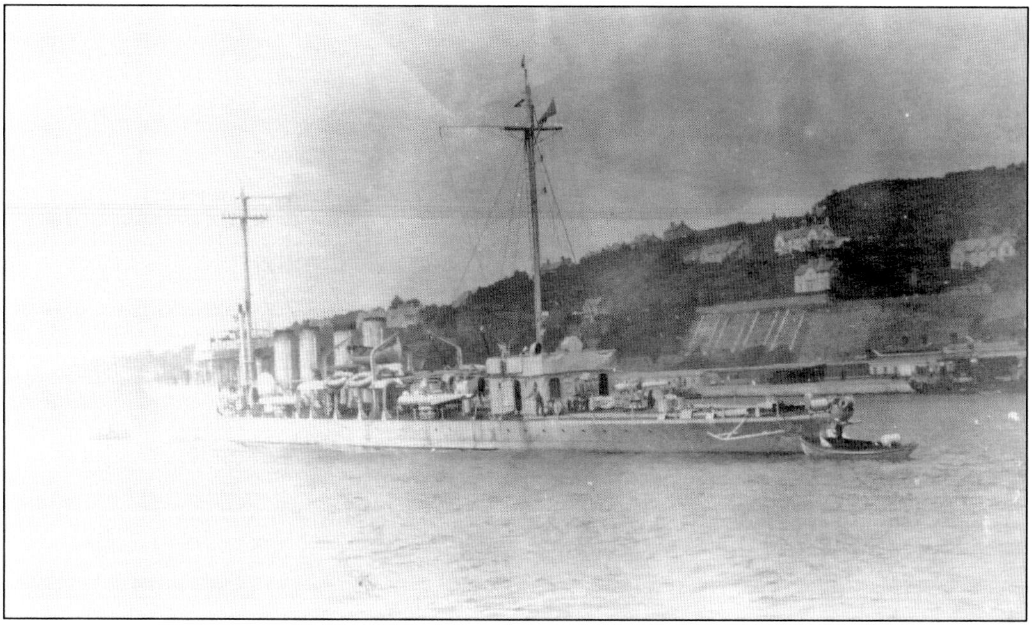

Commissioned in August 1915, destroyer USS *Cushing* (DD-55) patrolled the Irish Sea, where she was photographed at Queenstown, Ireland. *Cushing* escorted convoys, protected shipping, and rescued survivors of U-boat attacks. In April 1918, she dropped depth charges on German submarine *U-104*, damaging her severely. Later that day, HMS *Jessamine* finished off *U-104*, killing all but one of the crew. *Cushing* survived the war and was decommissioned in 1920.

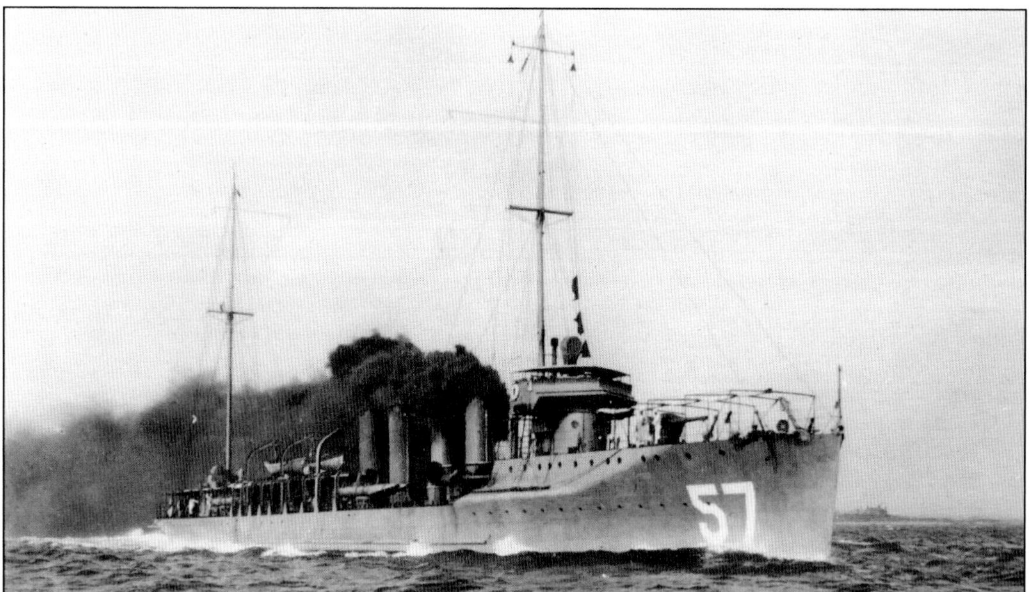

Launched in May 1915, USS *Tucker* (DD-57) was a classic four-stack destroyer. Only 315-feet long, *Tucker* could generate speeds of 29 knots very quickly. During World War I, she escorted ships and patrolled for U-boats in the Irish Sea and English Channel as well as rescuing survivors of sunken ships. In 1920, *Tucker* was assigned to the US Coast Guard "Rum Patrol," interdicting ships smuggling alcohol.

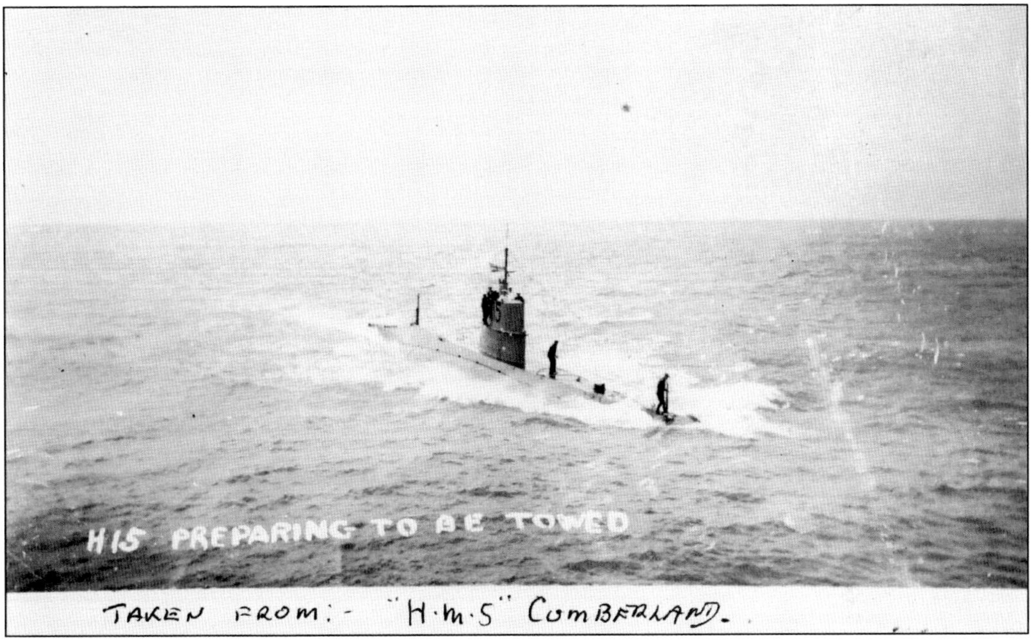

In 1915, the shipyard built 10 *H* class submarines for the Royal Navy. However, due to America's neutrality, the US government impounded the submarines until America entered the war in 1917. This view of *H-15* was taken from HMS *Cumberland* as the submarine was preparing to be towed. Transferred to Canada in 1919, *H-15* was scrapped in 1925 as HMCS *CH-15.*

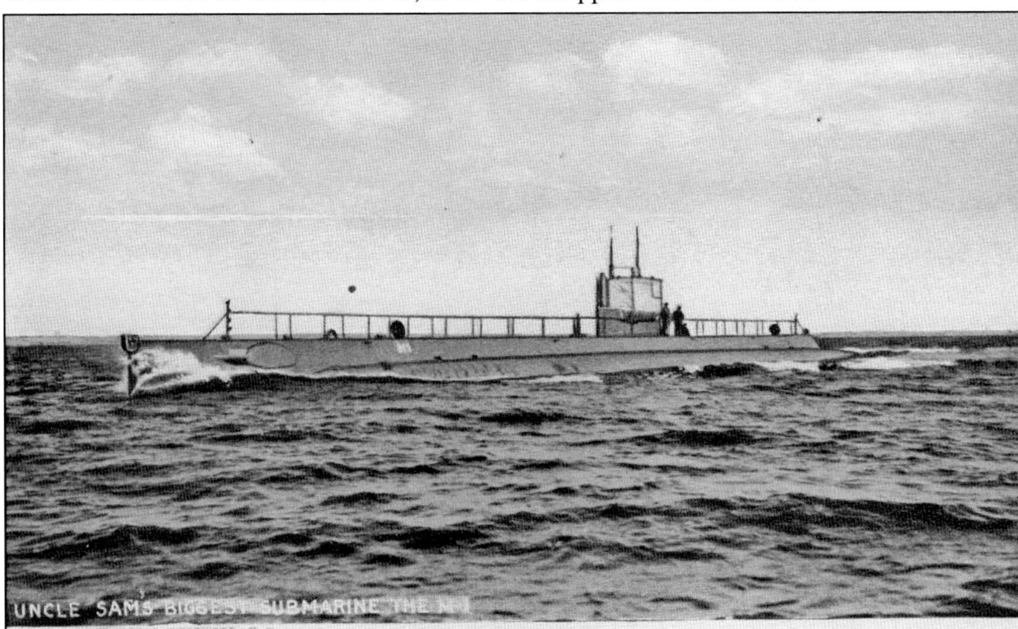

USS *M-1* (SS-47) was the first double-hull submarine built for the US Navy. When launched in September 1915, she became the largest American submarine at 185 feet in length, with a maximum steaming radius of 5,000 miles and a surface speed of 14 knots. She carried two officers and 26 enlisted men. Commissioned in February 1918, she trained submariners during World War I.

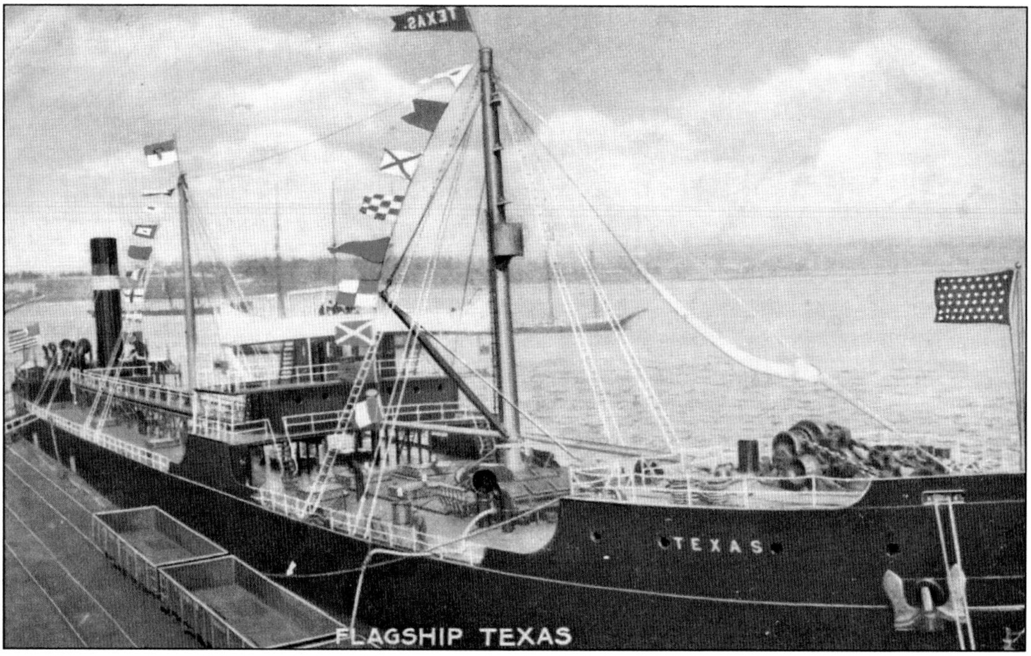

Texas was the first of four oil tankers built at the shipyard in 1916–1917. Sister ships were *New York*, *Pennsylvania*, and *Virginia*, all 432 feet long. Flagship *Texas* was waving more than a dozen flags in celebration of its completion and delivery to the Texas Oil Company. Founded in 1903, today the company is known as Texaco.

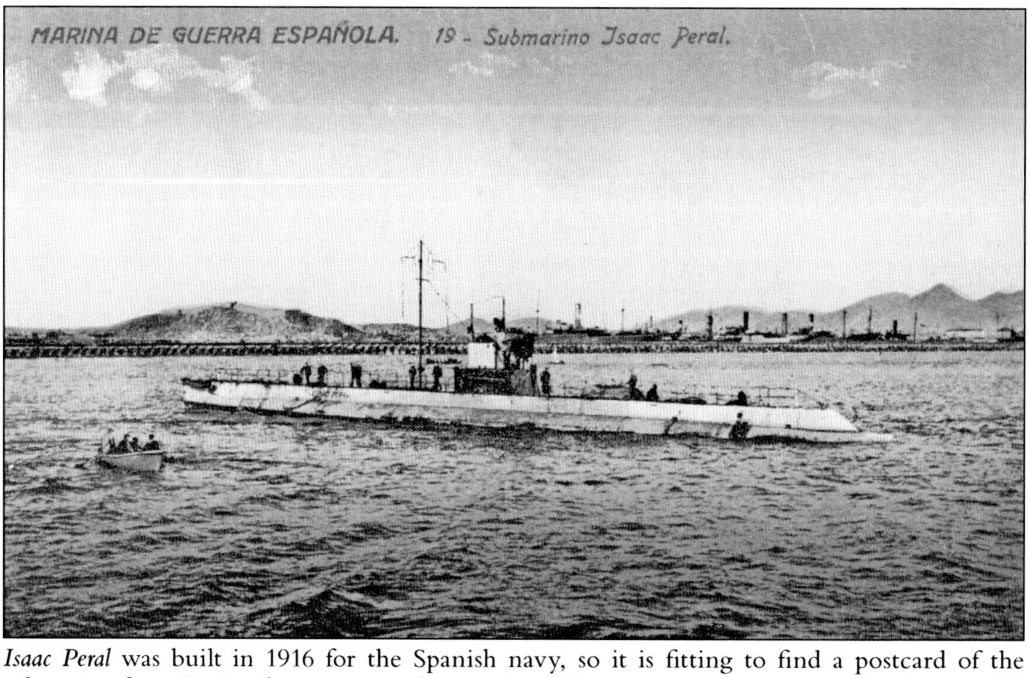

Isaac Peral was built in 1916 for the Spanish navy, so it is fitting to find a postcard of the submarine from Spain. She was an *M* class, very similar to *M-1* (SS-47) but with an innovative three-inch deck gun. The gun's disappearing mounting reduced underwater drag. *Isaac Peral* reached speeds of 15 knots on the surface and 10 knots submerged. She served until 1930.

Five

World War I
1917 to 1919

For three years, President Wilson tried to keep the United States out of World War I, but at his urging, Congress declared war against Germany on April 6, 1917. German U-boats were dominating the seas, so it should not be surprising that most of the work done at the shipyard from 1917 to 1919 was for the US Navy, and submarines were at the top of the list. Fore River Shipyard built eight *O* submarines (*O-3* through *O-10)* as well as 14 *R* submarines (*R-1* through *R-14*). Wickes and Clemson class destroyers were the other mainstays. Commercial work was on the back burner, but some oil tankers and freighters were delivered.

Due to the expansion of the workforce at the shipyard, there were critical shortages of housing along the South Shore. Sensing the need to aid areas with shipyards and munitions plants, Congress passed legislation creating the US Housing Corporation (USHC). The government built more than 200 houses at Quincy Point in 1918. The USHC also built a clubhouse and a restaurant with seating for 1,000 people. Streetcars made additional runs from the shipyard and surrounding points. Traffic around the shipyard was choked with vehicles day and night.

At the height of the war, there was a shipbuilding contest between two Bethlehem Steel–owned shipyards. Fore River Shipyard general manager S. Wiley Wakeman was approached by Joseph Tynan of the Union Ironworks in San Francisco to see which plant could deliver the most destroyers in 1918. Tynan suggested a $5,000 bet, but Wakeman was so convinced the Fore River Shipyard would win that he offered to double the bet, and Tynan accepted. Both shipyards printed bonds at $5 each, which were sold to workers. It was winner takes all, and the final tally was a big boost for morale in Quincy. It was Fore River Shipyard 18, Union Ironworks 6.

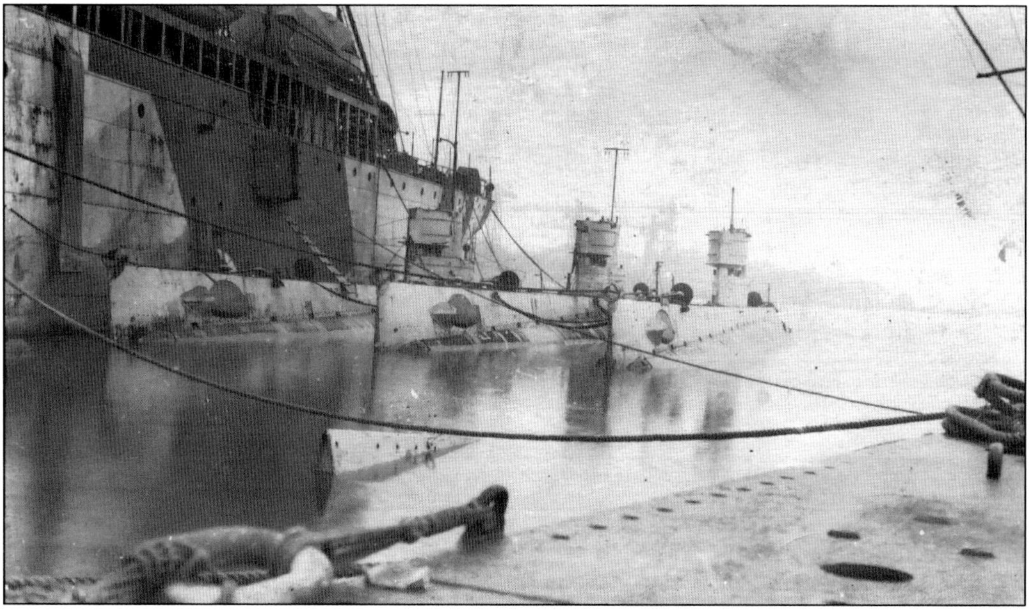

This real-photo postcard was taken from the dock as submarines USS *O-3* (SS-64), USS *O-7* (SS-68), and USS *O-8* (SS-69) were tied up to submarine tender USS *Savannah* (AS-8). Commissioned in 1918, the *O* class submarines were 173 feet long and had a range of 5,000 nautical miles. All three submarines served during World War II and were scrapped in 1946.

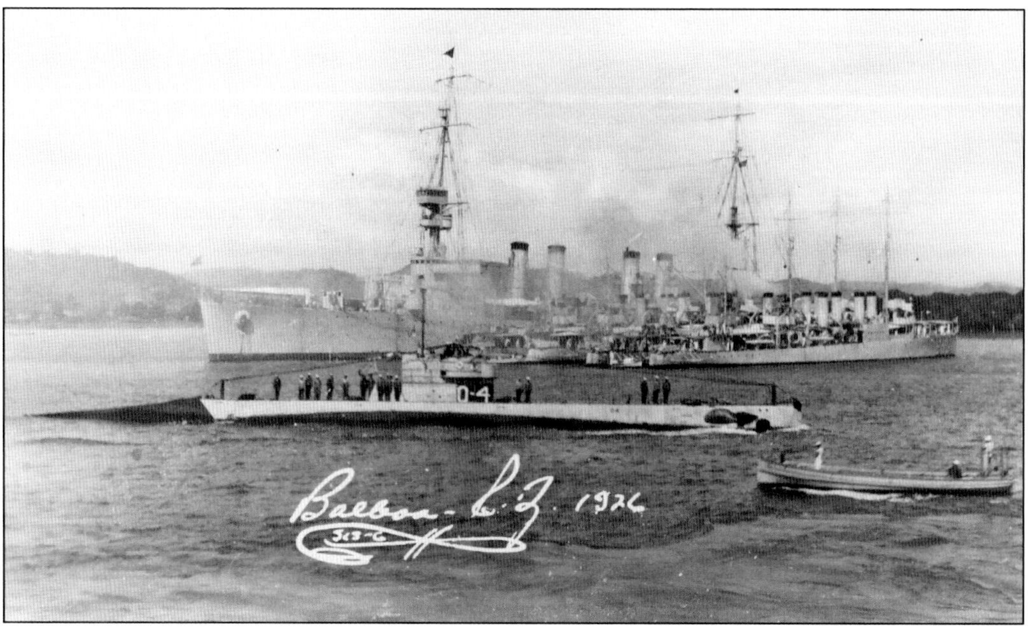

In 1926, submarine USS *O-4* (SS-65) joined the fleet in Balboa, Panama. The men of *O-4* were photographed as they were watching a large group of American destroyers transiting the Panama Canal. A trip through the new canal saved the destroyers over 7,500 miles on a voyage from New York City to Los Angeles.

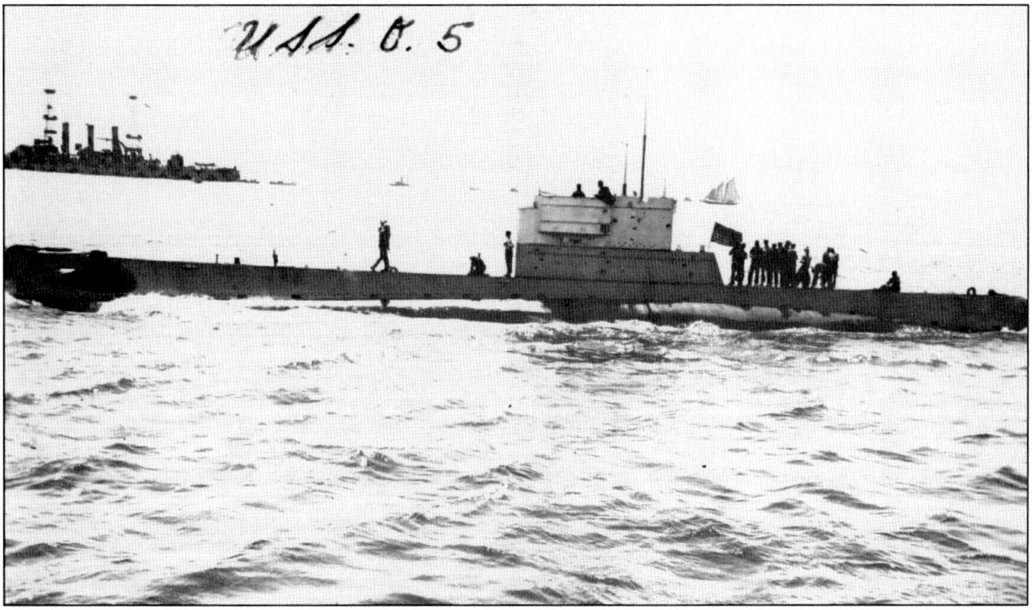

In 1923, USS *O-5* (SS-66) was rammed by the steamer *Abangarez* in Panama. Three crewmen were killed, and 16 men escaped. Henry Breault could have escaped, but he knew a shipmate was trapped inside the torpedo room. He sealed the room against flooding as the submarine sank. Over a day later, the submarine was raised and the men were saved. Breault was awarded the Medal of Honor for his actions.

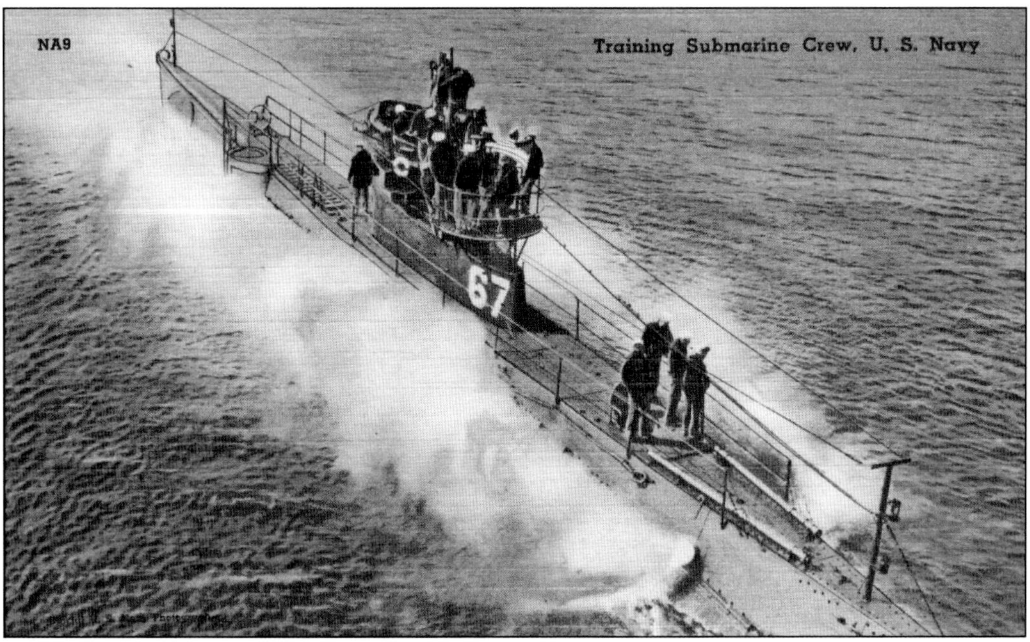

Commissioned in the late stages of World War I, USS *O-6* (SS-67) served along the Atlantic coast protecting ships against U-boats. She carried an all-volunteer crew of two officers and 27 enlisted men. Submarine applicants needed to graduate from the Submarine School at New London, Connecticut, before being assigned to a submarine. *O-6* was used to train new submariners throughout World War II.

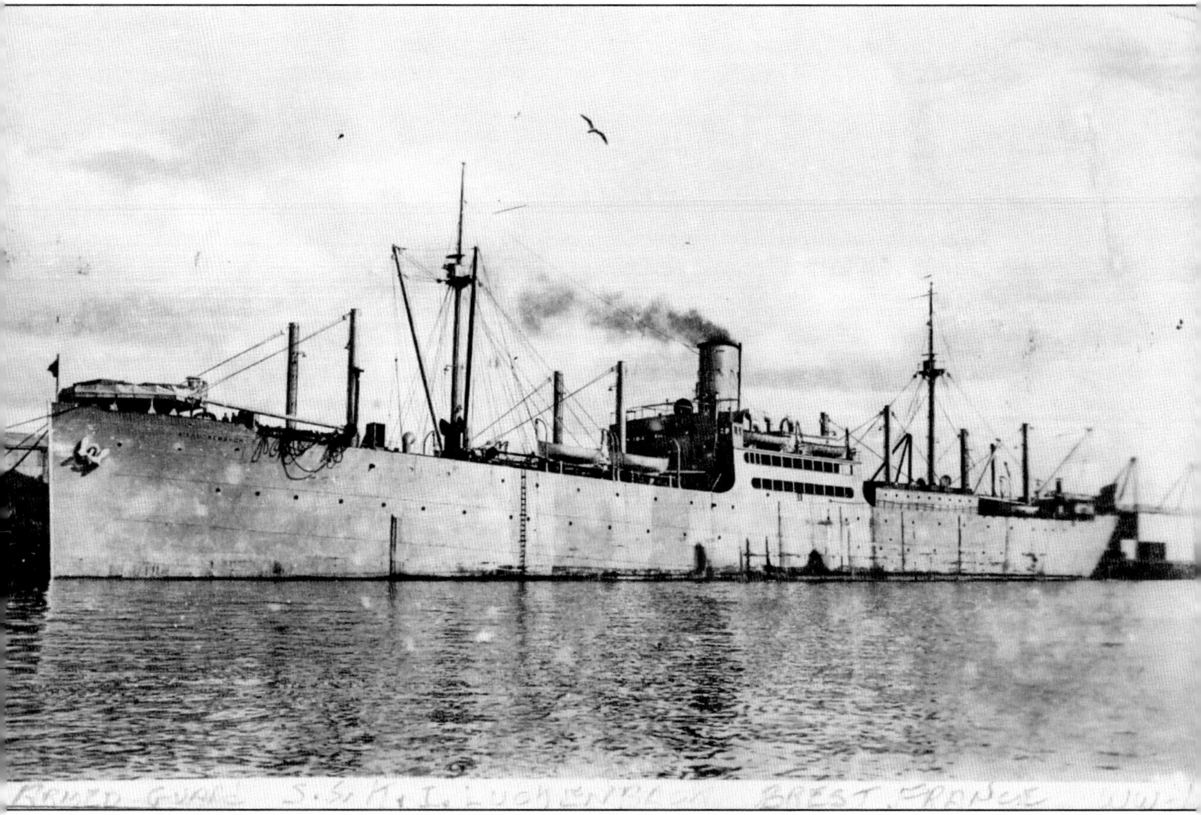

Between 1916 and 1919, the shipyard built seven freighters for the Luckenbach Steamship Company. Each was named for a member of the Luckenbach family. During World War I, the US Navy requisitioned five of the seven ships. After completing two trips to France with cargo, *K.I. Luckenbach* was used as a troop transport for the remainder of her war service. From December 1918 to September 1919, she completed three trips from Europe to the United States with returning soldiers. This real-photo postcard was taken by a member of the crew while the ship was docked at Brest, France. Located at the northwest corner of France, the port of Brest was frequently used for the arrival and departure of troops. After the war, *K.I. Luckenbach* was returned to civilian use, serving until 1954 when she was scrapped.

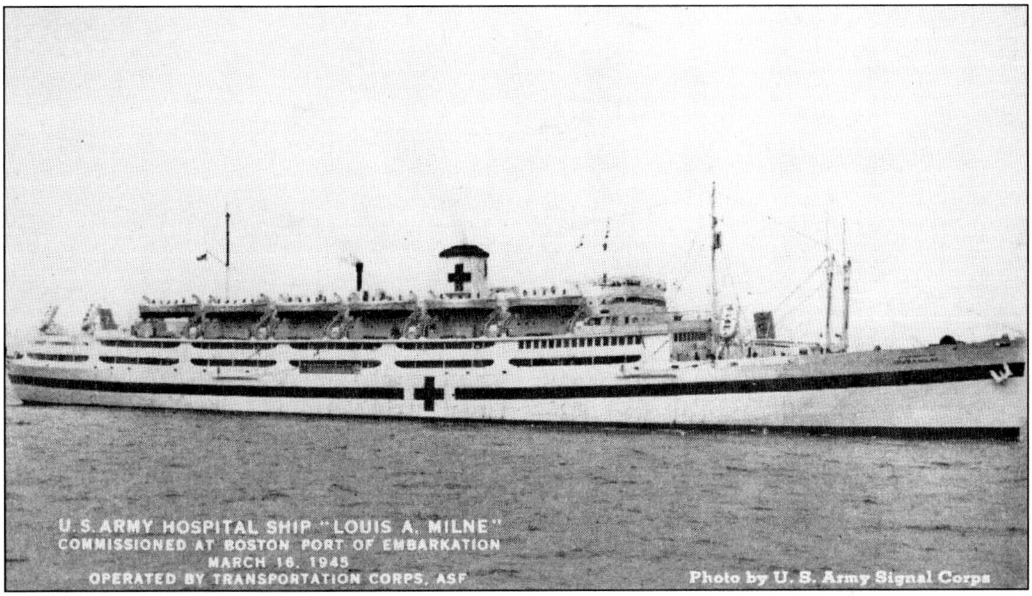

The American National Red Cross issued this postcard in an effort to raise funds for the organization during World War II. It featured *Louis A. Milne*, a US Army hospital ship that served in the Atlantic and Pacific theaters in 1945–1946. She was originally built at Quincy in 1919 as SS *Lewis Luckenbach*, a 527-foot cargo carrier.

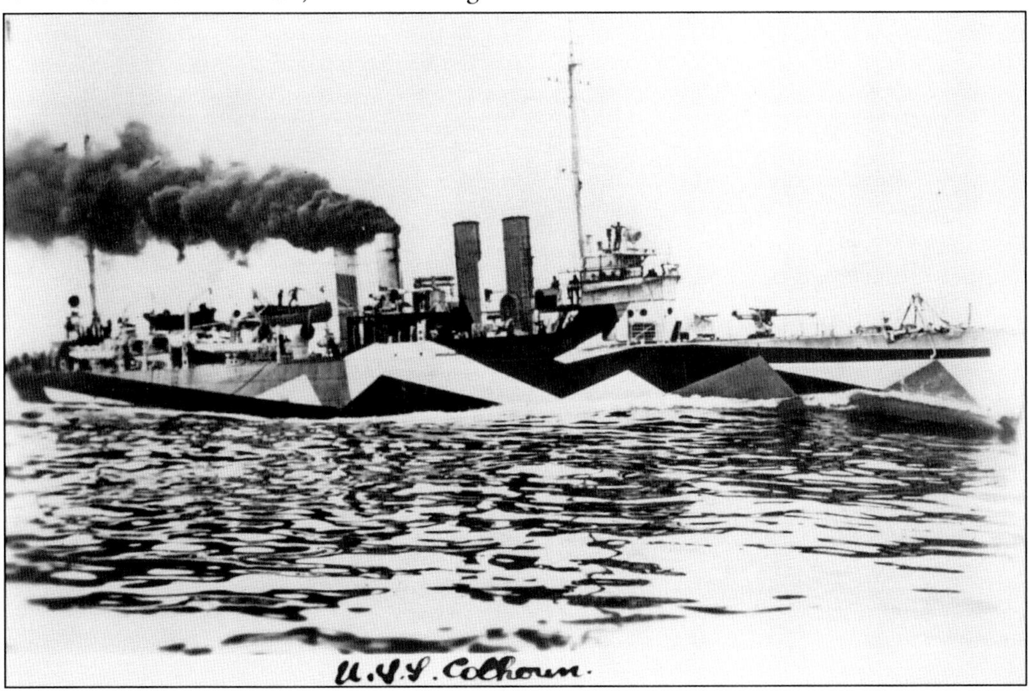

Wickes class destroyer USS *Colhoun* (DD-85) was launched in February 1918 and commissioned four months later. She was photographed in her dazzle camouflage, which was painted on the ship to confuse the enemy. Decommissioned for 18 years, she was converted to a high-speed transport (APD-2) in 1940 and was sunk by the Japanese off Guadalcanal on August 30, 1942, with a loss of 51 men.

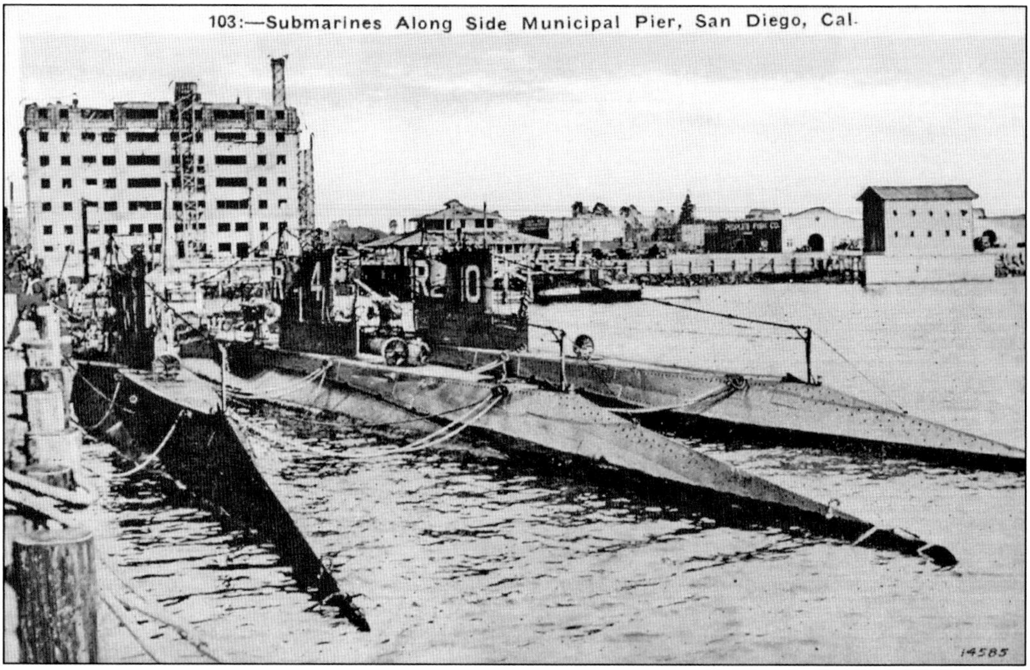

The *R* submarines arrived in California for the first time in June 1921. They were depicted in this early-1920s postcard while the submarines were docked in San Diego. Leaving California in 1923, they were based at Pearl Harbor until late 1930. All but two of the *R* submarines built at Quincy survived until the end of World War II. They were decommissioned shortly after the war.

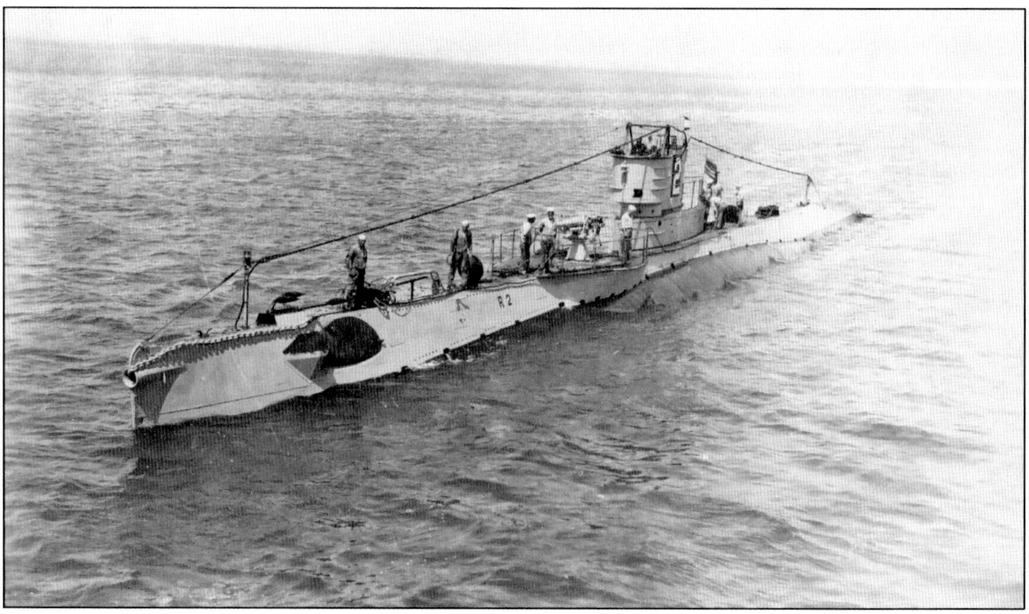

USS *R-2* (SS-79) was commissioned January 1919 with a complement of two officers and 27 enlisted men. This photograph provides a good view of the three-inch/50-caliber deck gun to the left of the bridge and crewmen performing maintenance on the submarine. The *R* submarines were 186 feet long with a surface speed of 13.5 knots and 10.5 knots submerged.

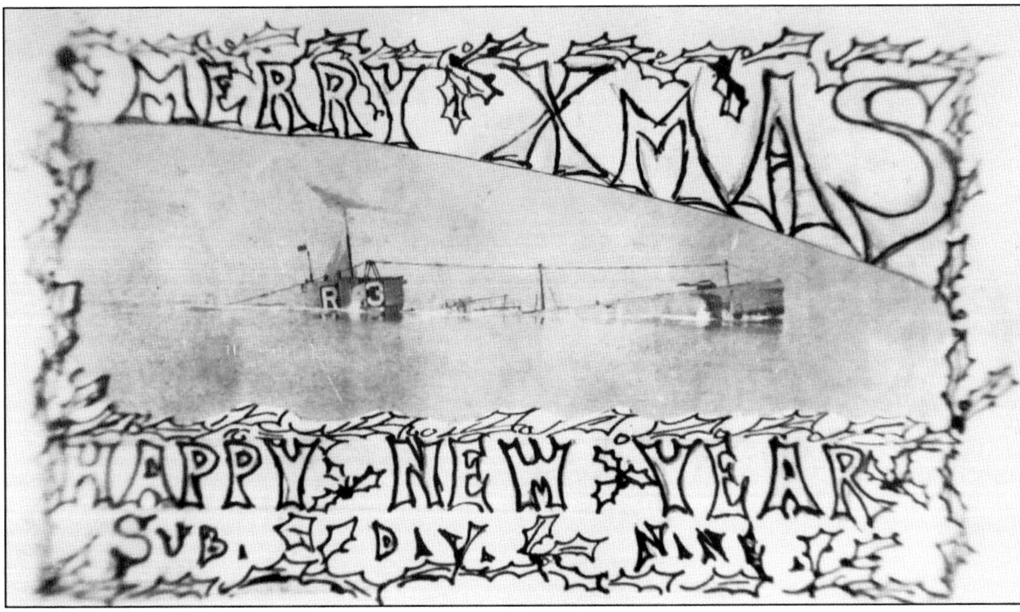

This Christmas postcard was issued not long after USS *R-3* (SS-80) was commissioned in April 1919. She was assigned to Submarine Division Nine at New London, Connecticut. In 1941, *R-3* was transferred to the Royal Navy, serving as HMS *P-511*. Returned to the US Navy in 1944, *R-3* was scrapped in Scotland in 1948.

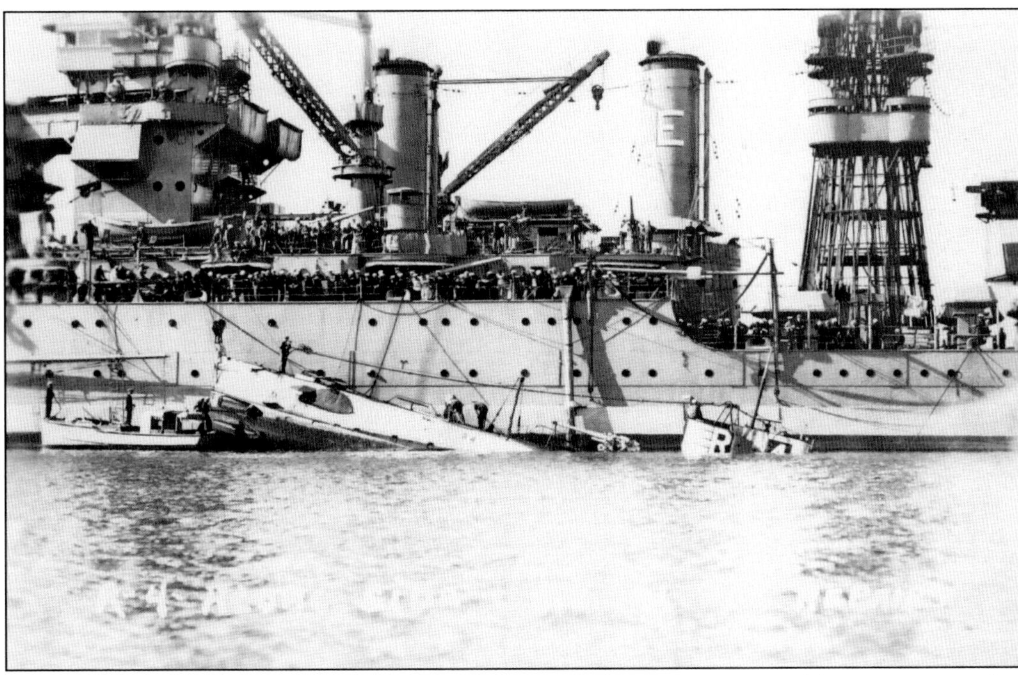

In the early 1920s, USS *R-4* (SS-81) was photographed alongside USS *California* (BB-44) when the submarine needed repairs. It must have been an unscheduled stop, as it would have been highly unusual for a submarine to be tied up to a battleship. Perhaps that explains why the deck of *California* was filled with sailors watching the action.

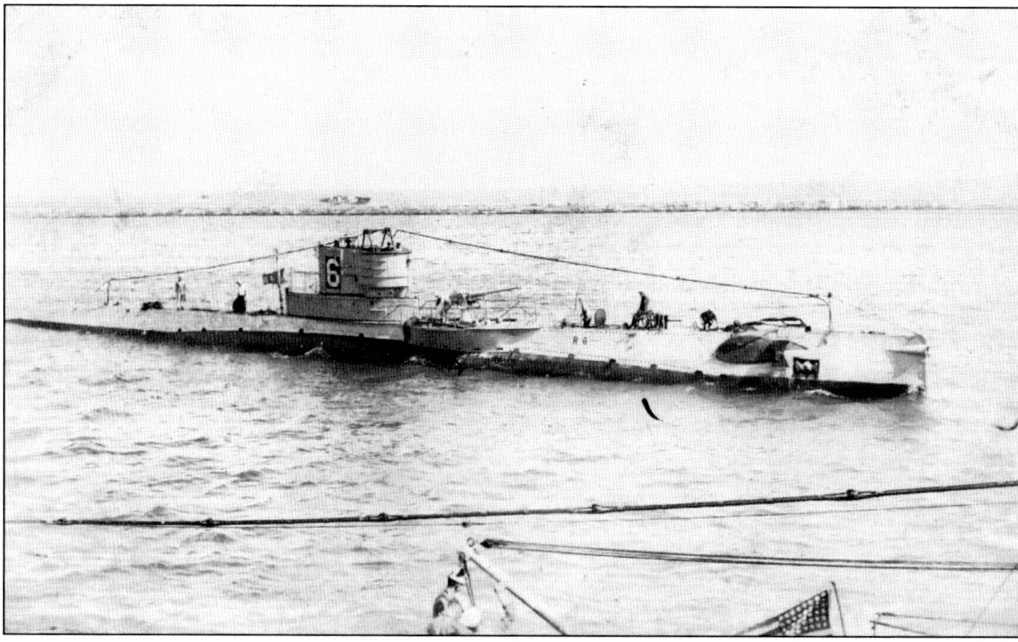

USS *R-6* (SS-83) was a hard luck submarine. Shortly after being commissioned in May 1919, she ran aground in a gale at the entrance to New London Harbor. In 1921, while based in San Pedro, California, *R-6* sank due to a malfunction in one of her torpedo tubes. She was raised with the help of *R-10*, submarine tender USS *Alert*, and tug *Cardinal*. Two of the crew died in the incident; they were the only men on board at the time. After successful repairs, *R-6* was used in a 1923 silent movie, *The Eleventh Hour*, starring Buck Jones and Alan Hale. During World War II, she patrolled the Atlantic coast for German U-boats. A real survivor, *R-6* was finally scrapped in 1946.

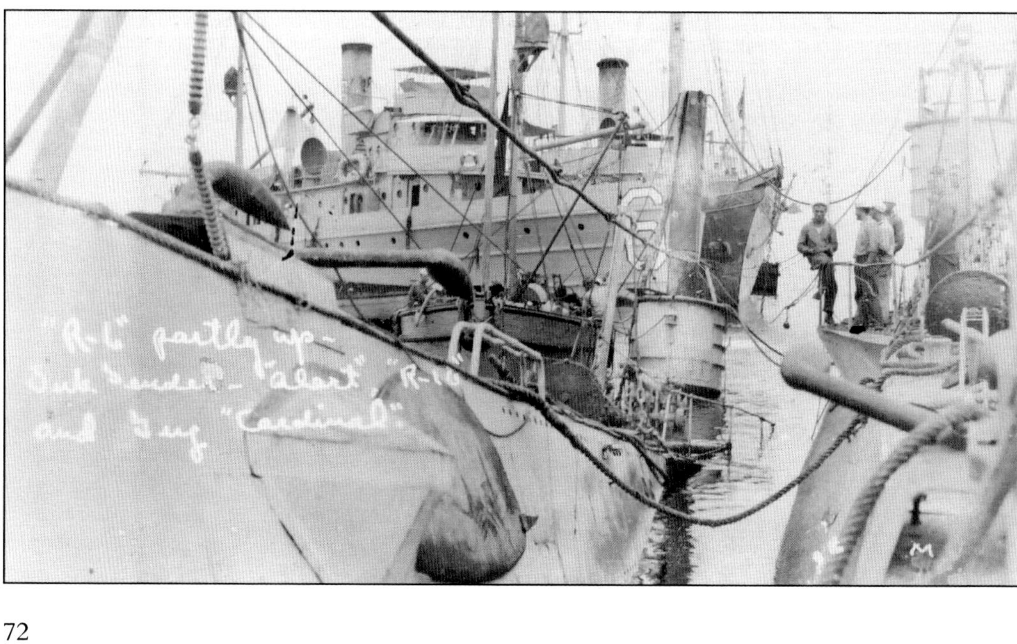

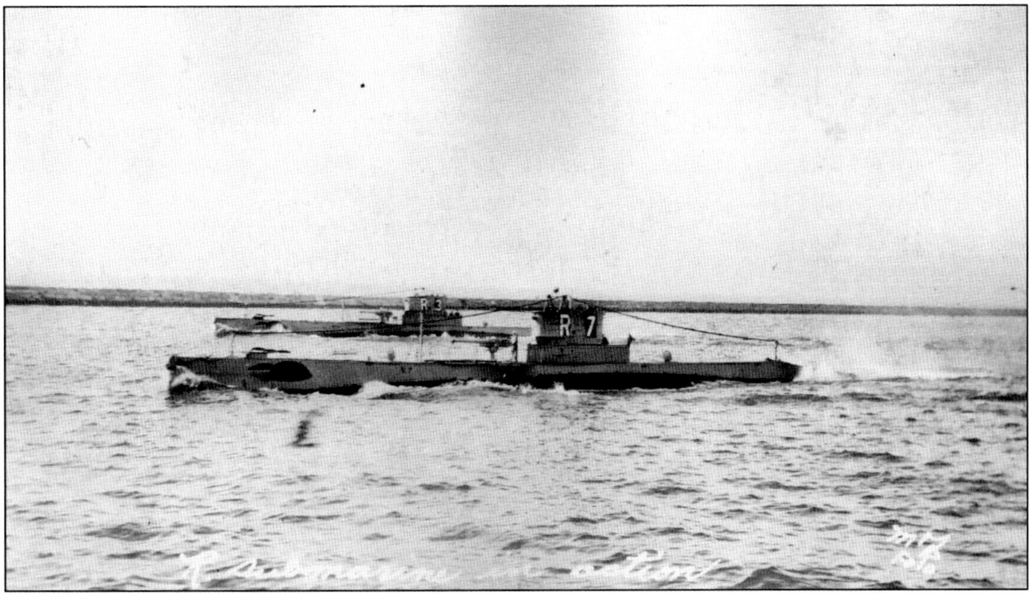

This real-photo postcard is entitled "R Submarines in Action." The photograph captured USS *R-7* (SS-84) and USS *R-3* (SS-80) in the open ocean. In May 1942, *R-7* patrolled the waters between Bermuda and New England. She spotted a U-boat and fired four torpedoes but did not score a hit, eventually losing contact with the enemy.

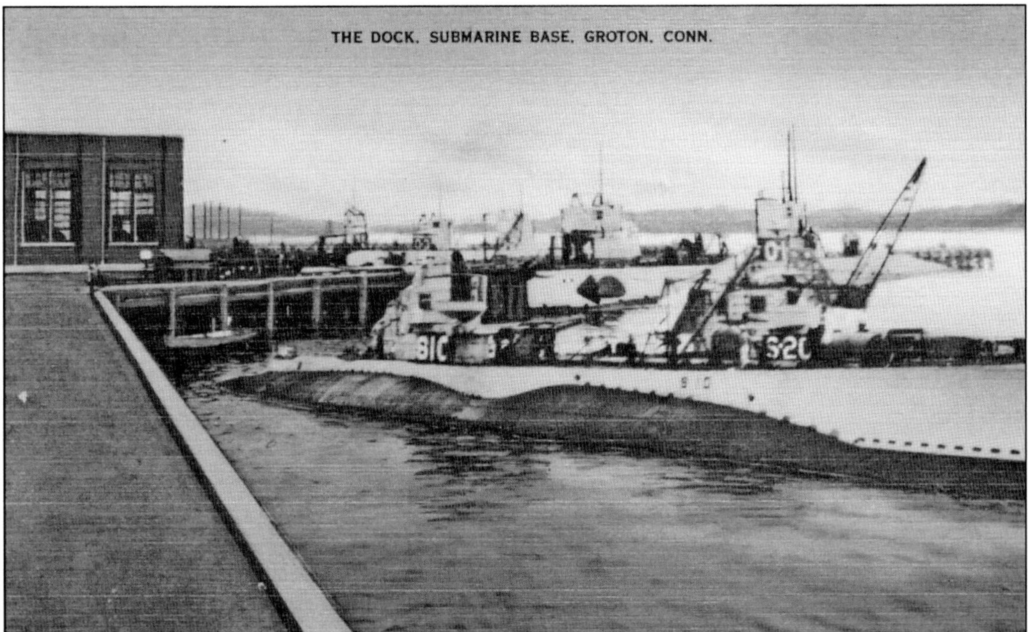

For most of the 1920s, USS *S-20* (SS-125) was stationed in New London, Connecticut. During the 1930s, she divided her time between Hawaii, the Panama Canal, and Guantanamo. *S-20* served during World War II, mostly as a patrol and training ship. In this view, *S-20* was docked at the Groton Connecticut Submarine Base with two other Quincy-built submarines, *O-3* and *O-4*.

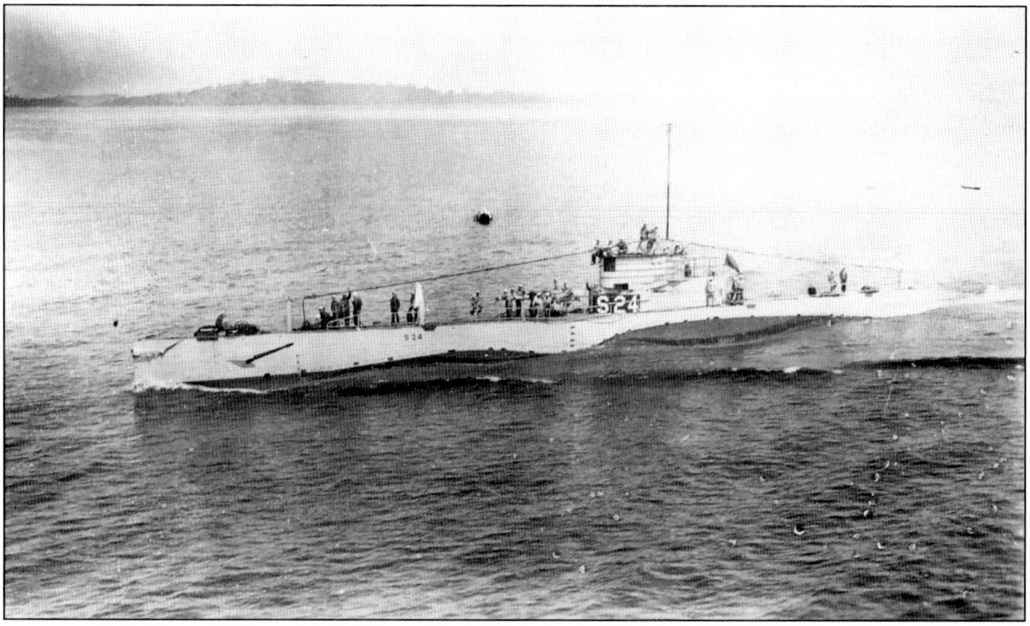

The keel of submarine *S-24* (SS-129) was laid down in November 1918. Commissioned in August 1923, *S-24* operated in the Caribbean and Panama Canal area until 1925. From 1931 to 1938, *S-24* was based at Pearl Harbor. She was transferred to the Royal Navy in 1942 and renamed HMS *P555*. Returned to the US Navy after the war, *S-24* served until 1947.

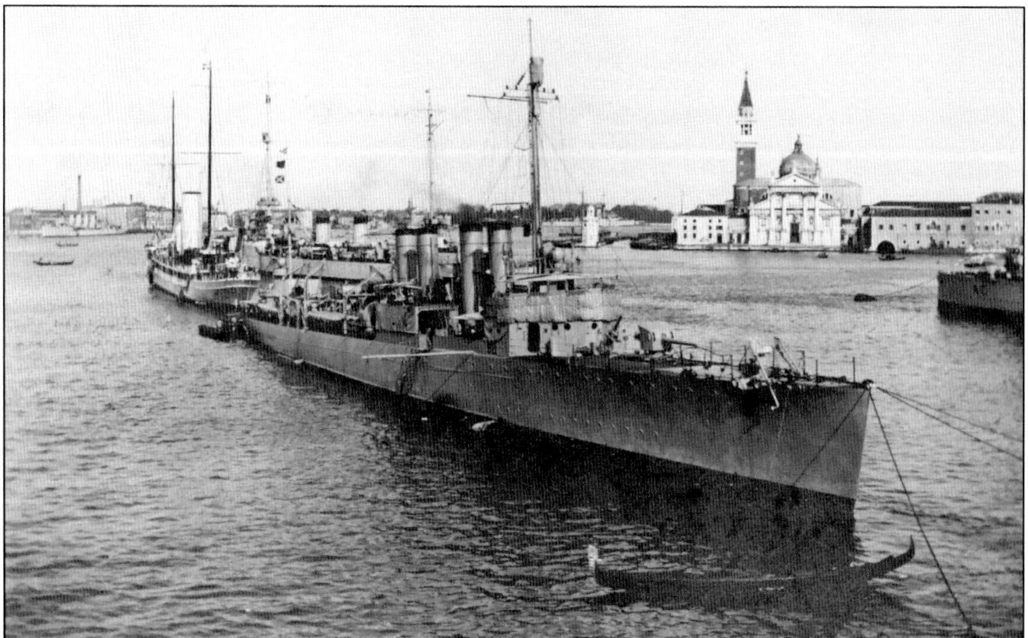

If a man joined the Navy to see the world, he could not ask for a better place than Venice, Italy. A gondola passed the bow of destroyer USS *Israel* (DD-98) as she was anchored in the harbor. Commissioned in September 1918, *Israel* operated out of Venice transporting men and supplies. In 1920, she was refitted as a light minelayer (DM-3), serving until 1922 when she was decommissioned.

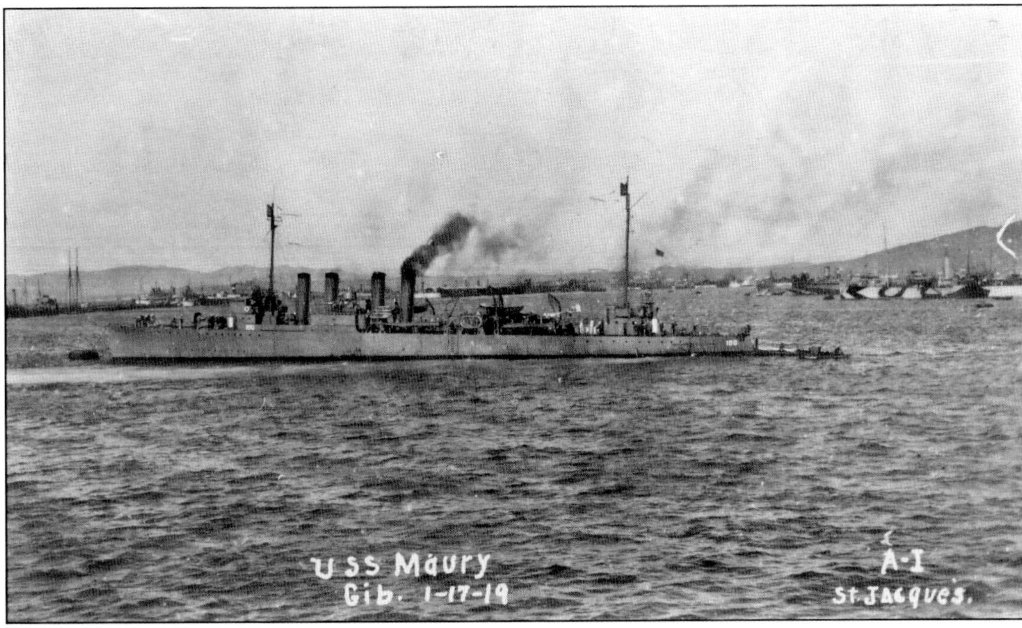

Wickes class destroyer USS *Maury* (DD-100) was commissioned in September 1918. This view was taken in Gibraltar on January 17, 1919, before she reported for duty in the Adriatic. *Maury* cleared mines that were a threat to shipping as well as distributing food to the Balkans. In 1920, she was overhauled and reclassified as a light minelayer (DM-5). She was decommissioned in 1930 and scrapped in 1934.

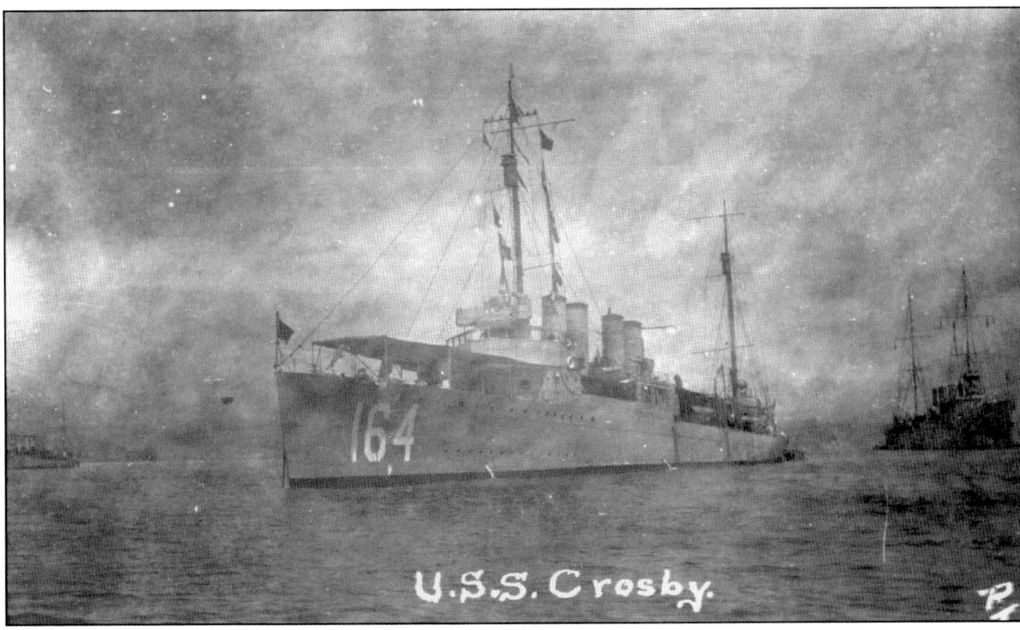

In May 1919, USS *Crosby* (DD-164) participated with dozens of American destroyers in aiding the Navy Curtiss NC-4 Flying Boat on the first successful transatlantic flight. After World War I, she was decommissioned for 17 years, then converted to a high-speed transport (APD-17). During World War II, *Crosby* landed troops throughout the Pacific theater from 1943 to 1945.

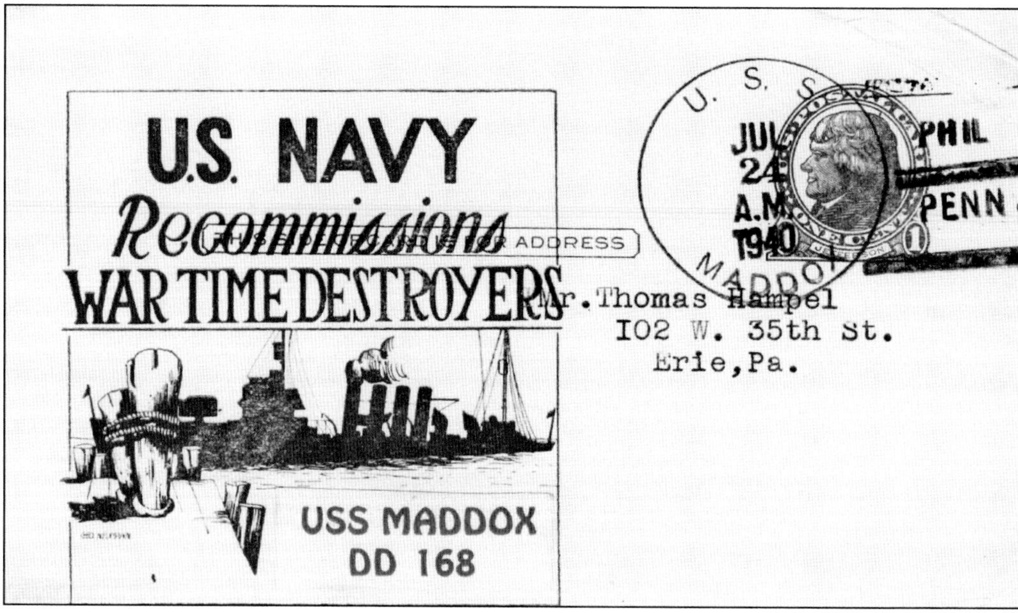

USS *Maddox* (DD-168) has a fascinating history as a ship with three distinct lives. Built as a Wickes class destroyer in 1918, she served during World War I but was inactive from 1922 to 1940. This postcard marked the recommissioning of *Maddox* in 1940. Only three months later, she was transferred to Great Britain and renamed HMS *Georgetown*. In August 1944, the Soviet Union took possession, renaming her *Doblestny*.

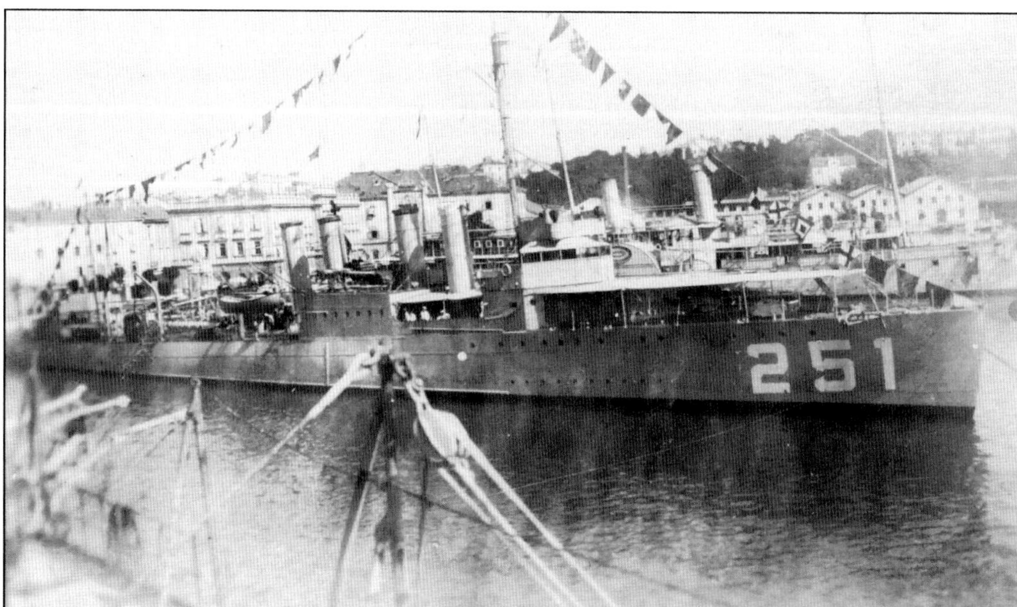

Commissioned in April 1919, USS *Belknap* (DD-251) was the first Clemson class destroyer built at the shipyard. During World War II, *Belknap* was converted into a high-speed transport (APD-34). On January 11, 1945, she was damaged beyond repair by a Japanese kamikaze attack in Lingayen Gulf in the Philippines and scrapped at the end of the war.

Six

Squantum Victory Yard 1917 to 1920

In order to accommodate construction of all the destroyers ordered by the US Navy, Bethlehem Steel decided to expand the manufacturing capability of the Fore River Shipyard to Squantum, located at the northern end of Quincy. The subsoil in Squantum was suitable for shipbuilding, and it had the advantage of being close to Quincy Point and Boston. Operations at the new "Victory Yard" began in October 1917 on 70 acres of land. The US government spent $14 million getting the new shipyard up and running, a huge sum of money at that time.

The Victory Yard was created to build only one type of ship, the Clemson class destroyer. Thirty-five were built in a yard that was so efficient that it took Squantum less than half the time it took the Fore River Shipyard to complete the same class of destroyer. It was mass production at its best. Over one in five of all the Clemson class destroyers built at American shipyards were constructed at Squantum, quite an achievement considering the shipyard was built from scratch only two years before. The Squantum and Fore River Shipyards produced so many destroyers so quickly that the US Navy was forced to tie up many of the ships at the Boston Navy Yard because there were not enough crews available to staff them.

The first destroyer completed at the Victory Yard was commissioned by the US Navy on November 30, 1918, just 19 days after the end of Word War I. Without the war, there was no longer a need for the Squantum facility. Nearly 8,000 workers would have to be reassigned or face the prospect of unemployment. By June 1920, the Victory Yard was shuttered and scheduled for demolition. Such was the boom-bust cycle of the shipbuilding industry.

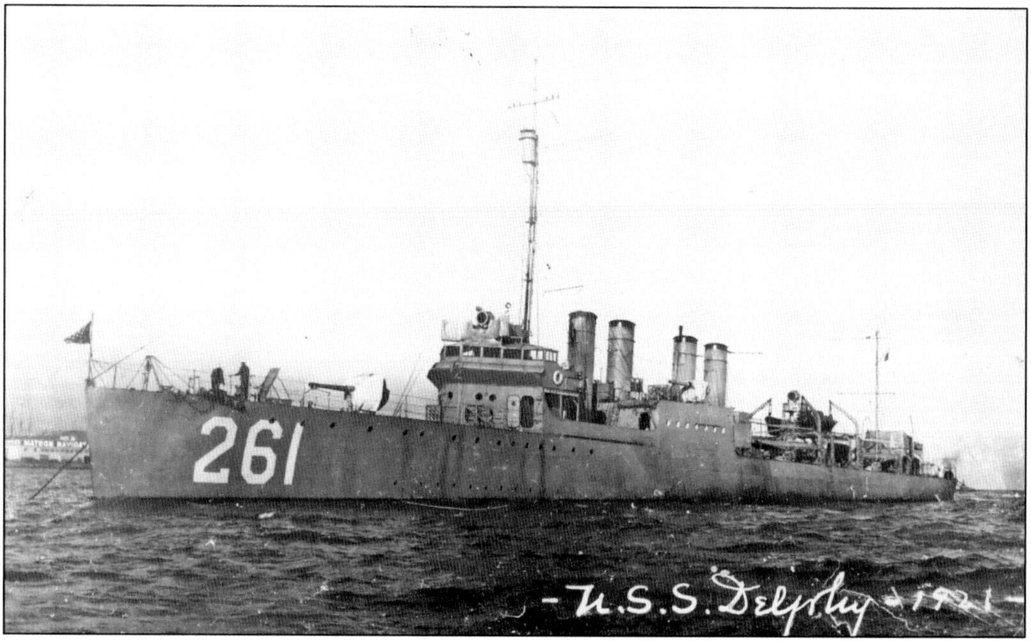

USS *Delphy* (DD-261) entered the US Navy as the first destroyer built at Squantum. She measured 314 feet long, carrying a complement of 114 men. Her speed was a brisk 35 knots. *Delphy* was photographed in 1921 while based in San Diego, California. Her quiet deployment ended on September 8, 1923. *Delphy* was the flagship of a destroyer convoy that ran aground in a dense fog near Santa Barbara, California. The tragedy, known as the Honda Point Disaster, resulted in the largest loss of US Navy vessels in peacetime. *Delphy* can be seen capsized in the lower right corner of the postcard. Seven ships and 23 crew were lost, including three crew from *Delphy*. Decommissioned the following month, she was scrapped in 1925.

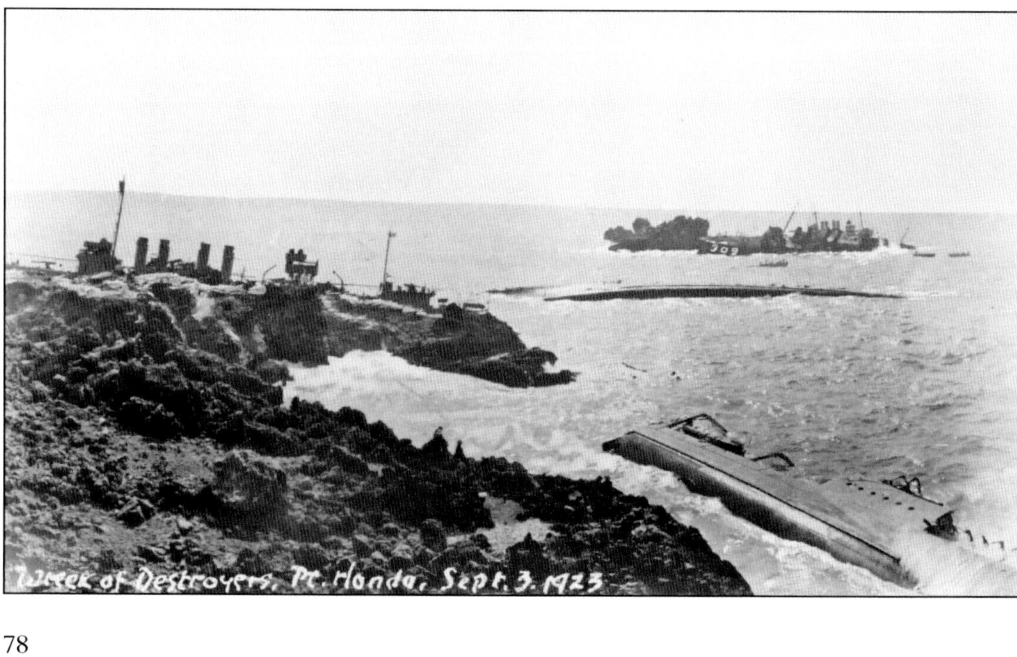

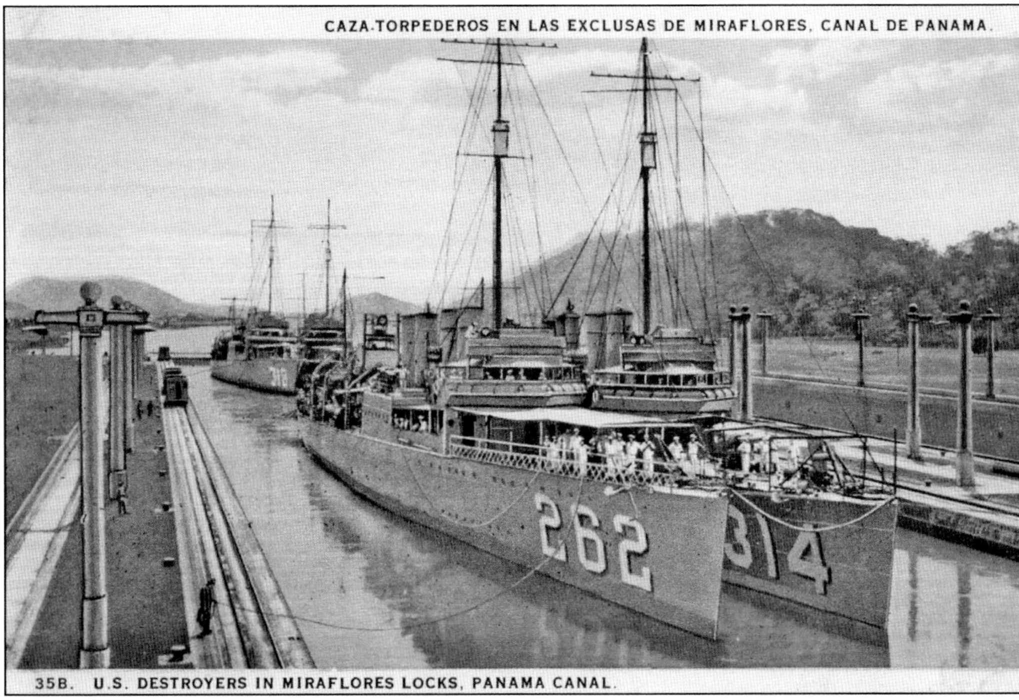

Commissioned in March 1919, USS *McDermut* (DD-262) was captured on this early-1920s postcard transiting the Miraflores Locks in the Panama Canal. In 1924, *McDermut* appeared in the Buster Keaton movie *The Navigator.* The following year she visited New Zealand and Australia. *McDermut* was decommissioned in 1929 and scrapped in 1932.

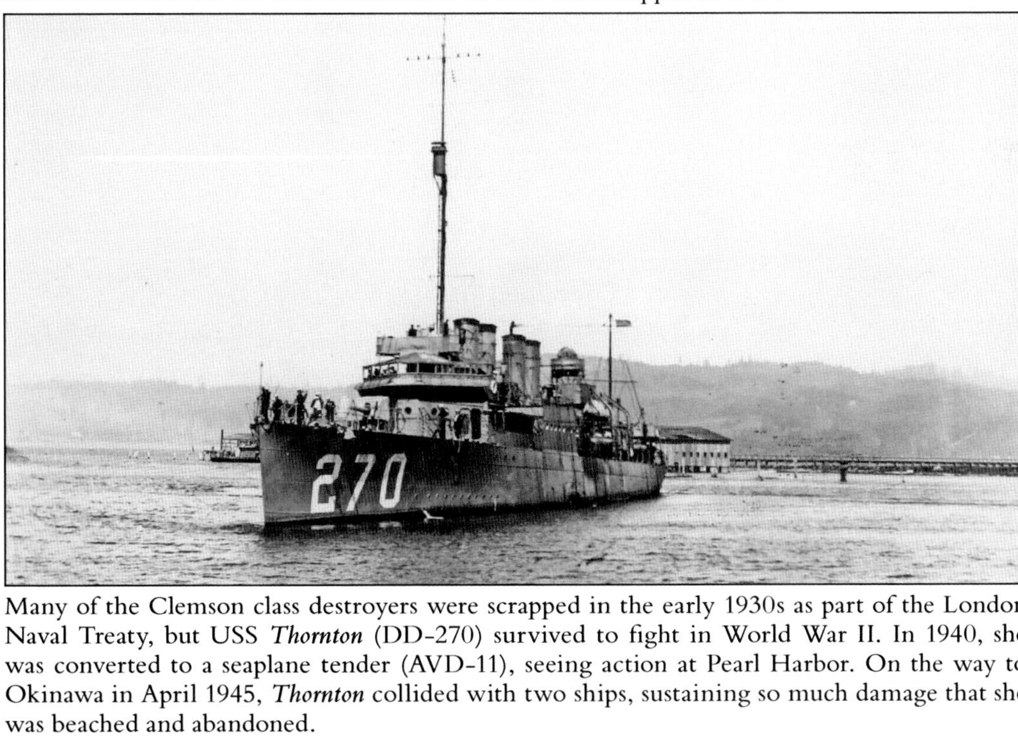

Many of the Clemson class destroyers were scrapped in the early 1930s as part of the London Naval Treaty, but USS *Thornton* (DD-270) survived to fight in World War II. In 1940, she was converted to a seaplane tender (AVD-11), seeing action at Pearl Harbor. On the way to Okinawa in April 1945, *Thornton* collided with two ships, sustaining so much damage that she was beached and abandoned.

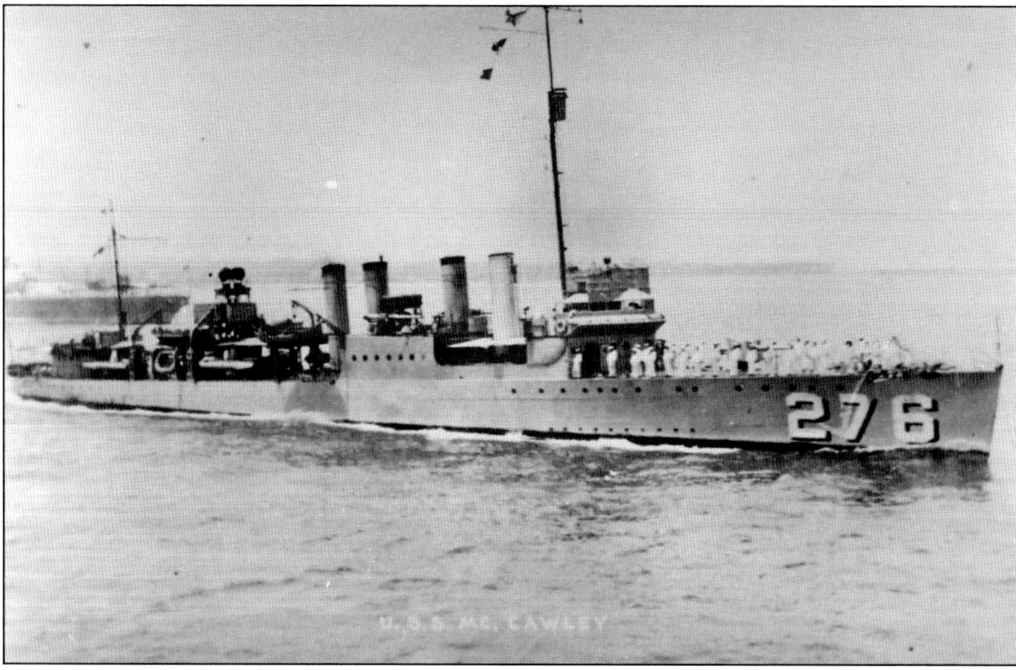

USS *McCawley* (DD-276) was named for Col. Charles McCawley, who chose "Semper Fidelis," Latin for "Always Faithful," as the official Marine Corps motto in 1883. After a shakedown cruise in 1919, *McCawley* sailed for San Diego, California, where she spent the better part of the next decade with the Pacific Fleet in exercises and training. She was scrapped in 1931.

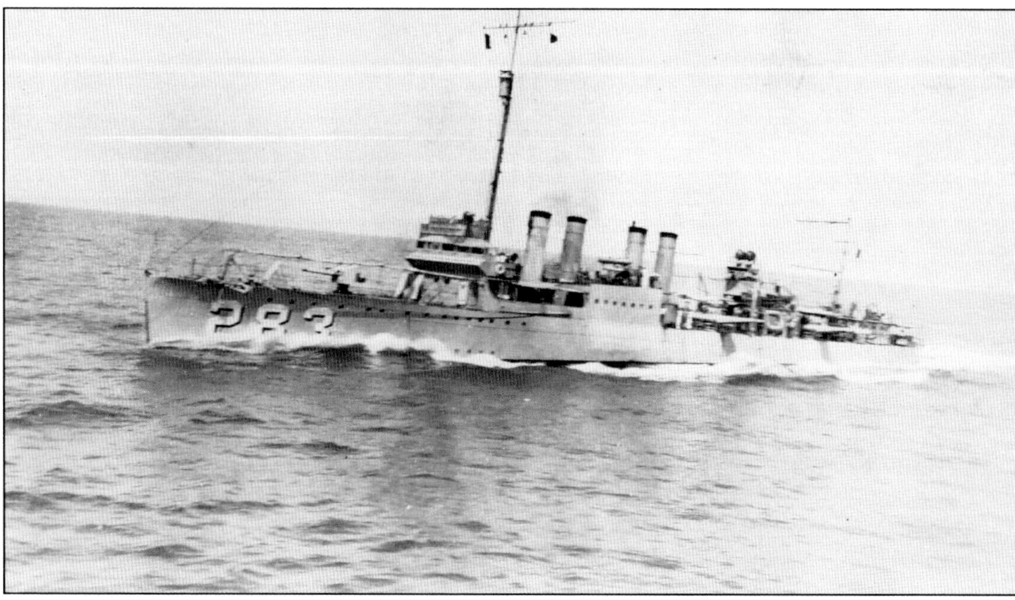

Commissioned in December 1919, USS *Breck* (DD-283) served with the Atlantic Fleet, Destroyer Squadron One out of Newport, Rhode Island. In 1926–1927, she engaged in target exercises on a trip to Europe and North Africa. Upon return to Newport, *Breck* participated in war games and fleet maneuvers until being decommissioned in 1930.

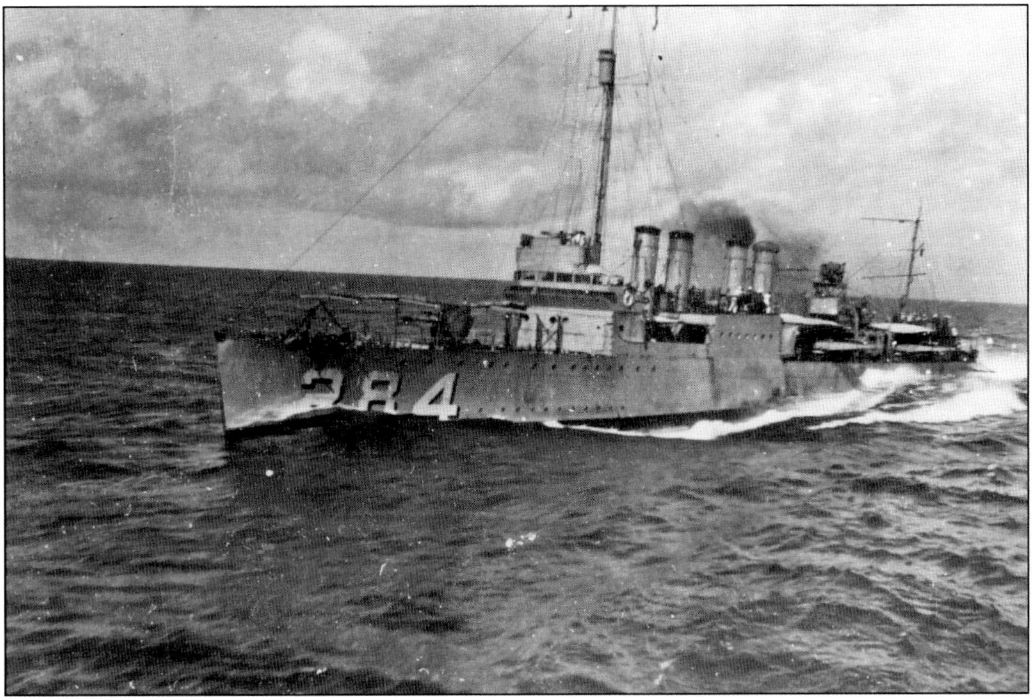

When Charles Lindbergh made his historic flight from New York to Paris in May 1927, USS *Isherwood* (DD-284) was off the coast of France on a goodwill tour to Europe. She provided escort to USS *Memphis* (CL-13), which carried Lindbergh back to the United States. Returned to Boston in July 1927, *Isherwood* was used in training and fleet maneuvers until 1929.

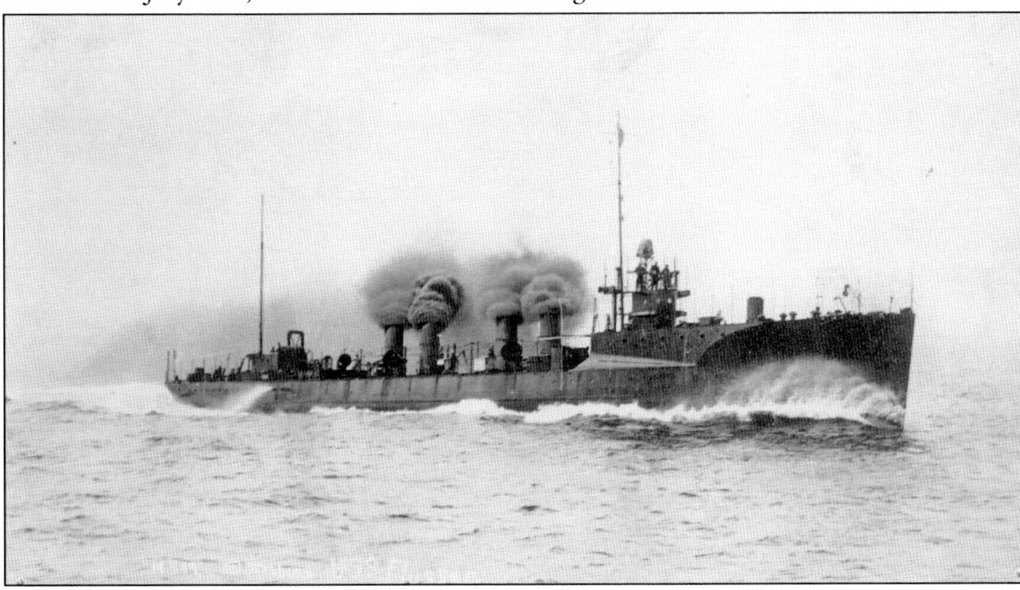

Nathaniel Stebbins took the photograph of USS *Flusser* (DD-289) that graces this postcard. Stebbins was famous for his photographs of American ships, working as a commercial photographer until his death in 1922. *Flusser* sailed for Europe in 1924, visiting Italy, Germany, Latvia, and several other countries before returning to the United States a year later. She was scrapped in 1930.

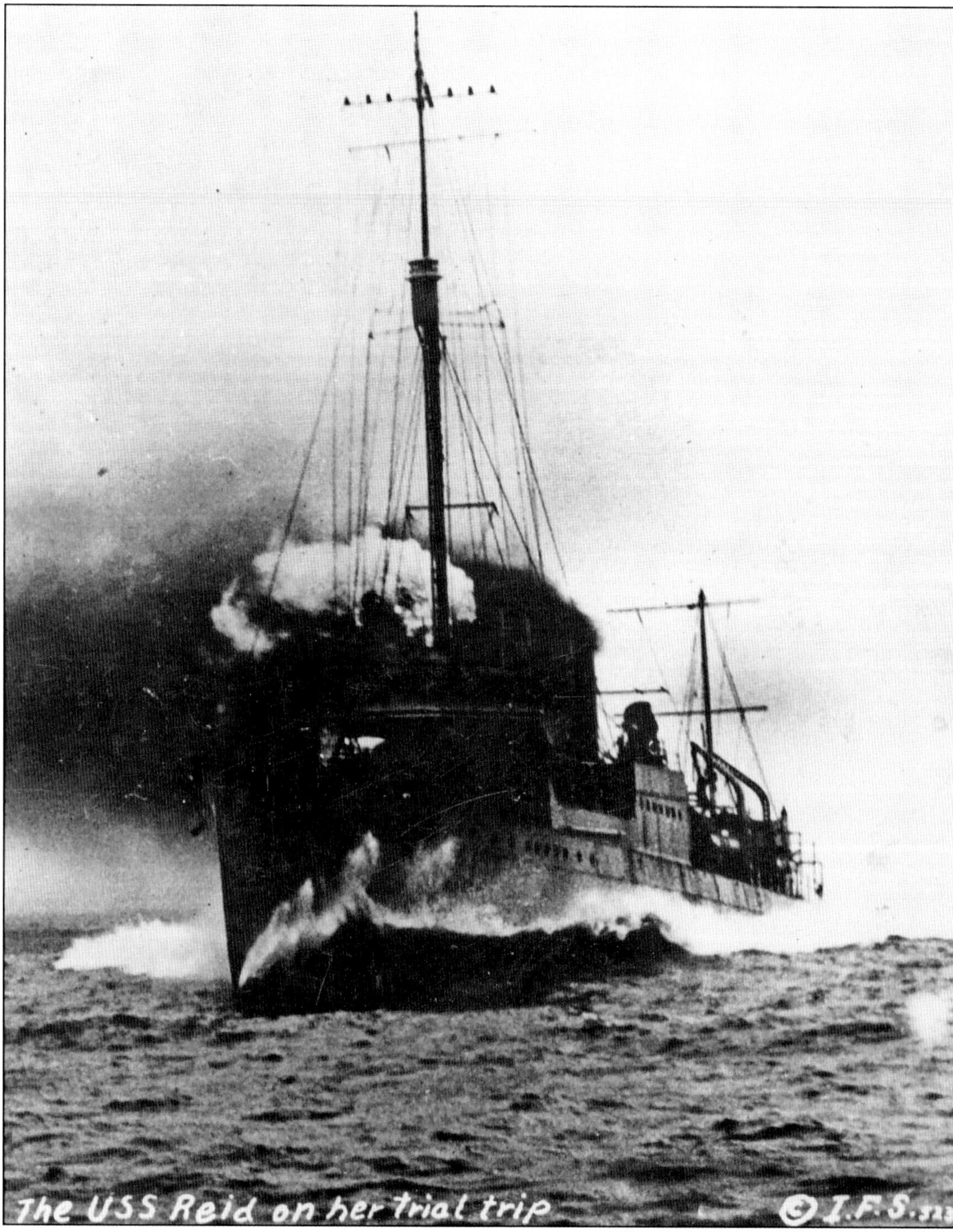

Construction of USS *Reid* (DD-292) established a world record—only 45.5 working days elapsed from laying the keel to delivery to the US Navy. The ship was commissioned in December 1919, assigned to Squadron Three of the Atlantic Fleet, and deployed mostly in the Caribbean and Atlantic coast. In 1924, *Reid* sailed to Europe, visiting the Baltics, Iceland, France, Greece, Turkey, Tunisia, and Egypt before returning home in 1925 for an overhaul. In 1927, *Reid* participated in the Second Nicaraguan Campaign, supporting Marines who were ashore protecting American citizens and seizing weapons. She was decommissioned in 1930 and scrapped in 1931.

Seven

Between the Wars
1920 to 1940

The end of World War I ushered in a 15-year slowdown at the shipyard. Work for the US Navy receded dramatically, but commercial work on ferries, cruise ships, and freighters saved the shipyard from certain doom. US Navy business would not pick up again until the mid-1930s.

Anticipating a major slowdown, Bethlehem Steel constructed a dry dock in 1919–1920 that would help reduce its dependence on building new ships. It was built at the mouth of Hayward Creek, which straddled Braintree and Quincy. The repair business enabled the shipyard to keep more people employed, as there were no contracts signed to build new ships from 1921 through 1924. In addition, a new building slip was erected for commercial ships and another for battleships that would eventually be critical for World War II production.

In 1931, there were fewer than 5,000 employees at the shipyard, a 67-percent decrease from 15 years earlier. It would get much worse as the Great Depression wore on, with employment declining to only 812 workers in 1933. The shipyard finally emerged from the doldrums after Franklin D. Roosevelt became president. Roosevelt had served as assistant secretary of the Navy from 1913 to 1920 during Woodrow Wilson's presidency. He knew the US Navy needed to be strengthened. Congress passed the Vinson-Trammell Act in 1934, which provided for the replacement of obsolete ships with new construction and an increase in ships up to levels permitted by international arms treaties. Because of this law, in 1936, the Fore River Shipyard won the contract to construct the aircraft carrier USS *Wasp* (CV-7). Finally, when Congress passed the Naval Expansion Act of 1938 calling for a 20-percent increase in the fleet, shipyards across the country recovered from the Great Depression, and the Fore River Shipyard once again produced ships that would help win a world war.

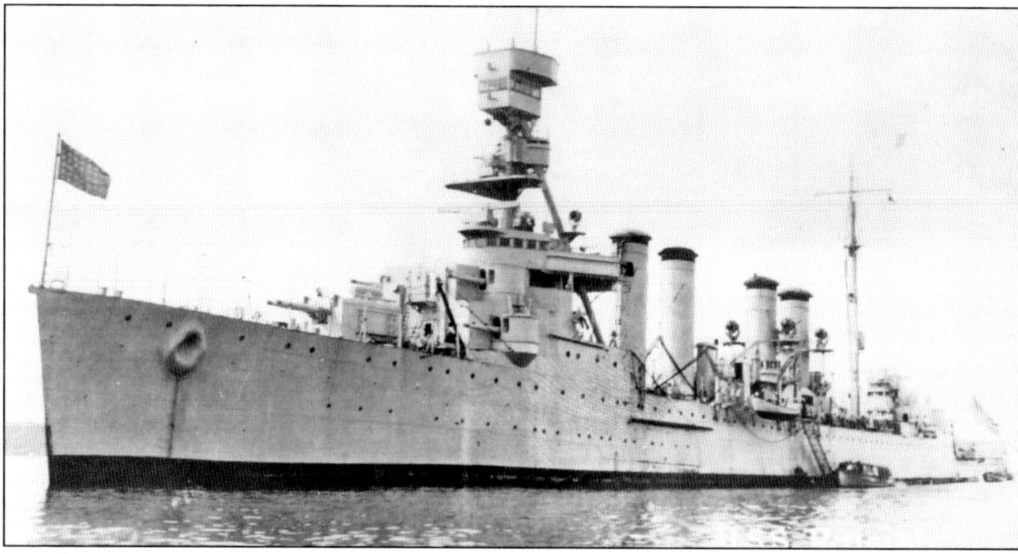

Omaha class light cruiser USS *Raleigh* (CL-7) was commissioned in February 1924. She was stationed at Pearl Harbor on December 7, 1941, and badly damaged in the attack, but miraculously no one was killed and only a few wounded. She was credited with downing five Japanese aircraft that day. *Raleigh* survived and after extensive repairs was sent to the Aleutians in July 1942.

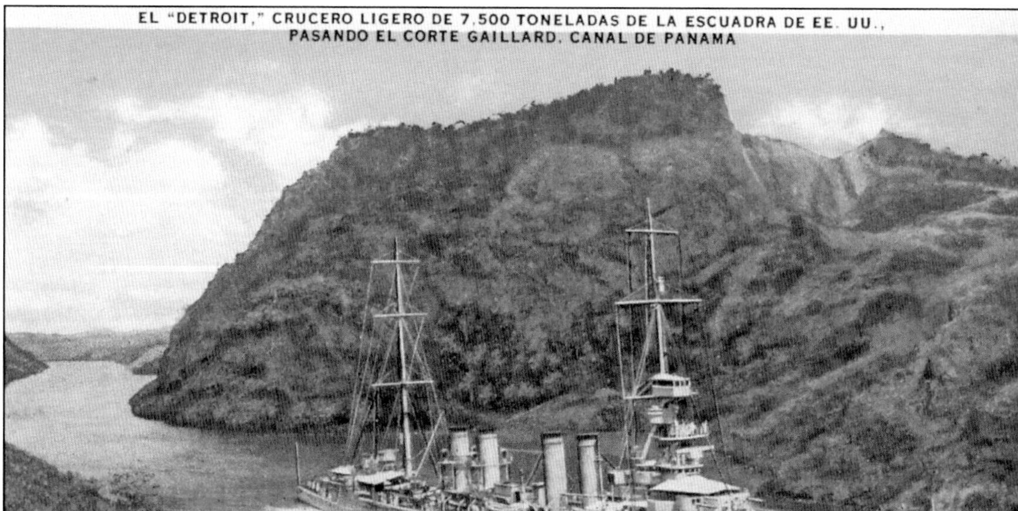

Commissioned in July 1923, USS *Detroit* (CL-8) was a sister ship to USS *Raleigh* (CL-7). As fate would have it, she was present at both Pearl Harbor on December 7, 1941, and Tokyo Bay on September 2, 1945, for the signing of the Japanese surrender. In 1942, *Detroit* was sent to Alaska to impede further penetration of the Aleutians by the Japanese. She spent almost two years in Alaskan waters.

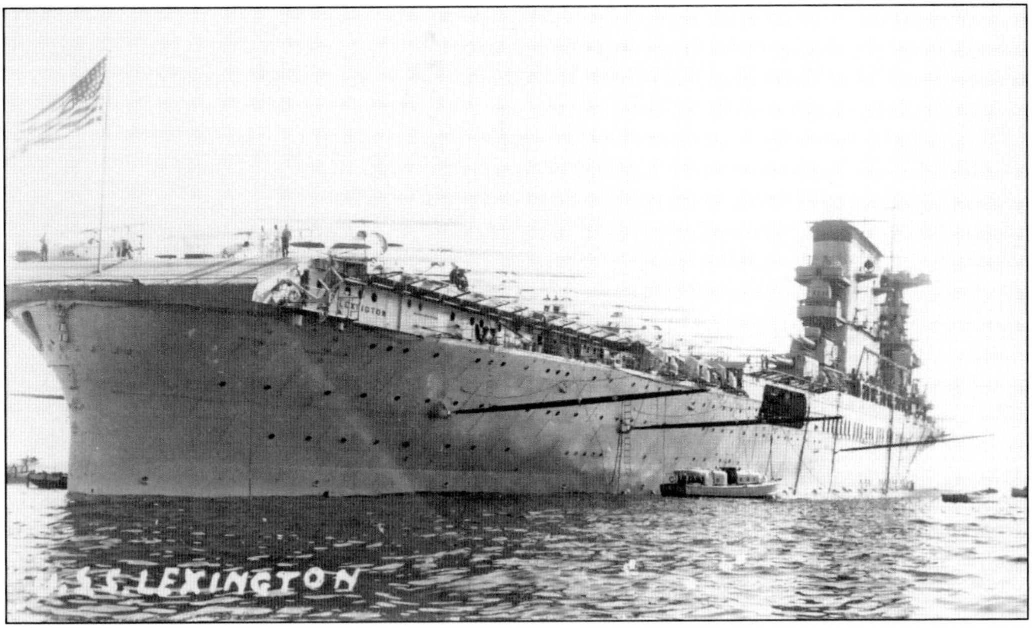

Nicknamed the "Gray Lady," USS *Lexington* (CV-2) entered the US Navy as one of its earliest aircraft carriers. Completed in 1927, *Lexington* was originally ordered as a battle cruiser in 1917. She was on the way to reinforce Midway Island when the Japanese attacked Pearl Harbor. Over the next five months, her airplanes shot down many enemy aircraft, until *Lexington* was sunk at the Battle of the Coral Sea. Since the invention of the picture postcard, nations have used it as a tool to communicate and influence public opinion. The 1942 propaganda postcard from Japan depicts the sinking of *Lexington* on May 8, 1942. The caption on the left reads, "US aircraft carrier Lexington attacked." Text on the bottom reads, "Hawaii westwards at sea, damage to navy ships resulting from battle attacks," followed by the date.

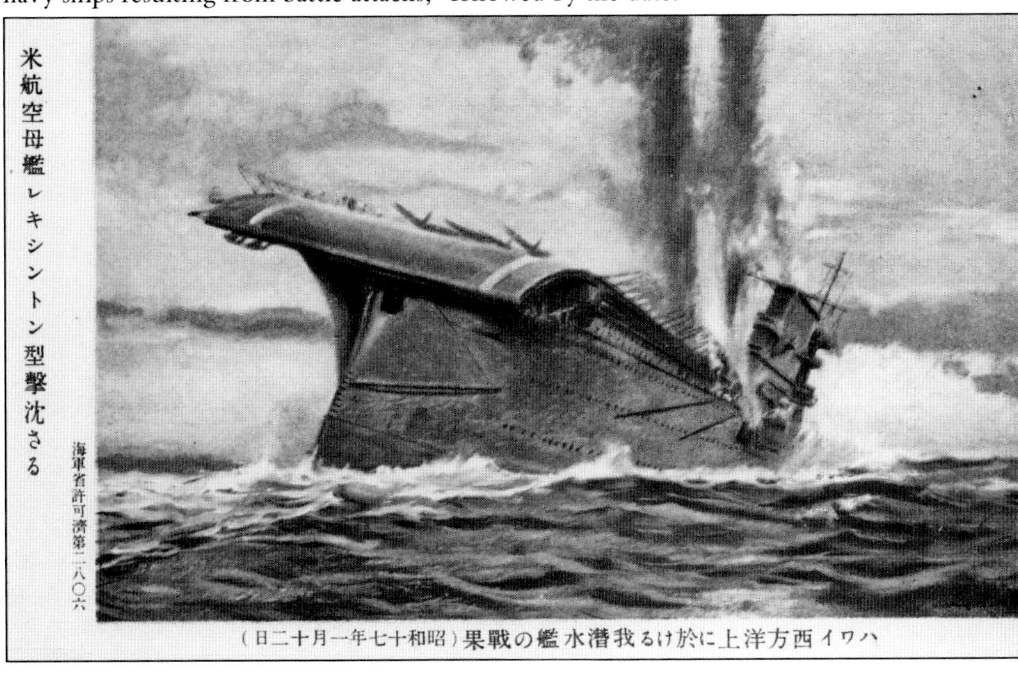

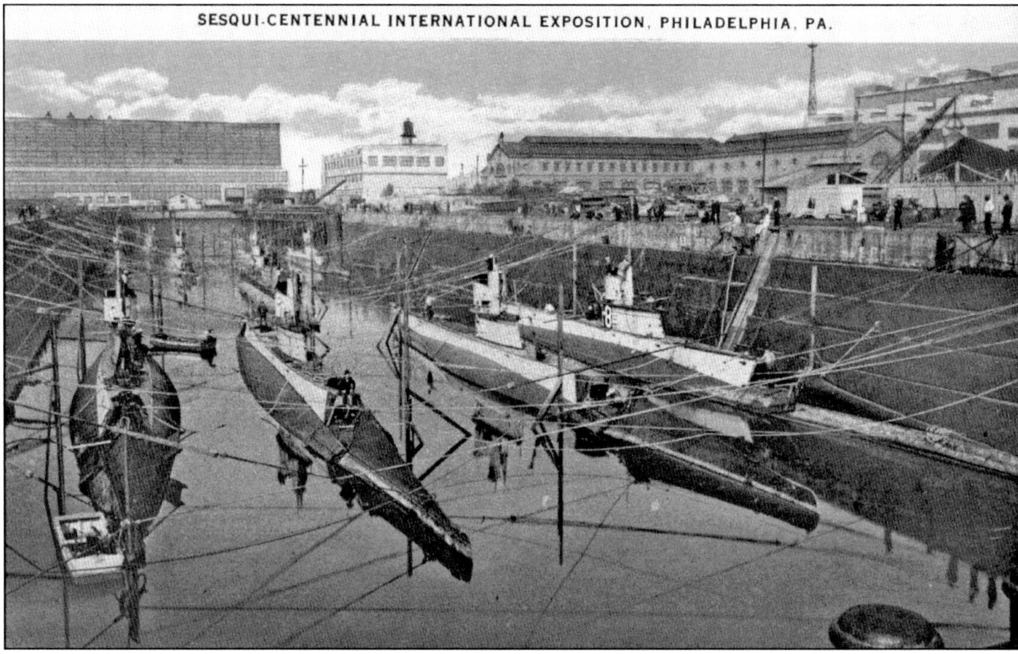

In 1926, the Sesquicentennial International Exposition at Philadelphia, Pennsylvania, published a series of commemorative postcards. One of the postcards featured 11 submarines docked at the League Island Navy Yard. When the Fore River–built submarines were decommissioned after World War I, they were sent to League Island. There was also a large dry dock at the yard, which the submarines frequented for repairs.

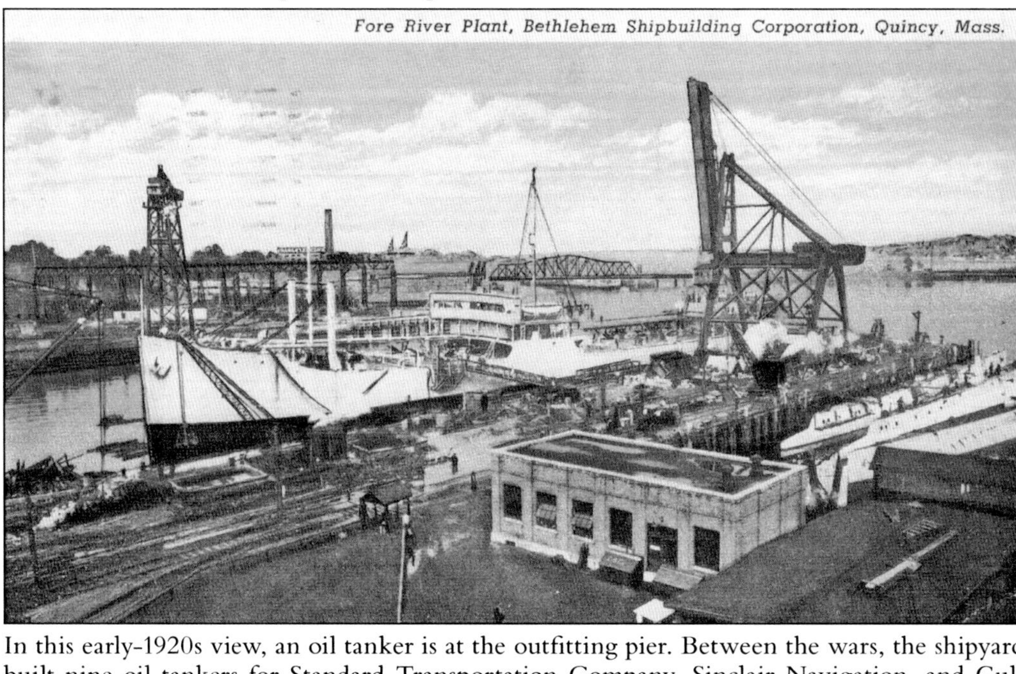

In this early-1920s view, an oil tanker is at the outfitting pier. Between the wars, the shipyard built nine oil tankers for Standard Transportation Company, Sinclair Navigation, and Gulf Refining. All the tankers were over 400 feet long. Four of the nine ships were sunk during World War II—*Wm. Boyce Thompson*, *Virginia Sinclair*, *China Arrow*, and *India Arrow*.

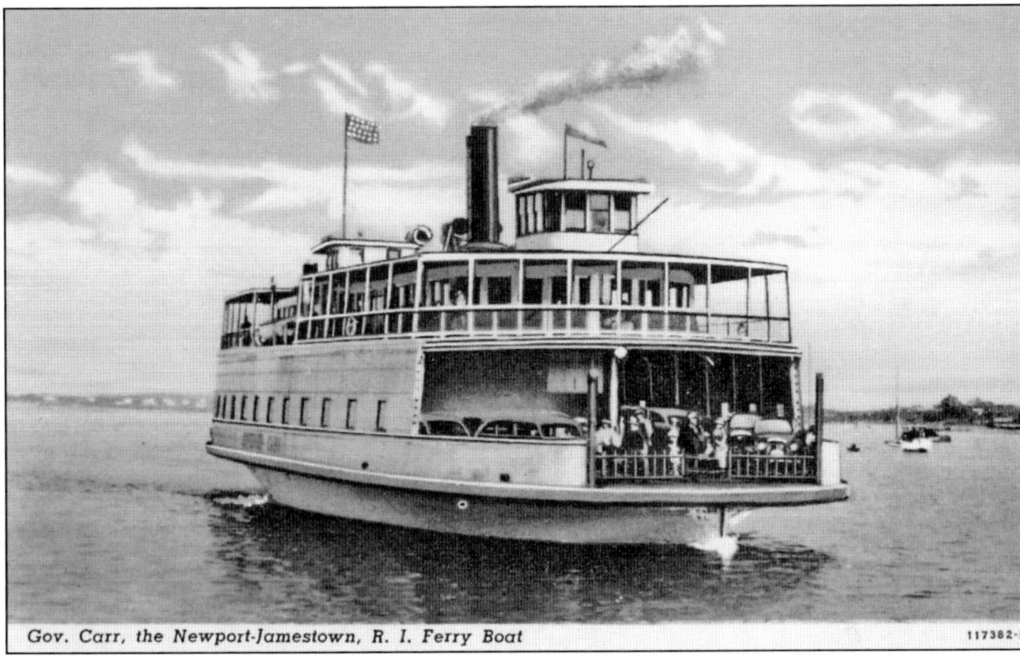

This postcard depicts a beautiful sunny day in Newport as harbor ferry *Governor Carr* steamed to Jamestown, a three-mile ride. The ferry is packed with automobiles, and the people standing at the railing are enjoying views of Narragansett Bay. Built in 1927 for the Jamestown and Newport Company, the ferry served the people of Rhode Island for 34 years.

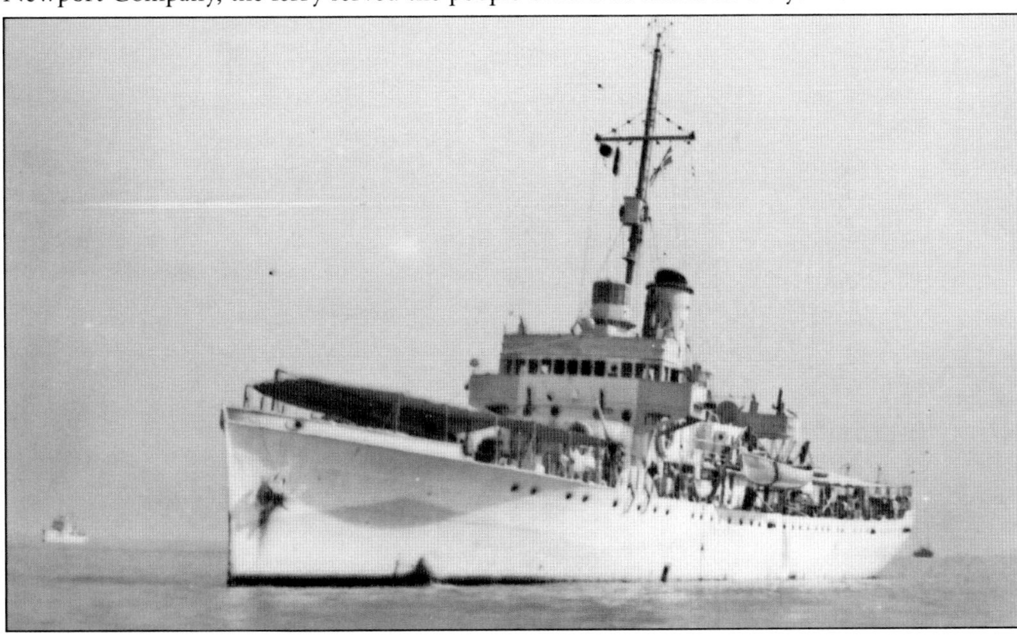

USCG *Chelan* (WPG-45) was the first of five Lake class Coast Guard cutters built at the shipyard in 1928–1929. Her sister ships were *Pontchartrain*, *Tahoe*, *Champlain*, and *Mendota*. Transferred to the Royal Navy in April 1941 and renamed HMS *Lulworth*, she received Battle Honours for service in the Atlantic, North Africa, and Burma. She sank the Italian submarine *Pietro Calvi* in 1942, taking many prisoners.

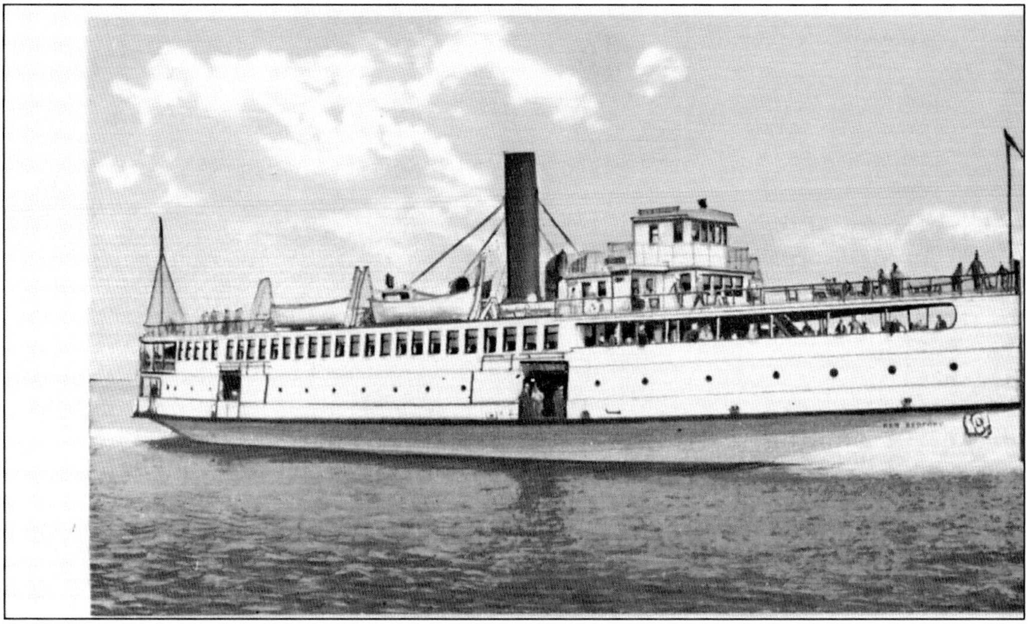

Steamer *New Bedford* joined the New England Steamship Company in 1928. The company was a subsidiary of the New Haven Railroad, the largest operator of steamships from New York City to destinations in New England, including Nantucket Island and Oak Bluffs on Martha's Vineyard. In addition to carrying several hundred passengers, this beautifully decorated steamer carried cargo in the hold to large industrial cities in the north. In 1942, she was requisitioned by the War Shipping Administration to serve as a hospital ship and troop carrier, finding herself at Normandy on D-Day. *New Bedford* returned to the United States after the war, resuming commercial operations.

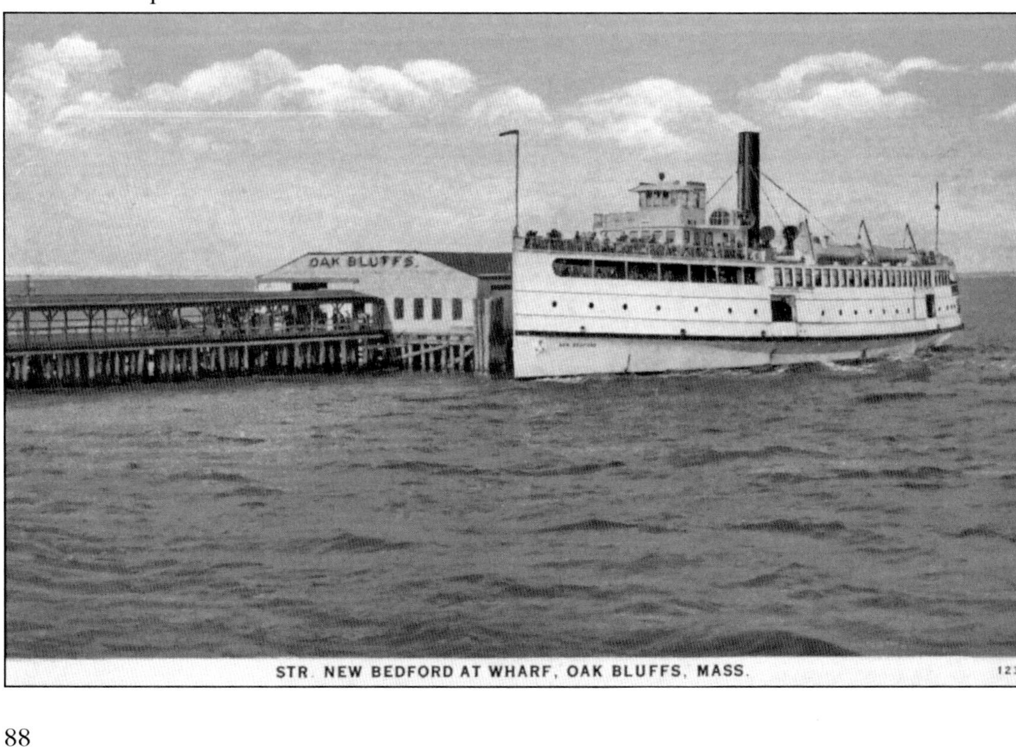

STR. NEW BEDFORD AT WHARF, OAK BLUFFS, MASS. 123

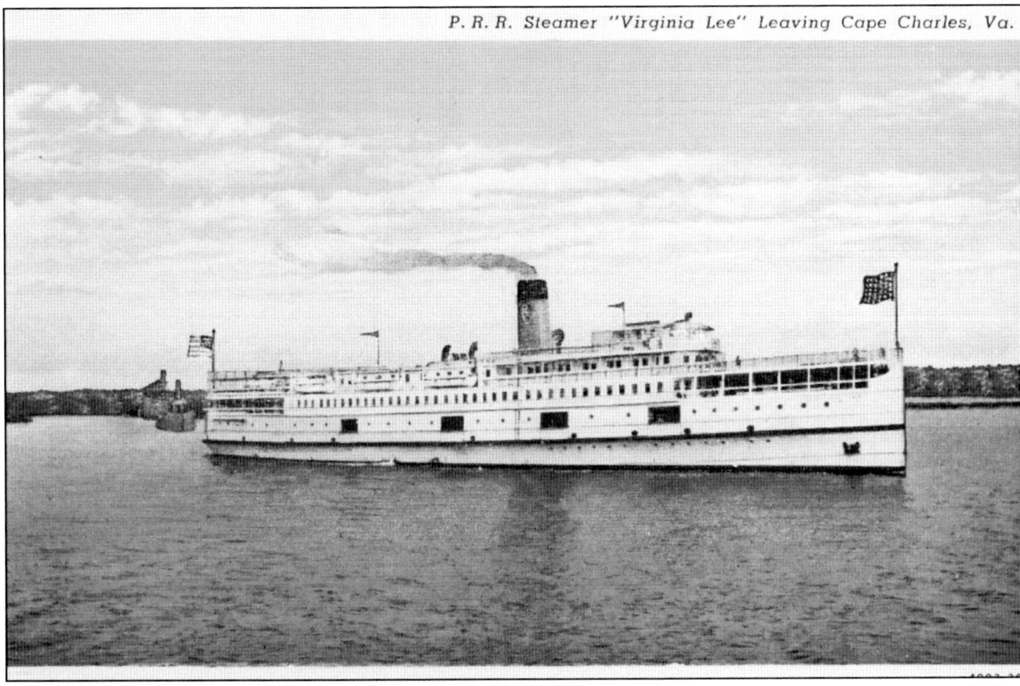

Built for the Pennsylvania Railroad in 1928, steamer *Virginia Lee* carried passengers, automobiles, and light trucks from Cape Charles on the Eastern Shore of the Chesapeake Bay to Old Point Comfort and Norfolk, Virginia. Equipped with dining rooms and staterooms, she was advertised as "the shortest route between north and south, save 130 miles." In 1942, she was taken over by the US Maritime Administration for service during World War II. After the war, *Virginia Lee* was returned to civilian service, refurbished, and renamed MS *Holiday*. She steamed the waters of Cape Cod Bay serving the people of Provincetown, Massachusetts.

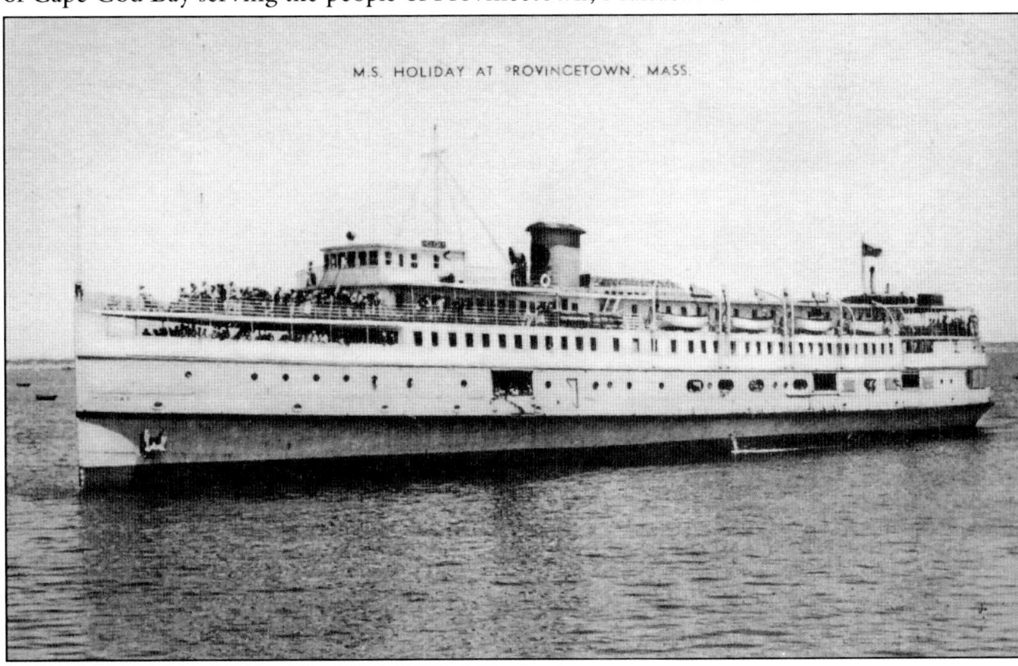

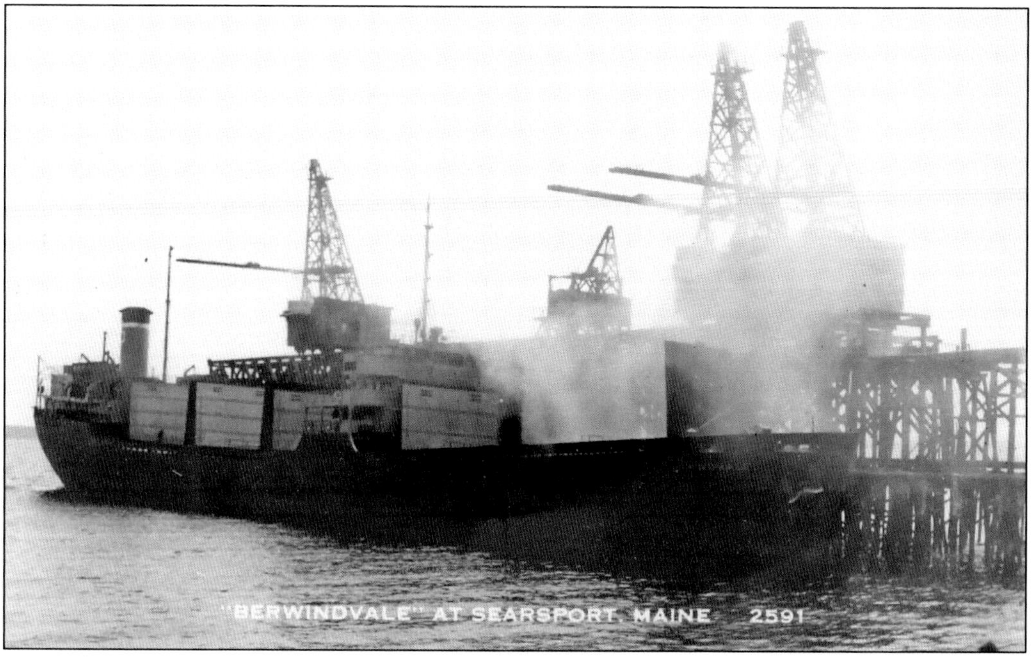

Berwindvale was built in 1929 for the Wilmore Steamship Company, a subsidiary of the Berwind-White Coal Mining Company in western Pennsylvania. In this view, *Berwindvale* unloaded coal at Searsport, Maine, a frequent stop for colliers. She was one of the last colliers built at Quincy, as the shipyard found a lucrative business building oil tankers. (Courtesy of Eastern Illustrating and Publishing Company.)

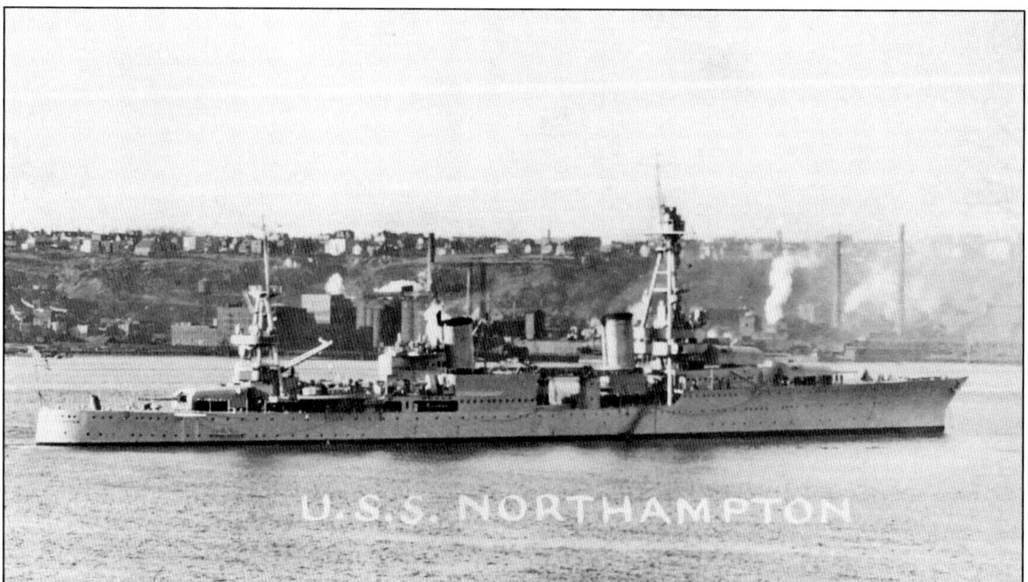

Commissioned in May 1930, cruiser USS *Northampton* (CA-26) was sunk by Japanese torpedoes at the Battle of Tassafaronga, off Guadalcanal, on November 30, 1942. Two great Hollywood actors have associations with *Northampton*. Jimmy Stewart played a seaman stationed on *Northampton* in the 1937 movie *Navy Blue and Gold*, and in real life, Jason Robards Jr. was a radioman onboard who survived the sinking.

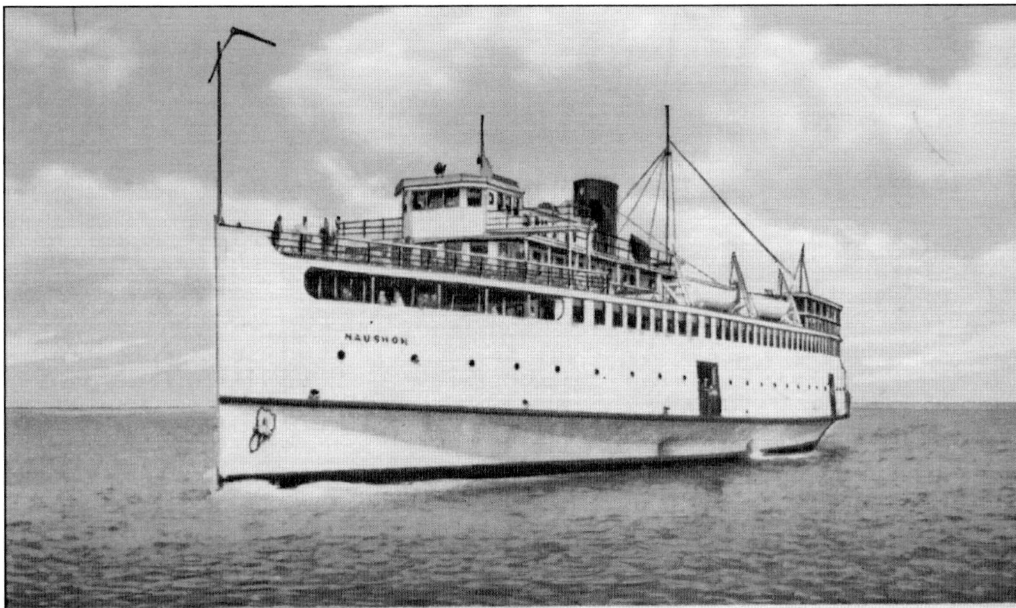

NEW BEDFORD, MARTHAS VINEYARD AND NANTUCKET STEAMBOAT LINE, MASS. 108

Naushon was a 250-foot steamer built in 1929 for the New England Steamship Company. She could carry up to 60 automobiles on a route from New Bedford to Martha's Vineyard and Nantucket Island. At the time, she was the largest steamer to serve the islands off Cape Cod. During World War II, *Naushon* was requisitioned by the War Shipping Administration to serve as a hospital ship and troop carrier in the European theater. In 1947, the Meseck Steamship line purchased *Naushon*. She was rebuilt as *John A. Meseck*, a 3,200-passenger excursion boat with service to the popular amusement park Playland in Rye Beach, New York.

Meseck Lines — Jersey City & New York to Rye Beach, N. Y. & Bridgeport, Conn.

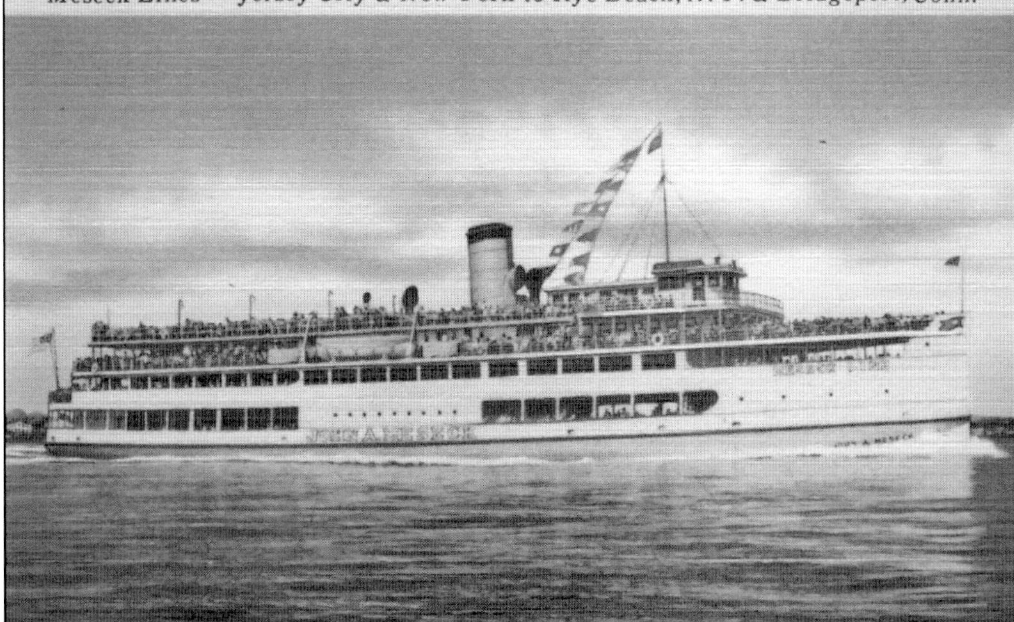

Steamer "John A. Meseck" 7988

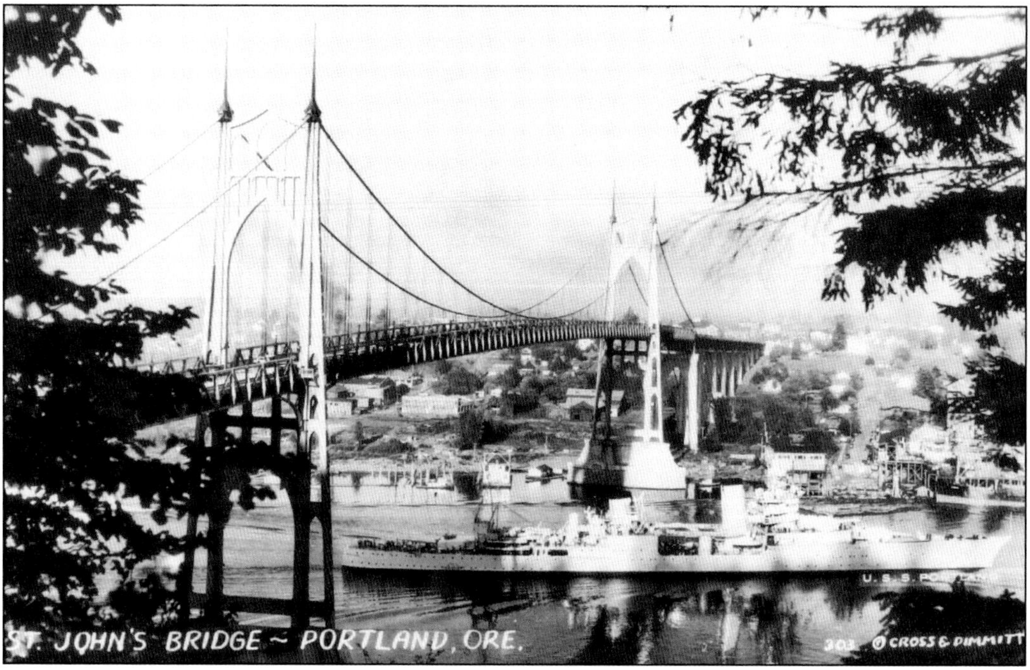

Commissioned in February 1933, heavy cruiser USS *Portland* (CA-33) was one of the most decorated ships of World War II, awarded 16 battle stars and a Navy Unit Commendation. She picked up 722 survivors from USS *Lexington* (CV-2) at the Battle of the Coral Sea and survived a torpedo hit at Guadalcanal. On September 2, 1945, the Japanese army surrendered the base at Truk, Caroline Islands, in ceremonies onboard *Portland*.

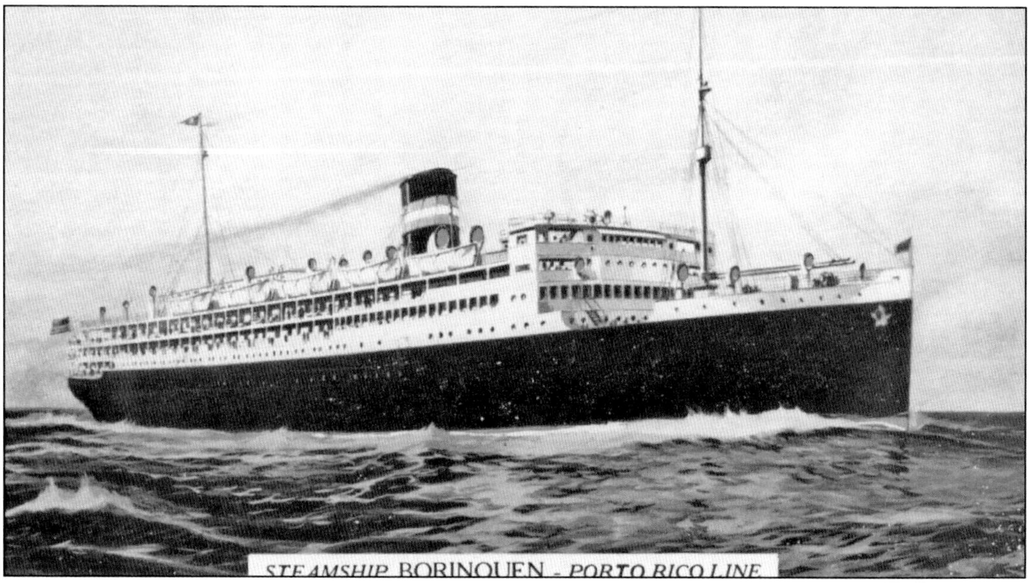

Built in 1931, cruise ship SS *Borinquen* sailed between New York, Puerto Rico, and the Dominican Republic. In 1942, she served as a troop transport, surviving World War II without being attacked. She had several owners and was subsequently named *Puerto Rico*, *Arosa Star*, *Bahama Star*, and *La Jenelle*. In 1970, she became beached at Port Hueneme, California, where the hull is now part of the breakwater.

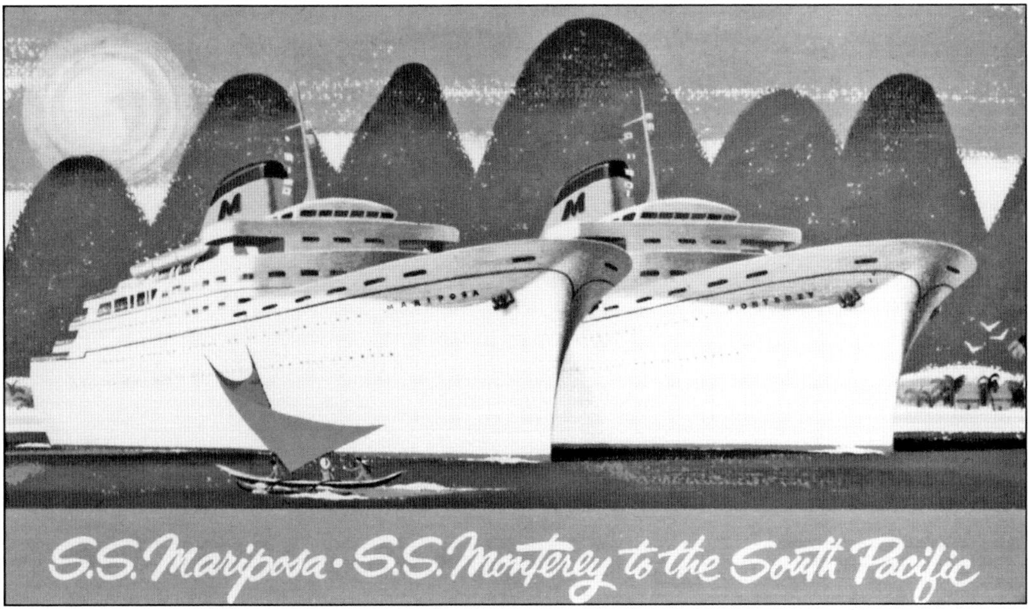

Sister ships SS *Mariposa* and SS *Monterey* were delivered to the Matson Lines in 1931 and 1932. They were ultramodern cruise ships, air-conditioned throughout, with accommodations for 365 passengers, all in first class. The ships cruised at 20 knots from San Francisco and Los Angeles to New Zealand and Australia via Hawaii, Tahiti, Samoa, and Fiji.

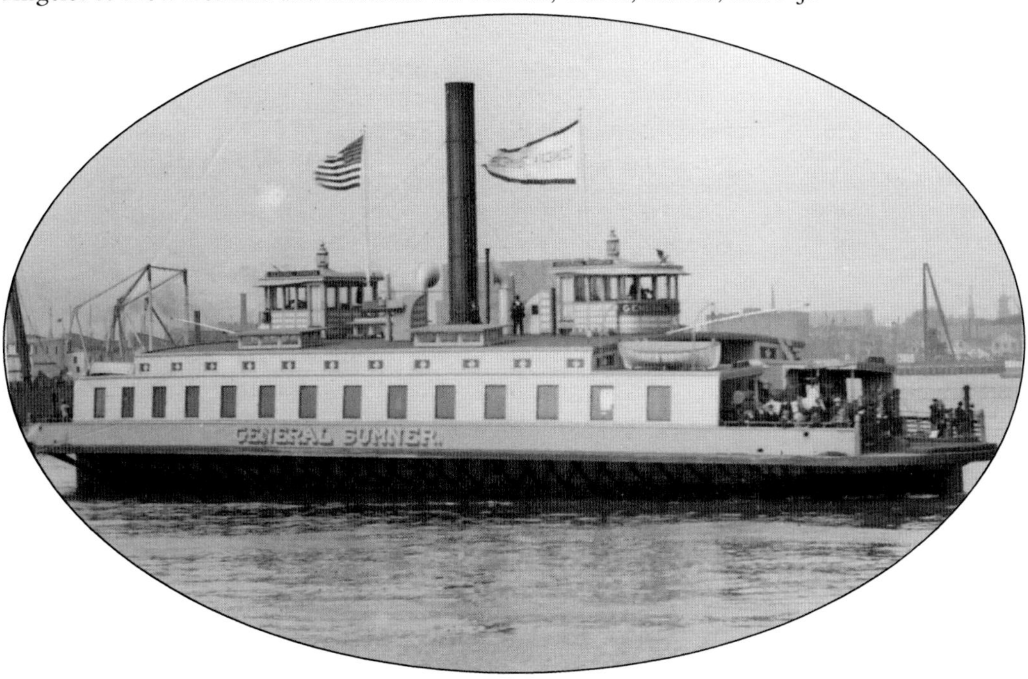

General Sumner was named for Gen. William H. Sumner, developer of Noddle Island and East Boston in the 1830s. The Sumner Tunnel, connecting the city of Boston to East Boston, is also named for him. This 174-foot harbor ferry was built for the city of Boston in 1931, three years before the tunnel. Standing among the people is a beautiful white horse, no doubt enjoying the cool sea breeze.

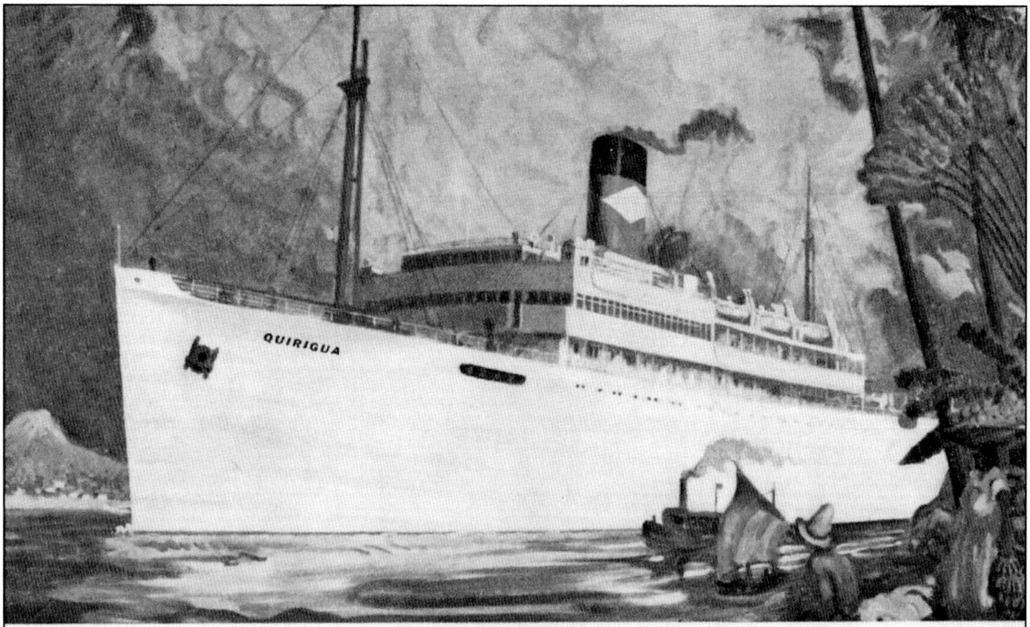

GREAT WHITE FLEET—UNITED FRUIT COMPANY

SS *Quirigua* and SS *Veragua* were 447-foot cruise ships/freighters built for the United Fruit Company in 1932. The company's ships were advertised as "The Great White Fleet." In 1932, one could cruise from New York to New Orleans and the Caribbean; the following year the company offered service along California's coast. They were also known as banana boats for carrying the fruit from Latin America for export to the United States. During World War II, both ships were acquired by the US Navy to transport men and supplies. *Quirigua* was commissioned as USS *Mizar* (AF-12) and served in the Pacific theater; *Veragua* was commissioned as USS *Merak* (AF-21) and served in the Atlantic and Caribbean. In 1946, the ships returned to commercial use, operating until 1964.

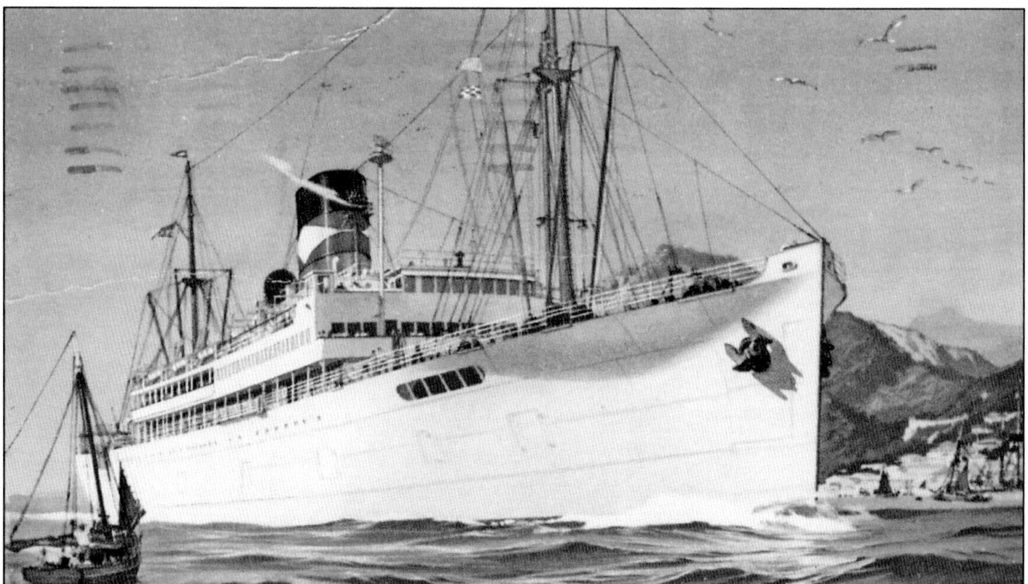

T.E.S. VERAGUA, one of six sister ships of the GREAT WHITE FLEET—UNITED FRUIT COMPANY

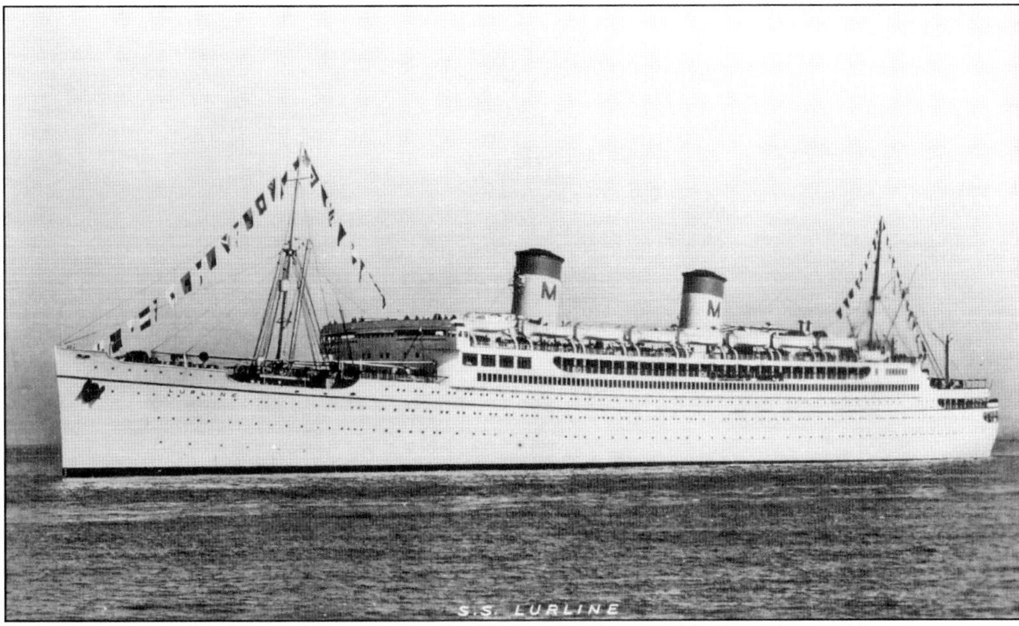

Delivered to the Matson Lines in 1933, SS *Lurline* appears to be on her maiden voyage with flags decorating the stem and stern. She cruised in air-conditioned comfort from ports in California to Hawaii. From the hairstyles, clothing, and Art Deco interior, one gets a glimpse of life in the 1930s in the "First Class Dining Salon." One could expect to be pampered in first class onboard a Matson Lines ship. Flowers adorned the dining room where busy waiters served well-dressed passengers. Following the attack on Pearl Harbor, *Lurline* served as a troop carrier throughout World War II, surviving intact to resume cruise service until 1981.

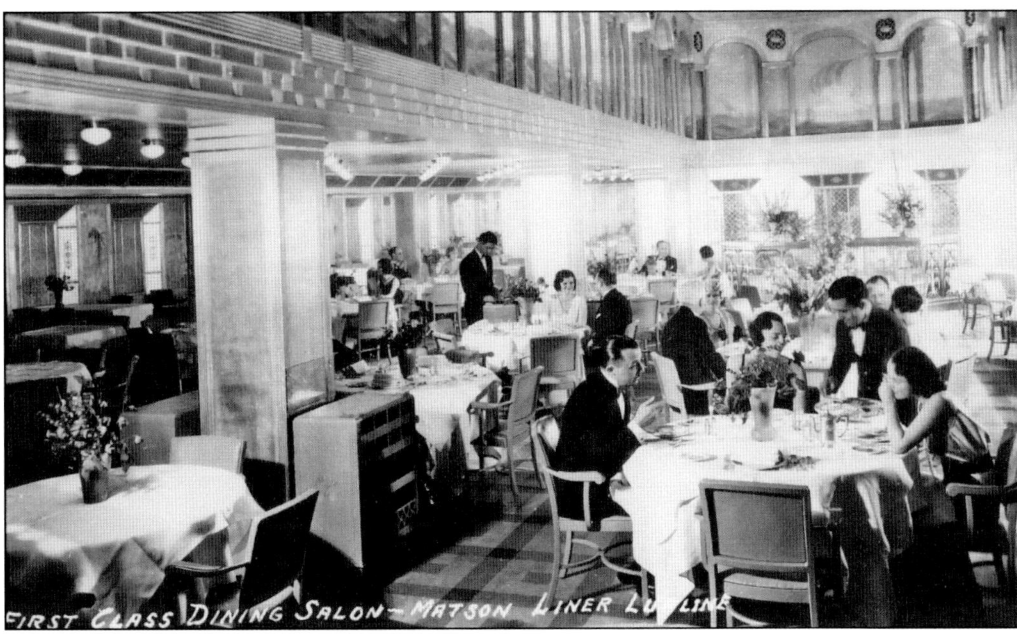

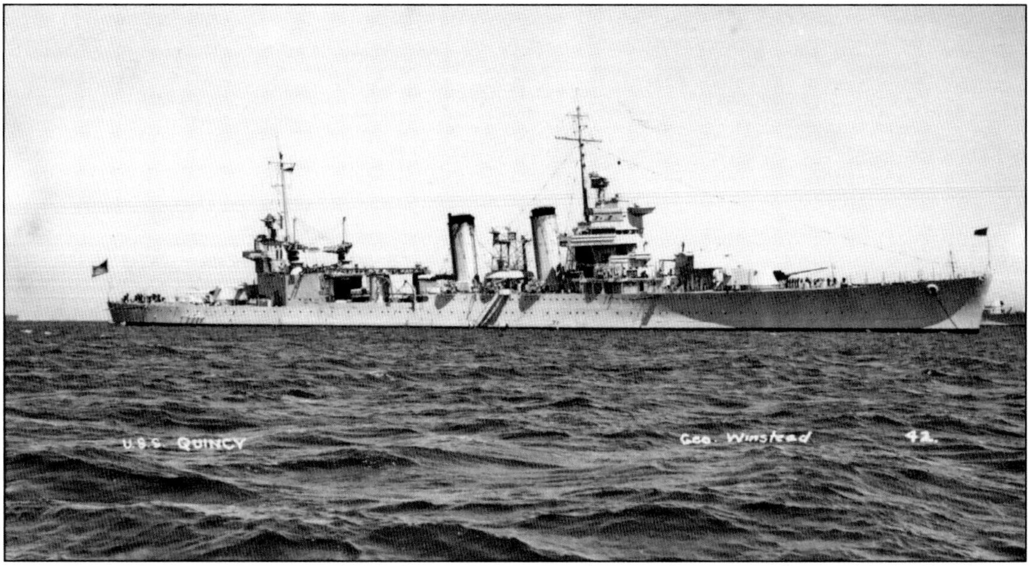

Commissioned in June 1936, USS *Quincy* (CA-39) immediately joined the Atlantic Fleet in the Mediterranean to protect American interests during the Spanish Civil War. She was in the last class of New Orleans heavy cruisers built before World War II, and the Washington Naval Treaty of 1922 regulated her armament. The ship carried nine eight-inch/55-caliber guns mounted in triple turrets. Each round weighed 260 pounds and had a range of 18 miles. In addition, there were eight five-inch/25-caliber antiaircraft guns and eight .50-inch water-cooled machine guns. On August 7, 1942, *Quincy* was positioned at Guadalcanal bombarding Japanese installations in advance of the Marines landing. The following evening she was attacked by a group of Japanese cruisers and sunk during the Battle of Savo Island on August 9, 1942. Nearly half the 800-man crew were killed.

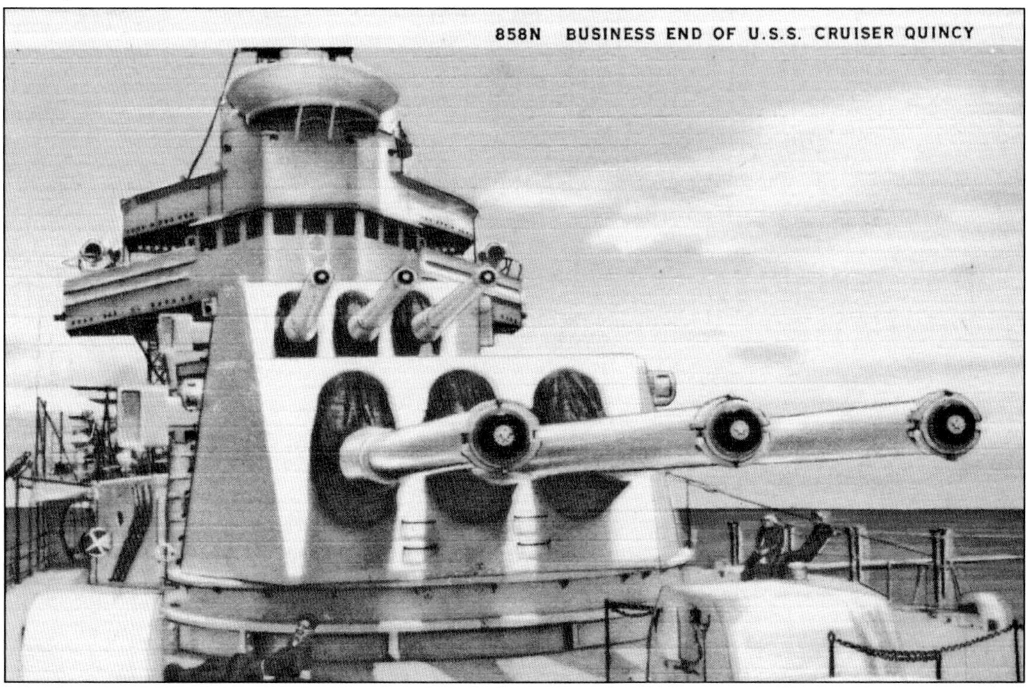

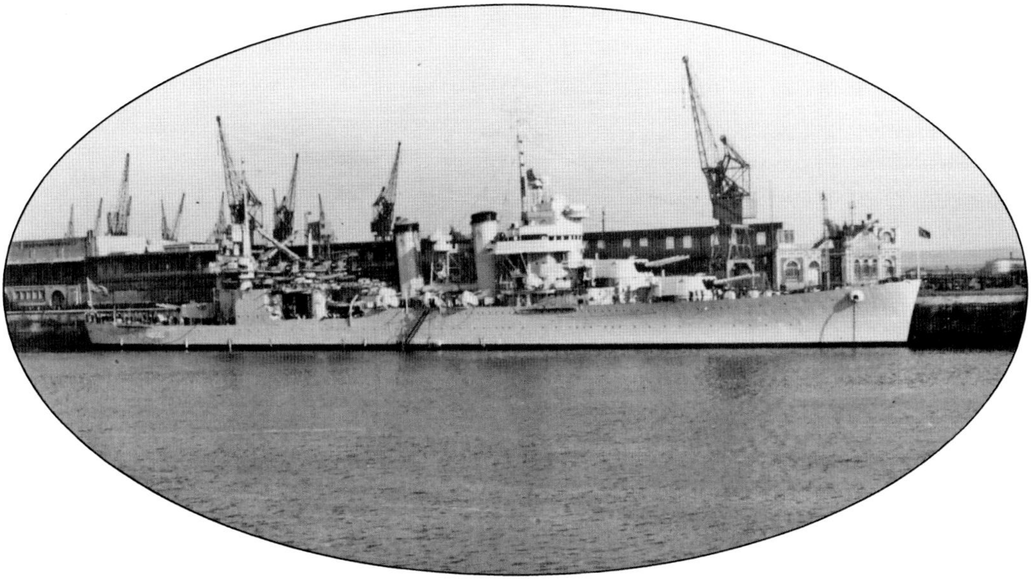

A sailor onboard USS *Vincennes* (CA-44) took the photograph on this postcard in 1937 while the ship was docked in Le Havre, France. *Vincennes* fought at the Battle of Midway and Guadalcanal before being sunk by the Japanese at the Battle of Savo Island on August 9, 1942. She rests in "Iron Bottom Sound" with sister ship USS *Quincy* (CA-39) and many other ships sunk there during the war.

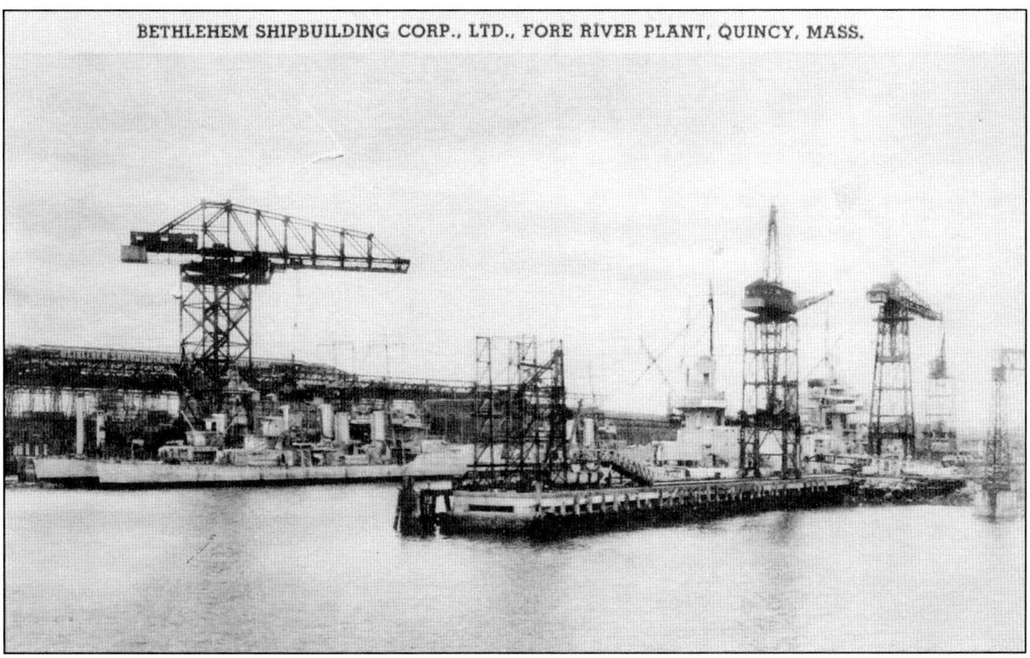

This 1936 view of the outfitting piers shows USS *Vincennes* (CA-44) and USS *Quincy* (CA-39) under the shadow of the McMylar Hammerhead Crane on the left. This crane could lift up to 120 tons, over three times that of the other cranes at the shipyard. At the pier to the right, two Porter class destroyers were in the final stages of production.

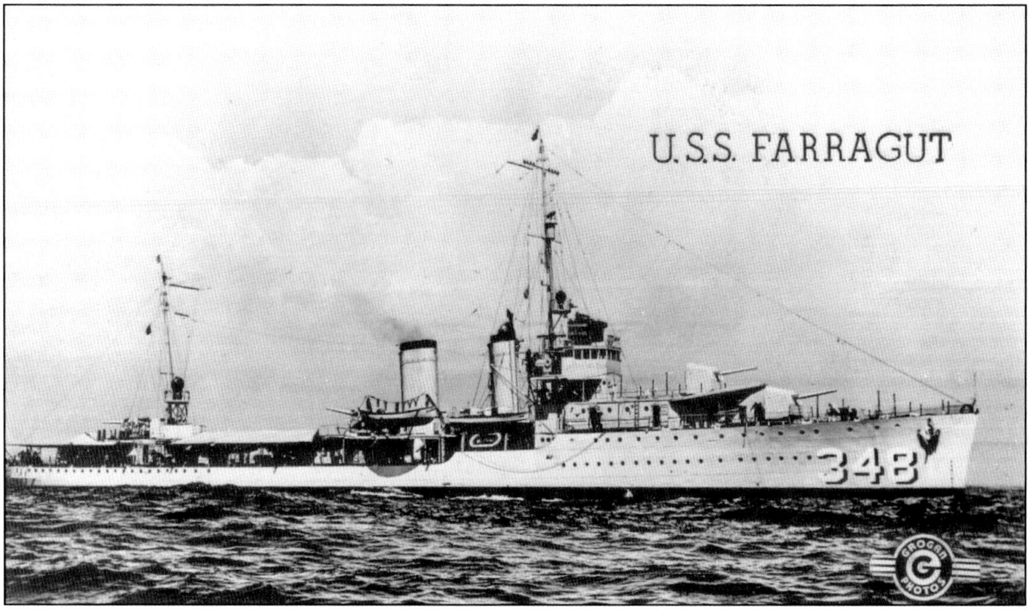

Commissioned in June 1934, destroyer USS *Farragut* (DD-348) was berthed at Pearl Harbor when the Japanese attacked but was able to get underway, escaping damage. *Farragut* fought in the biggest battles of World War II, including the Battle of the Coral Sea, Guadalcanal, the Marshall Islands, Tarawa, Guam, Iwo Jima, Okinawa, and Saipan. Awarded 14 battle stars for service, she was decommissioned at the war's end.

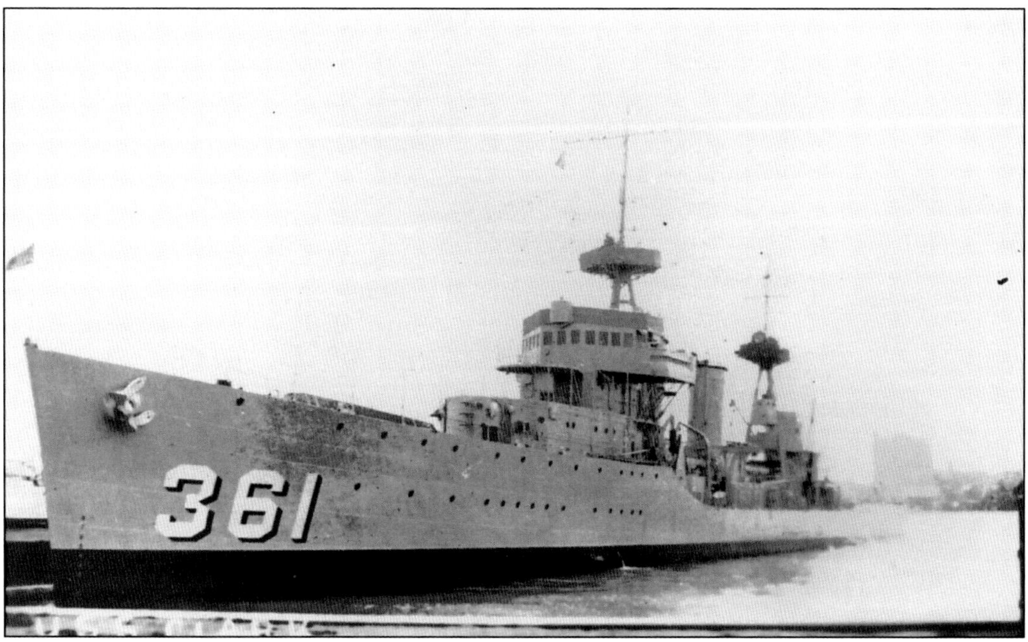

Porter class destroyer USS *Clark* (DD-361) was commissioned in May 1936. After the attack on Pearl Harbor, *Clark* escorted a convoy to Wellington, New Zealand. From September 1944 to April 1945, she guarded convoys sailing from the United States to ports in the United Kingdom and France. Like many destroyers that survived World War II, *Clark* was decommissioned in late 1945 and scrapped in 1946.

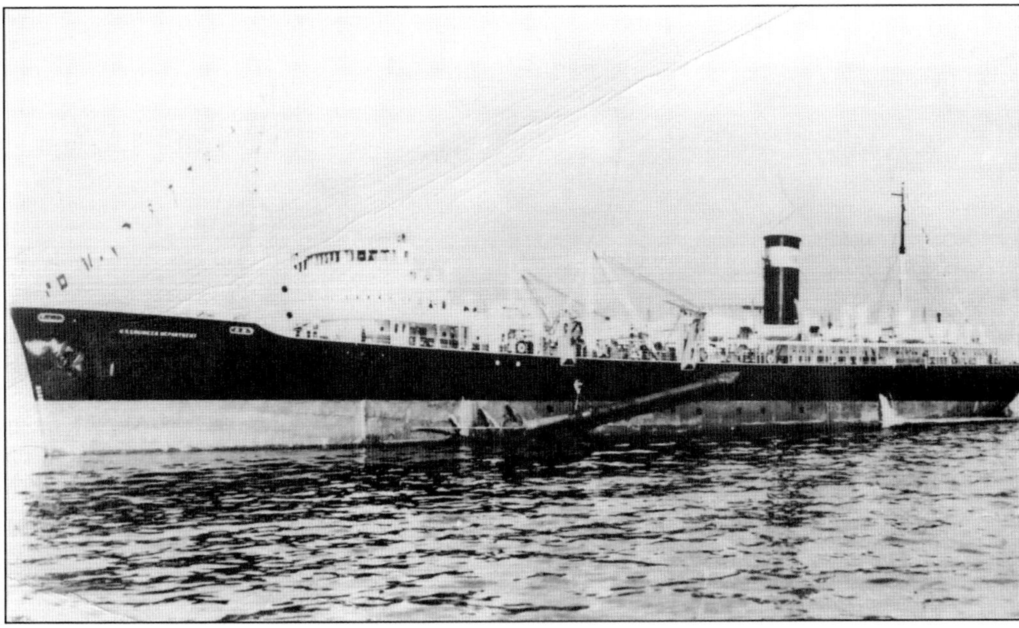

US dredge *Goethals* was built for the US Army Corps of Engineers in 1937. Billed as "The World's Largest Seagoing Hopper Dredge," *Goethals* was turbo-electric powered and 476 feet long; she carried a crew of 100 men. She would dredge channels and rivers, storing material onboard and later transporting it for disposition at a designated location.

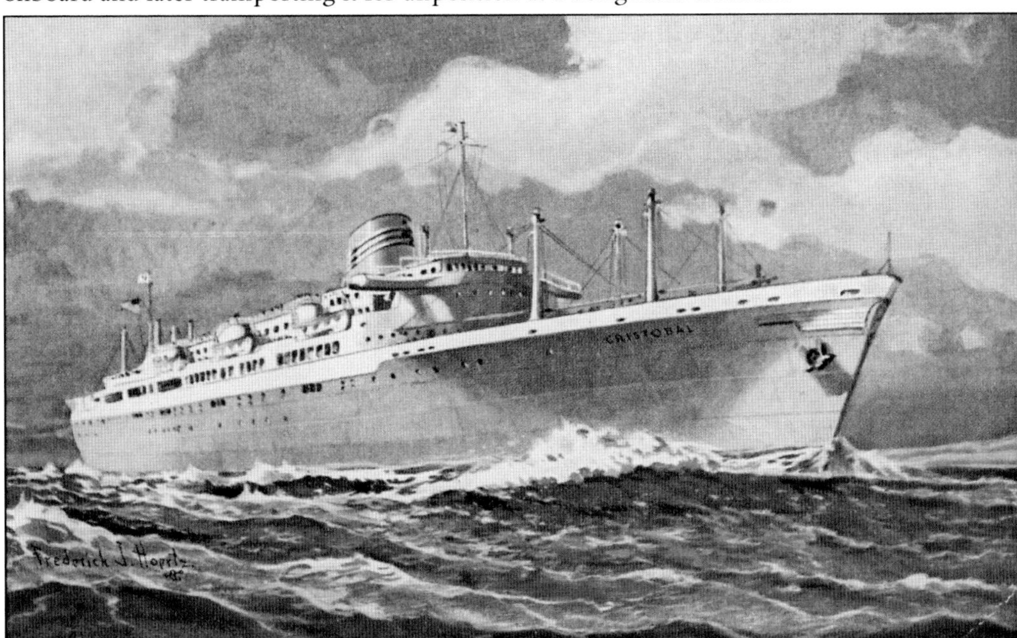

In 1939, the shipyard built three identical 493-foot cruise ships for the Panama Railroad Company. Named *Panama*, *Ancon*, and *Cristobal*, they were delivered as the Panama Canal was celebrating its 25th anniversary. Each had 70 staterooms, air-conditioned dining rooms, and outdoor swimming pools and provided service from New York to Port-au-Prince, Haiti, and the Canal Zone. All three ships were appropriated for World War II service.

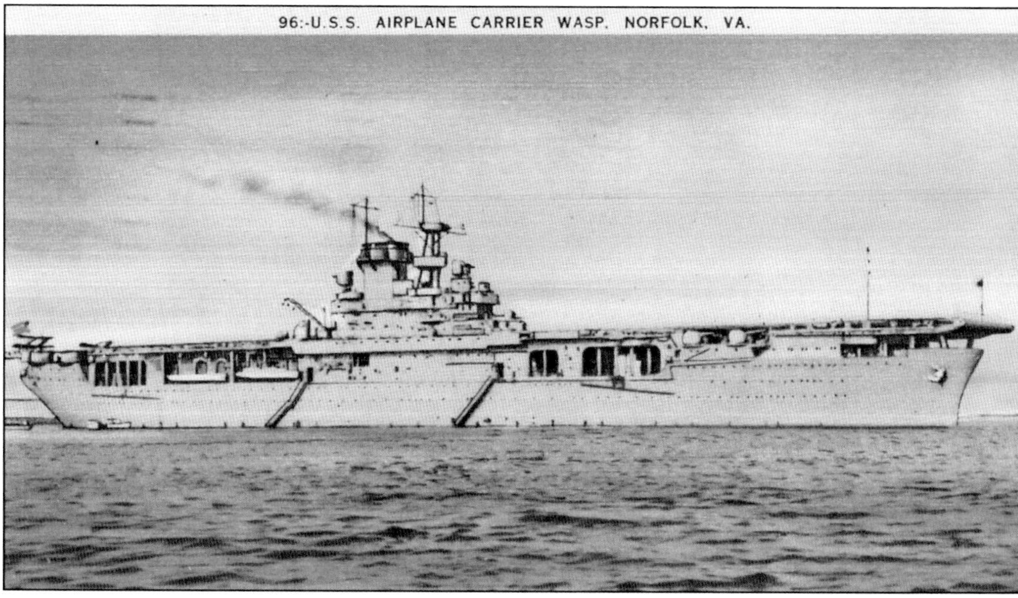

Aircraft carrier USS *Wasp* (CV-7) was launched in April 1939 and commissioned one year later. She could carry over 80 airplanes. *Wasp* was sunk by the Japanese submarine *I-19* near Guadalcanal on September 15, 1942. The workers at the shipyard took the news very hard and lobbied for a new ship to be named *Wasp*. They got their wish when USS *Oriskany*, then under construction, was renamed USS *Wasp* (CV-18).

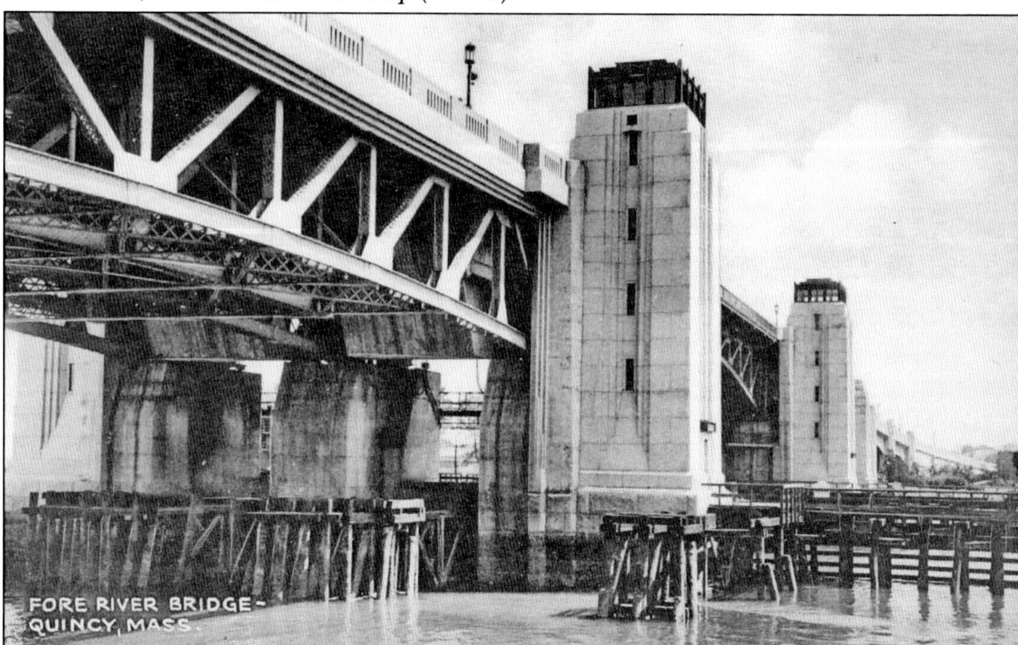

For many, the Fore River Bridge was the symbol of the Fore River Shipyard. When the great ships that fought in World War II sailed out to sea, traffic stopped on the bridge to cheer the ships on their way. Built in 1936 as a Works Progress Administration project, the $2.5 million bascule bridge replaced Watson's iron swing bridge. Unfortunately, the bridge was demolished in 2004 after many years of disrepair.

Eight

World War II
1941 to 1945

The Fore River Shipyard broke all of its production records during World War II. From the attack on Pearl Harbor to the surrender of Japan, the shipyard delivered 92 ships to the US Navy, or better than one ship every 15 days. This was a staggering amount of production considering that the shipyard constructed less than 30 ships for the US Navy and Coast Guard over the prior 20 years!

Employment at the shipyard was 17,000 on December 7, 1941, reaching a peak of 32,000 in January 1943. Once again Bethlehem Steel needed additional space to build all the ships ordered by the US Navy. Instead of turning to Squantum as in World War I, Bethlehem Steel constructed a new shipyard in Hingham, three miles south of Quincy Point, breaking ground early in 1942. The Bethlehem-Hingham shipyard mass-produced destroyer escorts (DE), with landing ship tanks (LST) eventually added to production. Bethlehem-Hingham built a total of 227 ships in 39 months of operation, setting a world record by delivering five ships in 50 hours.

There were many accomplishments at the Fore River Shipyard during World War II. Battleship USS *Massachusetts* was built 15 months ahead of schedule, aircraft carrier USS *Hancock* was completed in a record 14.5 months, a Cleveland class light cruiser in 16.5 months, and a Baltimore class heavy cruiser in just 20.5 months.

On May 15, 1942, the Fore River Shipyard was honored with the coveted Navy "E" award for excellence in production. Secretary of the Navy William Franklin Knox came to Quincy to present the award and a pennant with the "E" to fly over the shipyard. The shipyard subsequently received four stars for a total of five consecutive awards. The stars were added to the pennant each year in recognition of the shipyard's superior contribution to the war effort.

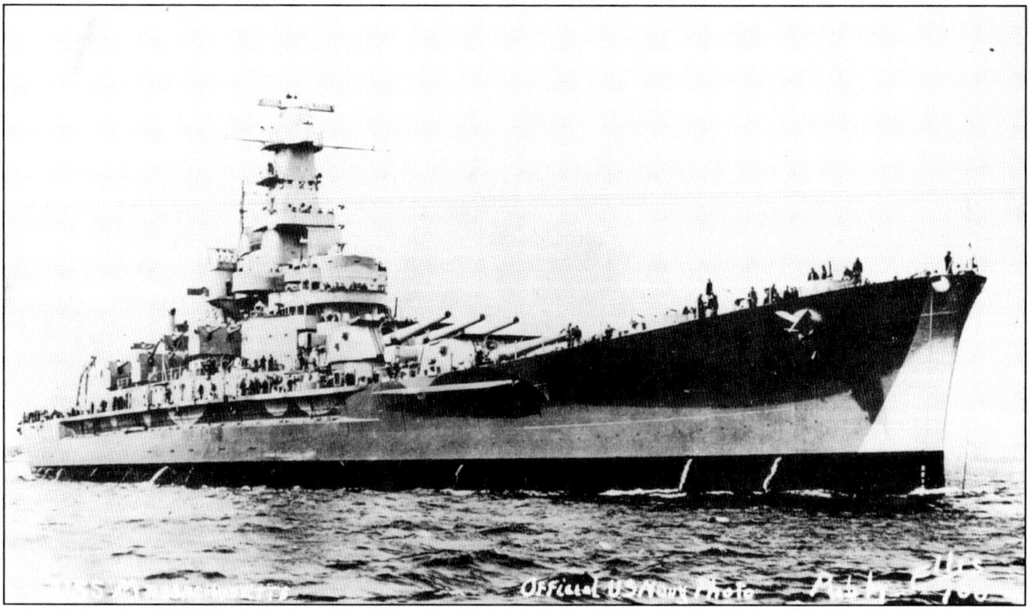

Battleship USS *Massachusetts* (BB-59) was the last battleship built in Quincy, commissioned in May 1942. Famous for her massive 16-inch guns, her nickname was "Big Mamie." In November 1942, she fired the first American 16-inch shell of World War II as part of the invasion of North Africa, defeating the battleship *Jean Bart* (a French ship previously captured by the Germans) in a gun duel. Joining the action in the Pacific in February 1943, *Massachusetts* fought at Tarawa, the Marshall Islands, Saipan, Guam, Leyte Gulf, Iwo Jima, and Okinawa. She fired the last American 16-inch shell of the war at Kamaishi, Japan, on August 9, 1945. Decommissioned in 1947, *Massachusetts* was declared a National Historic Landmark. Since 1965, she has welcomed the public as a museum ship at Battleship Cove in Fall River, Massachusetts.

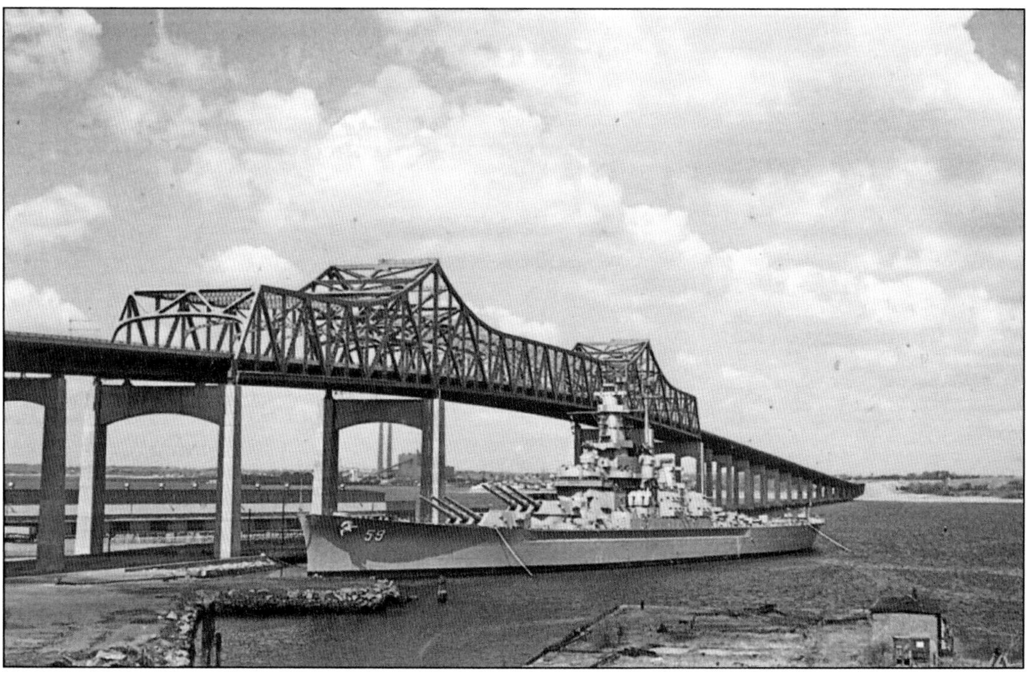

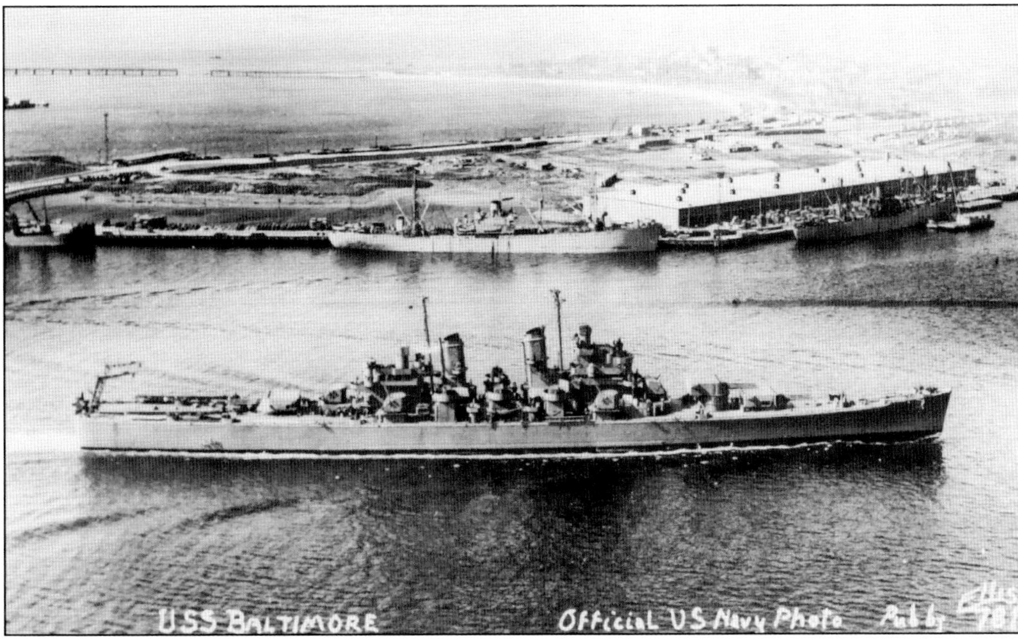

Heavy cruiser USS *Baltimore* (CA-68) survived World War II unscathed despite fighting at Luzon, the Marianas, Wake Island, Saipan, Formosa, Okinawa, and Iwo Jima. In July 1944, Pres. Franklin Roosevelt boarded *Baltimore* for an historic meeting with Adm. Chester Nimitz and Gen. Douglas MacArthur at Pearl Harbor. The result of the meeting was the decision to attack the Japanese in the Philippines.

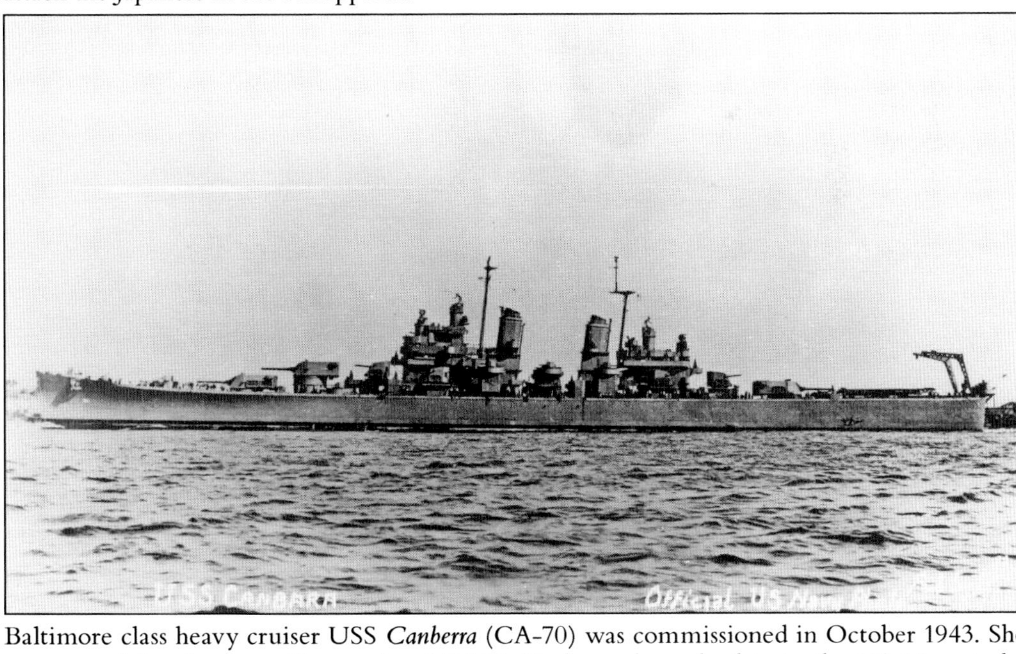

Baltimore class heavy cruiser USS *Canberra* (CA-70) was commissioned in October 1943. She was named for the Australian cruiser HMAS *Canberra*, the only ship in the US Navy to be named for a foreign warship and foreign capital city. On October 13, 1944, near Formosa, an aerial torpedo struck *Canberra*, killing 23 men. She survived World War II to serve five tours in Vietnam.

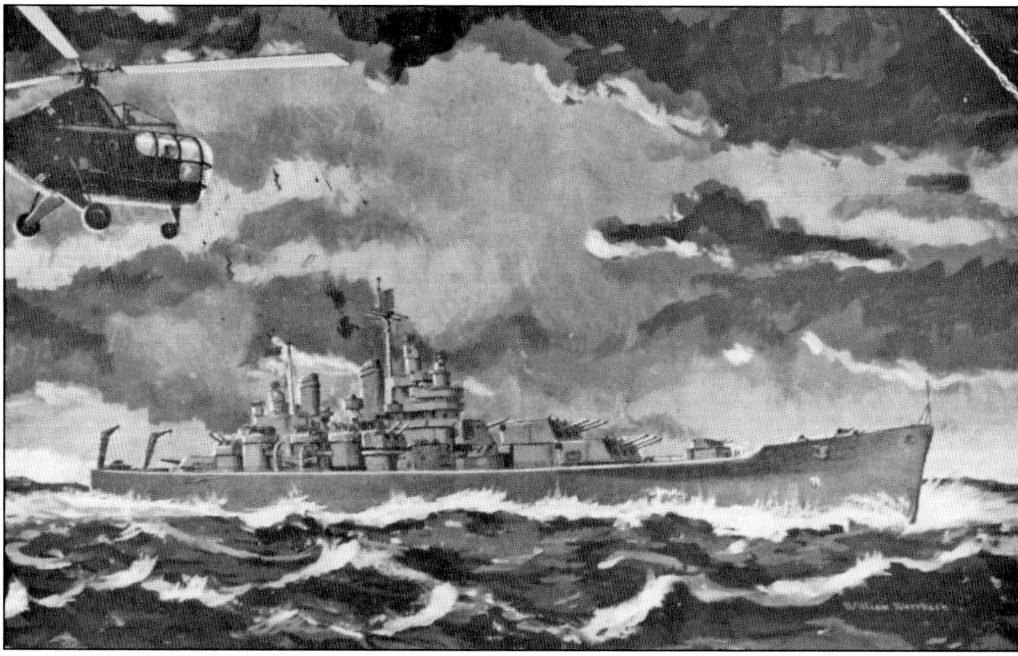

Heavy cruiser USS *Quincy* (CA-71) joined the Twelfth Fleet in May 1944. She fired upon shore batteries at Utah Beach on D-Day, hosted an historic conference between President Roosevelt and the king of Saudi Arabia in February 1945, and supported aircraft carriers at Okinawa in April 1945. *Quincy* was scrapped in 1974, but her bell has a place of honor next to Quincy's city hall.

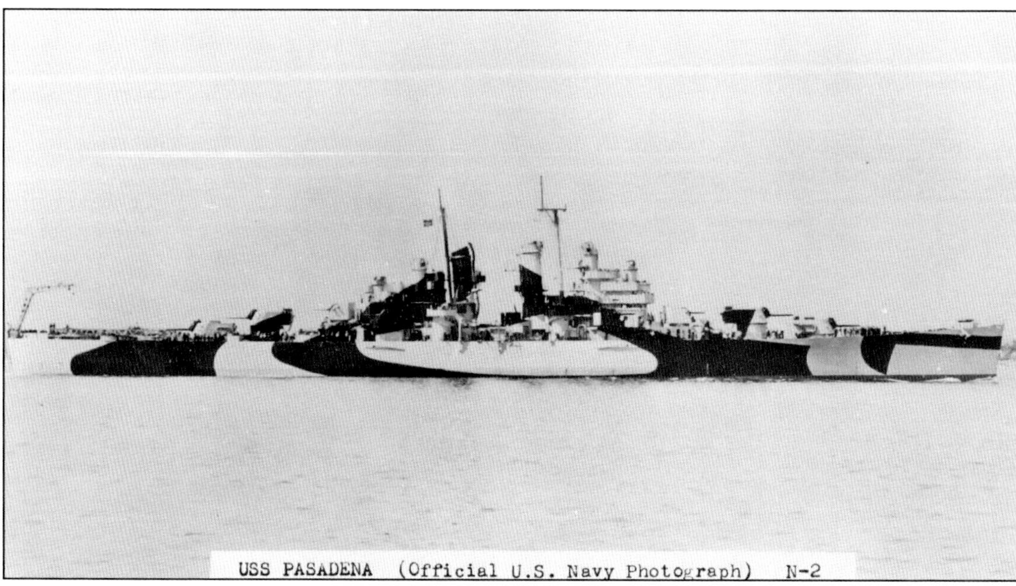

Commissioned in June 1944, Cleveland class light cruiser USS *Pasadena* (CL-65) earned five battle stars for service during World War II, participating in operations against Luzon, Formosa, Iwo Jima, Ryukyu Islands, and Okinawa, finally striking the coast of Japan in anticipation of an invasion. After the war, *Pasadena* conducted exercises and training in the Pacific until being decommissioned in 1950.

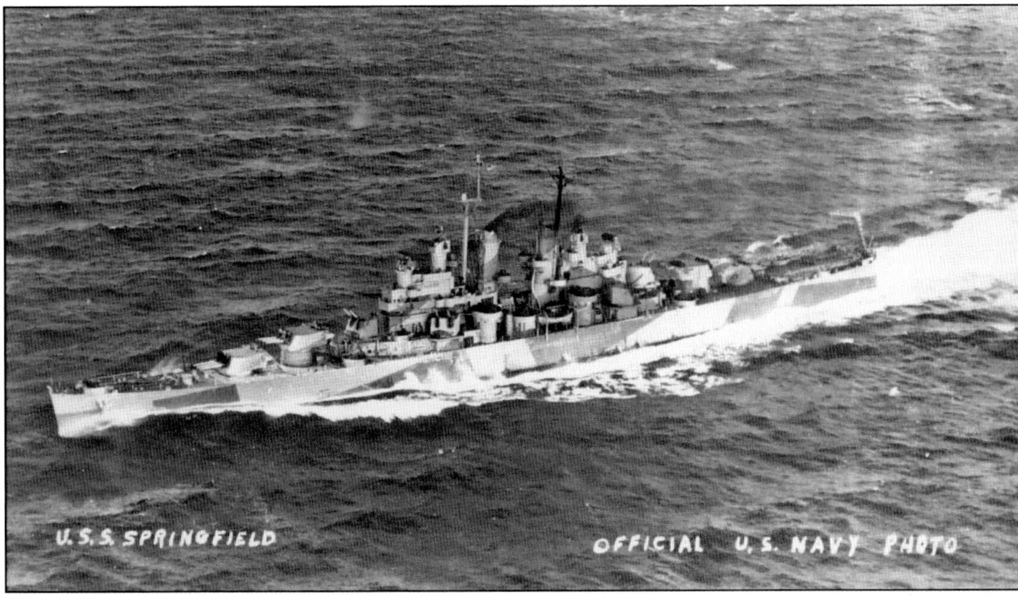

Light cruiser USS *Springfield* (CL-66) was commissioned in September 1944. She served in the Pacific, bombing the coast of Japan in the final stages of World War II. In 1957, she was overhauled at Quincy and reclassified as a guided missile cruiser (CLG-7), thereafter operating as the flagship of the Second Fleet and later the Sixth Fleet in the 1960s. She was sold for scrap in 1980.

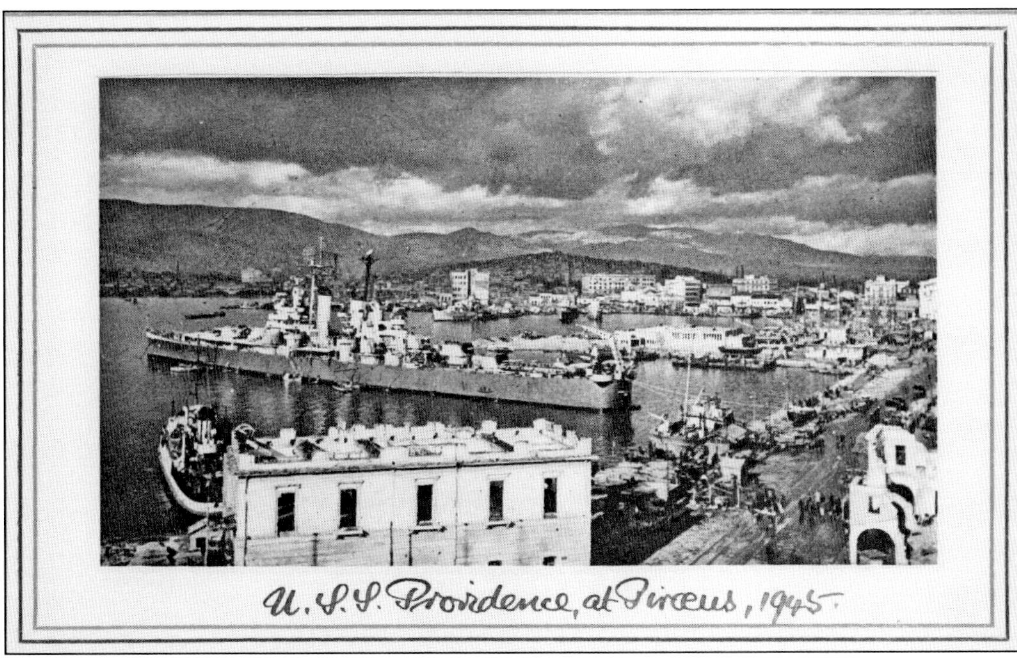

Commissioned in May 1945, light cruiser USS *Providence* (CL-82) visited Piraeus, Greece, and other Mediterranean ports in late 1945 and early 1946. *Providence* served several tours in Vietnam from 1967 through 1972, receiving the Navy Unit Commendation in 1968 and 1972 for exceptionally meritorious service in combat operations off the coast of North and South Vietnam.

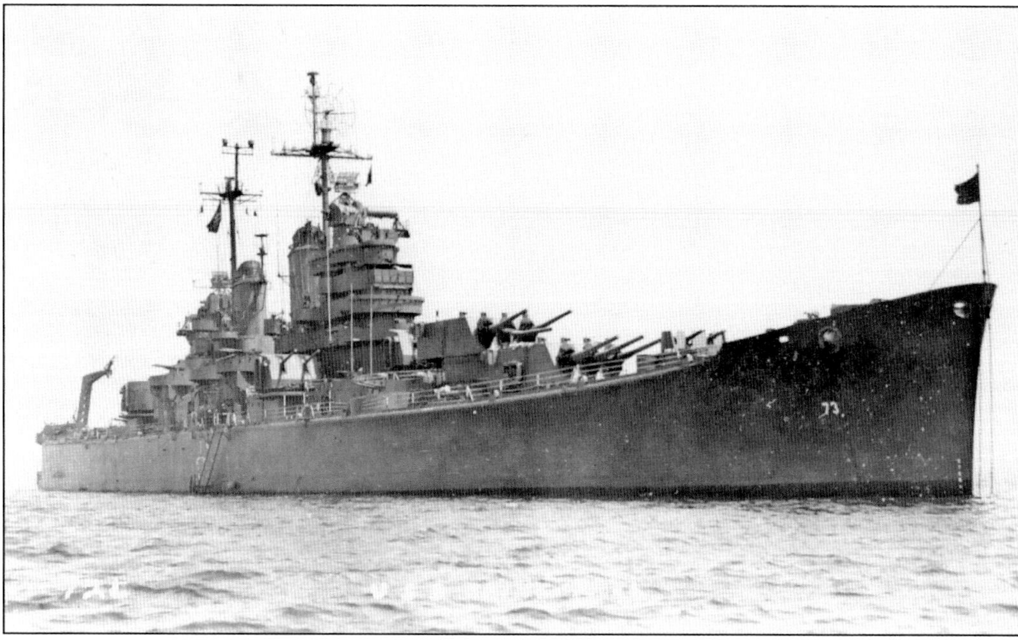

Known as "The Fighting Saint," USS *Saint Paul* (CA-73) was commissioned in February 1945. A Baltimore class heavy cruiser, she was a workhorse, serving in World War II, Korea, and Vietnam and earning 18 battle stars in the three wars. After World War II, *Saint Paul* sailed up the Whang-poo River on a visit to Shanghai, China. She became the flagship of Task Force 73, remaining in China until early 1946. She spent her entire 26-year career in the Pacific Ocean, firing more rounds than any other cruiser in the history of the US Navy. On July 4, 1960, during a special ceremony, *Saint Paul* became the first ship in the US Navy to fly the new 50-star flag.

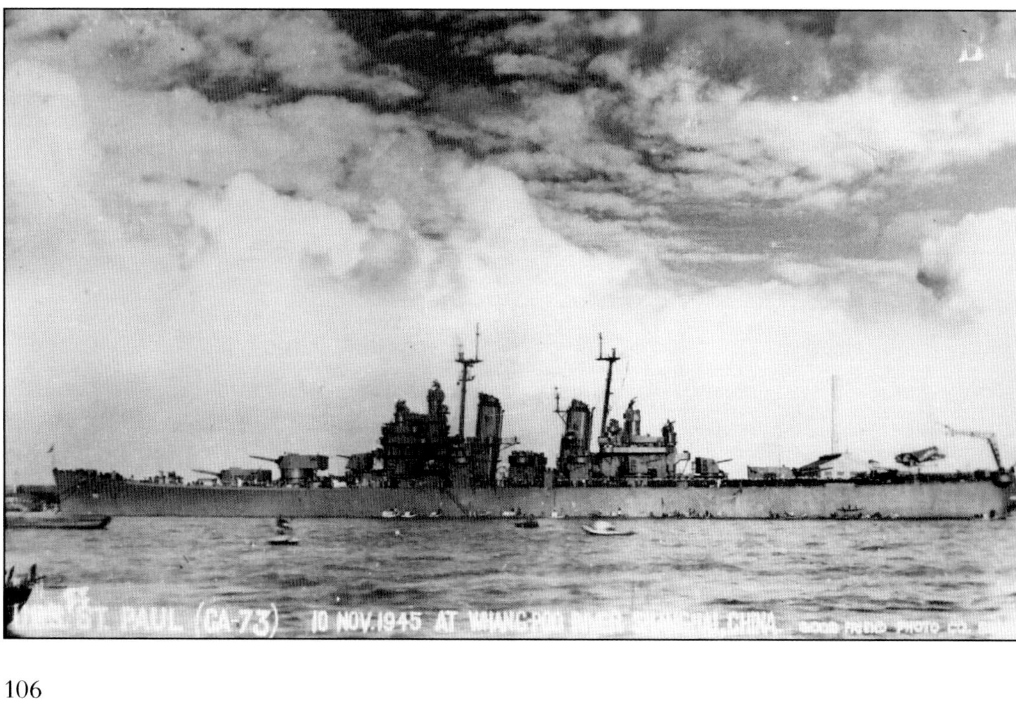

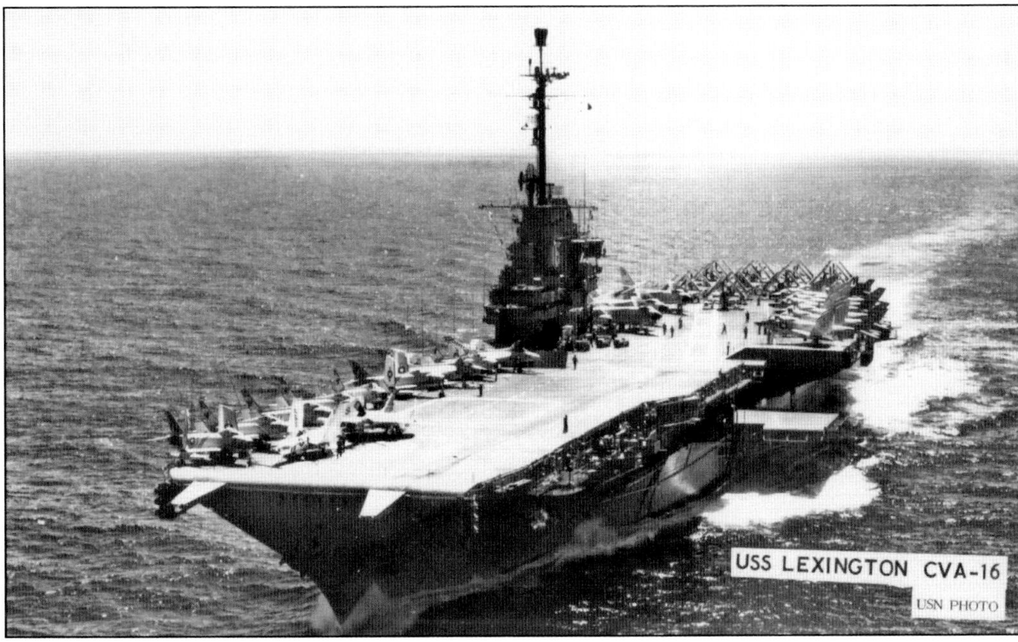

USS *Lexington* (CV-16) and USS *Bunker Hill* (CV-17) were Essex class aircraft carriers, commissioned in February and May 1943, respectively. *Lexington* earned 11 battle stars for World War II service, fighting at the Marianas, Guam, Okinawa, Leyte Gulf, and Formosa. Painted dark blue and nicknamed "The Blue Ghost" by Tokyo Rose, she was reported sunk many times by Japanese propaganda only to reappear and devastate the enemy. Today, she is a museum ship in Corpus Christi, Texas. USS *Bunker Hill* (CV-17) fought at Tarawa, the Marshall Islands, Palau, Guam, Iwo Jima, Saipan, and the Battle of the Philippine Sea. She was badly damaged by two kamikaze aircraft during the invasion of Okinawa on May 11, 1945, losing 389 crew. After repairs, *Bunker Hill* participated in returning troops to the United States from the Pacific theater.

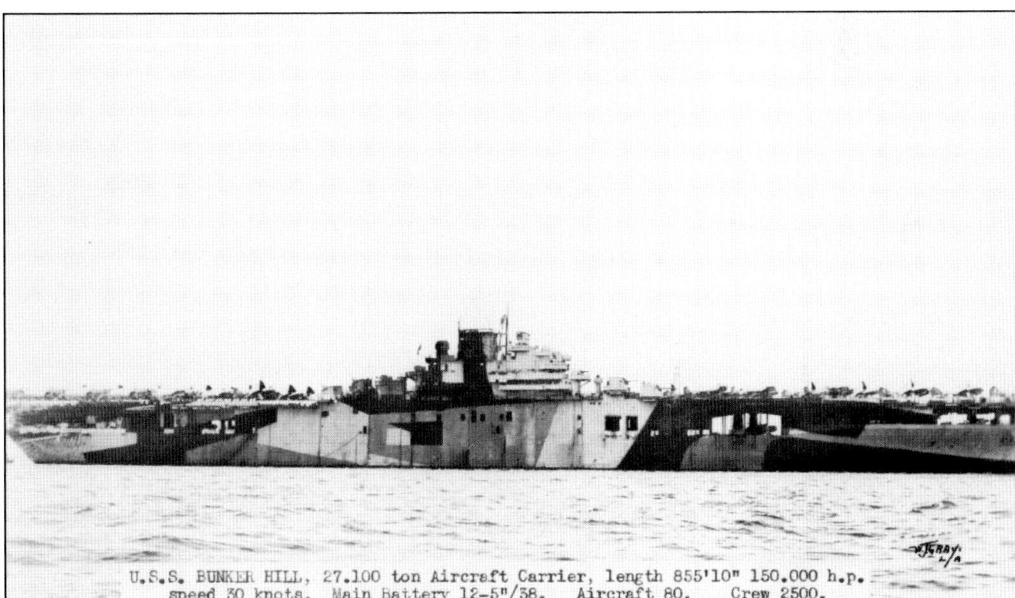

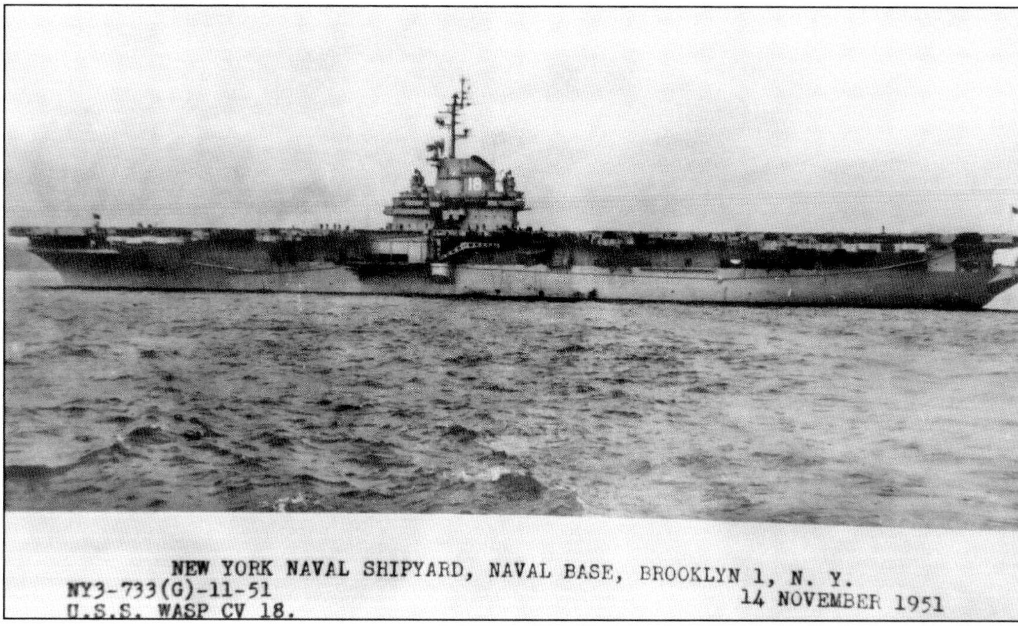

Working at breakneck speed, it took the shipyard 28 fewer months to build the much larger USS *Wasp* (CV-18) than the 1930s-built USS *Wasp* (CV-7) she replaced. Commissioned in November 1943 as an Essex class aircraft carrier, she served in the Pacific theater at Western New Guinea, the Marianas, Western Carolina Islands, Leyte, Luzon, Iwo Jima, and Okinawa as well as in operations against Japan, earning eight battle stars. In late 1952, she was remodeled as an attack carrier (CVA-18), eventually becoming an antisubmarine carrier in 1956 (CVS-18). In 1965–1966, *Wasp* worked as a recovery ship during the Gemini program. She was decommissioned in 1972. (Below, courtesy of Atlantic Fleet Sales.)

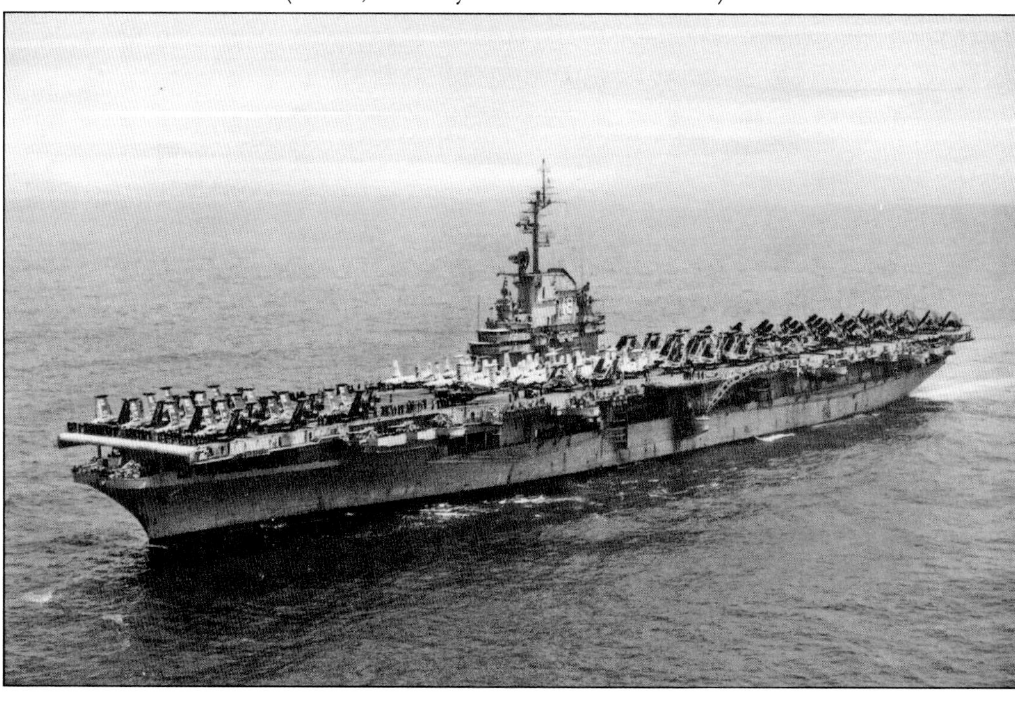

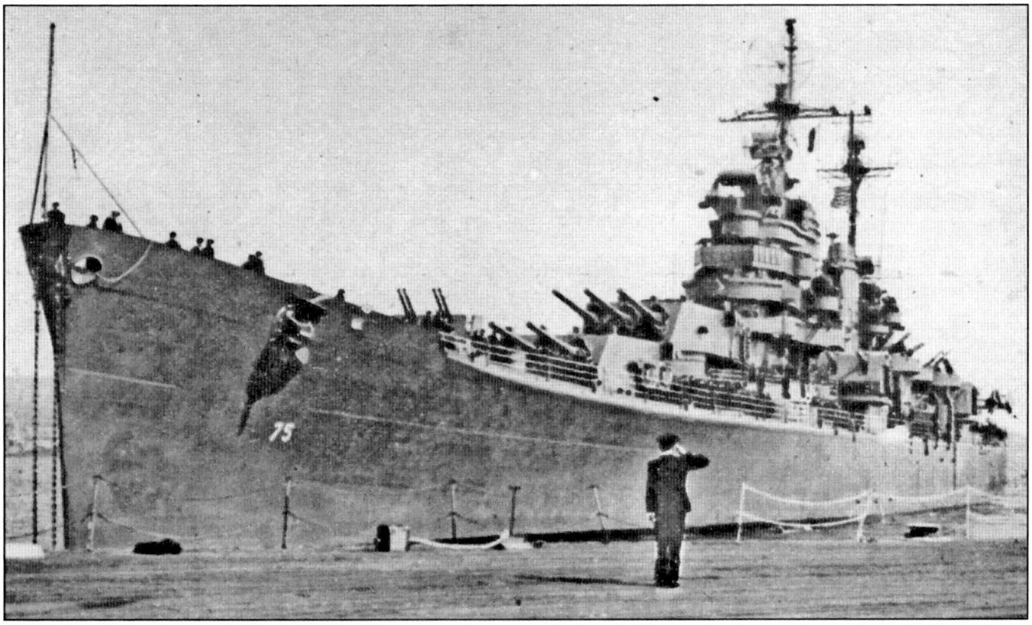

Baltimore class heavy cruiser USS *Helena* (CA-75) was launched in April 1945 and commissioned five months later. Just missing out on the action in World War II, she fought in the Korean War from 1950 to 1952. In December 1952, she carried President-elect Eisenhower and several prospective cabinet members from Guam to Pearl Harbor for policy discussions. *Helena* was decommissioned in 1963.

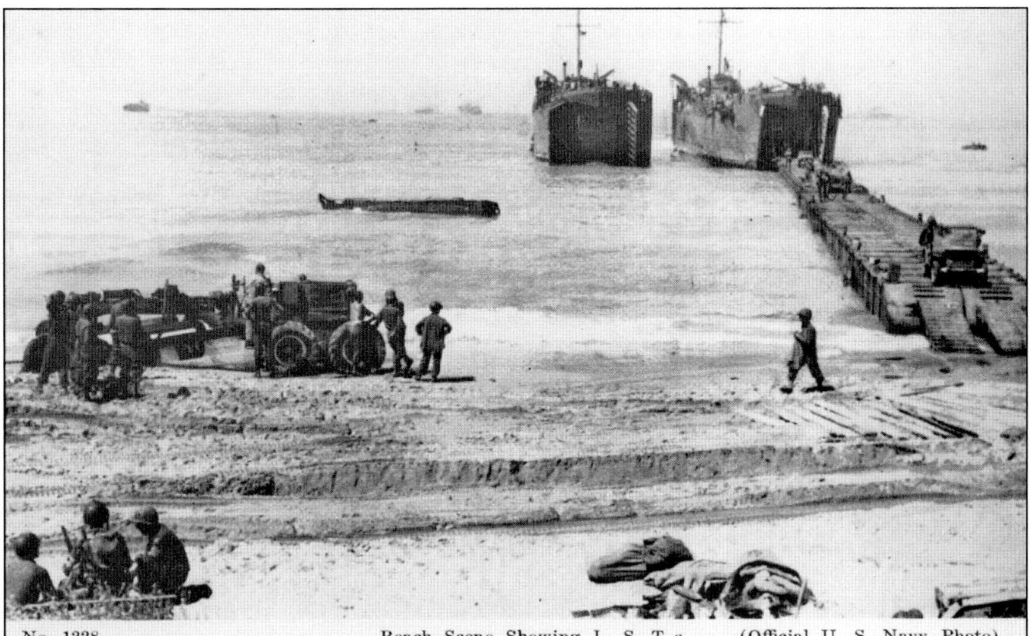

The shipyard built 22 *LST 1* class landing ship tanks in 1942 and 1943. Most of those built were an integral part of the assault on the Normandy beaches on D-Day, delivering tanks, jeeps, and supplies. The Germans sank *LST 376* in the English Channel on June 9, 1944. However, most of the *LST*s survived World War II but were decommissioned shortly after the war's end.

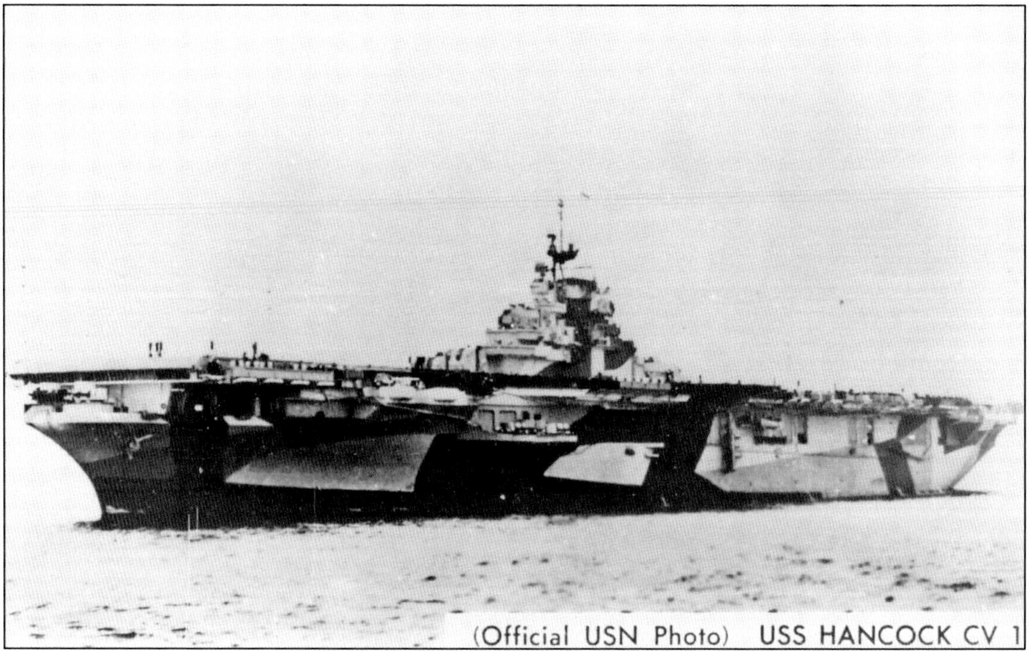

Essex class aircraft carrier USS *Hancock* (CV-19) appeared in dazzle camouflage shortly after launching in January 1944. Originally laid down as USS *Ticonderoga*, she was renamed USS *Hancock* in 1943 after the John Hancock Life Insurance Company conducted a bond drive to raise money for the ship. She earned four battles stars for World War II service and the Navy Unit Commendation for service during the Vietnam War.

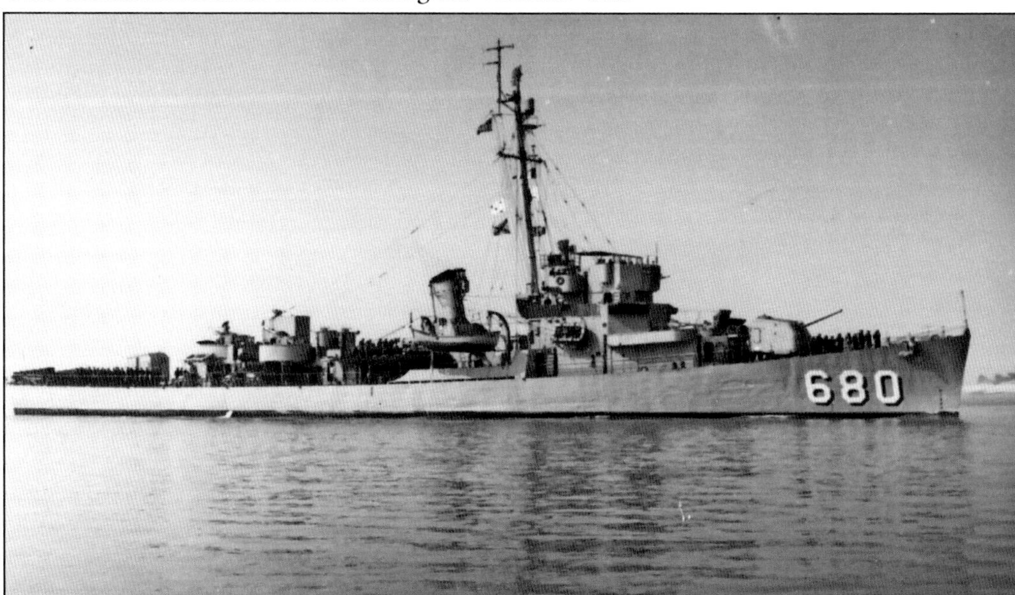

USS *Loeser* (DE-680), a Buckley class destroyer escort, was commissioned in October 1943. During World War II, she served at Lingayen Gulf, Guam, and Iwo Jima, patrolling for Japanese submarines and escorting troop transports. She survived the war only to be sunk in target exercises in 1969. (Courtesy of Wright and Logan, National Museum of the Royal Navy.)

Nine

Post–World War II 1946 to 1963

As expected, once World War II ended, work for the US Navy diminished very quickly and orders for several heavy cruisers were cancelled. The shipyard completed one Essex class aircraft carrier, two Des Moines heavy cruisers, and four Gearing class destroyers, but now the most promising opportunity for the shipyard was in the oil tanker business. From 1949 to 1963, the Fore River Shipyard produced 45 tankers for Texaco, Gulf Oil, Niarchos, Onassis, the US Maritime Administration, and others. At the time of construction, many of these tankers were the largest in the world.

In the early 1950s, the shipyard would build its last cruise ships, SS *Independence* and SS *Constitution*. In the late 1950s, there was a spurt of US Navy work, as the shipyard produced five Forrest Sherman class destroyers. These were to be the final destroyers built in Quincy, ending a 60-year run for a shipyard that made its reputation building destroyers. However, the shipyard would be at the forefront of nuclear-powered ships, winning contracts from the US Navy for the first nuclear guided missile cruiser, USS *Long Beach*, and the first nuclear frigate, USS *Bainbridge*. These were the most complex ships ever built in Quincy.

There were strikes at the shipyard in 1947 and 1952, but labor relations hit an all time low when, in 1960, there was a bitter five-month strike over work rules and pay. After difficult negotiations, the result was a new three-year contract that increased payroll costs and nullified many of the work rules. Although there were many successes in the 1950s and early 1960s, Bethlehem Steel found itself with high costs and an antiquated facility, despite spending tens of millions of dollars upgrading the plant and equipment after World War II. Unable to compete with the larger, more modern shipyards, something would have to give.

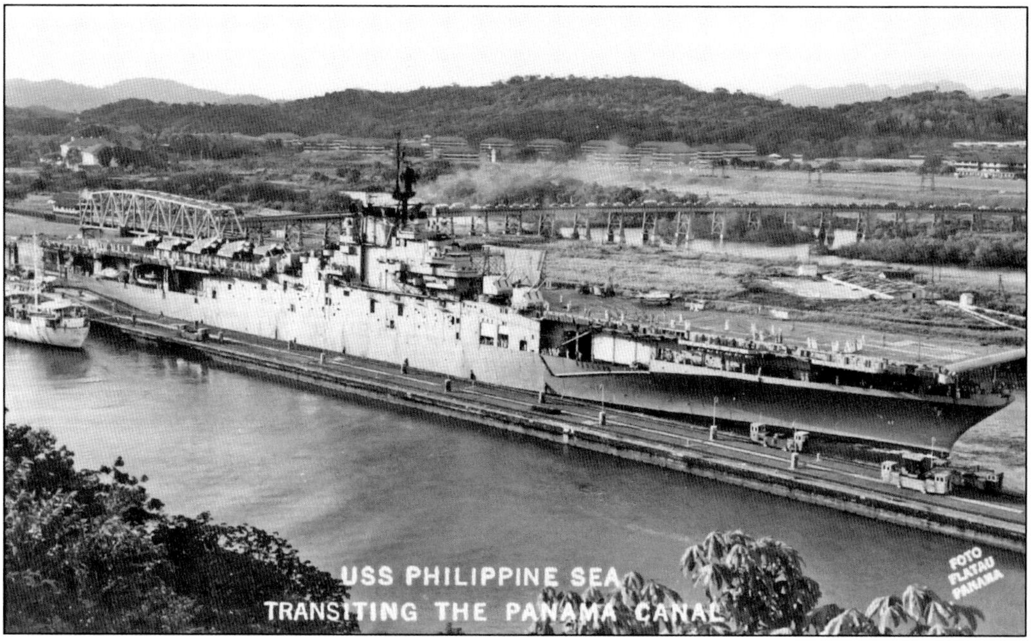

Commissioned in May 1946, USS *Philippine Sea* (CV-47) was the last of the Essex class aircraft carriers built for the US Navy and the last aircraft carrier built in Quincy. Early in 1947, Rear Adm. Richard E. Byrd boarded the ship for an expedition to Antarctica. *Philippine Sea* was relied on heavily during the Korean War, spending the better part of three years there and earning nine battle stars.

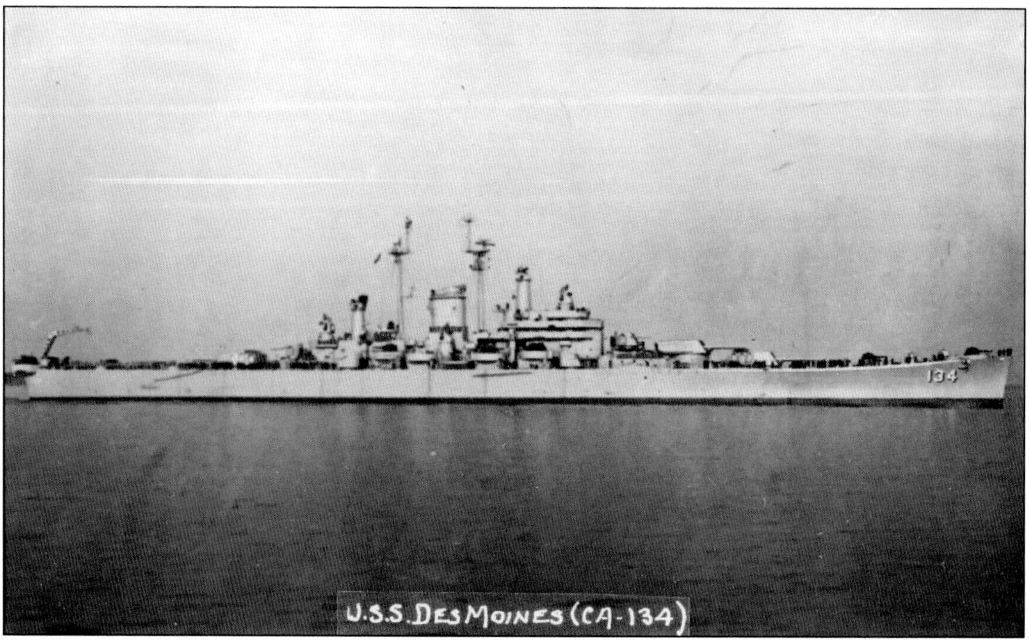

USS *Des Moines* (CA-134) was the first of her class of post–World War II heavy cruisers and the first to mount a battery of fully automated eight-inch guns. From 1950 to 1956, she served as the flagship of the Sixth Fleet. Sold for scrap in 2007, two of her gun mounts are on display at the USS *Lexington* Museum in Corpus Christi, Texas.

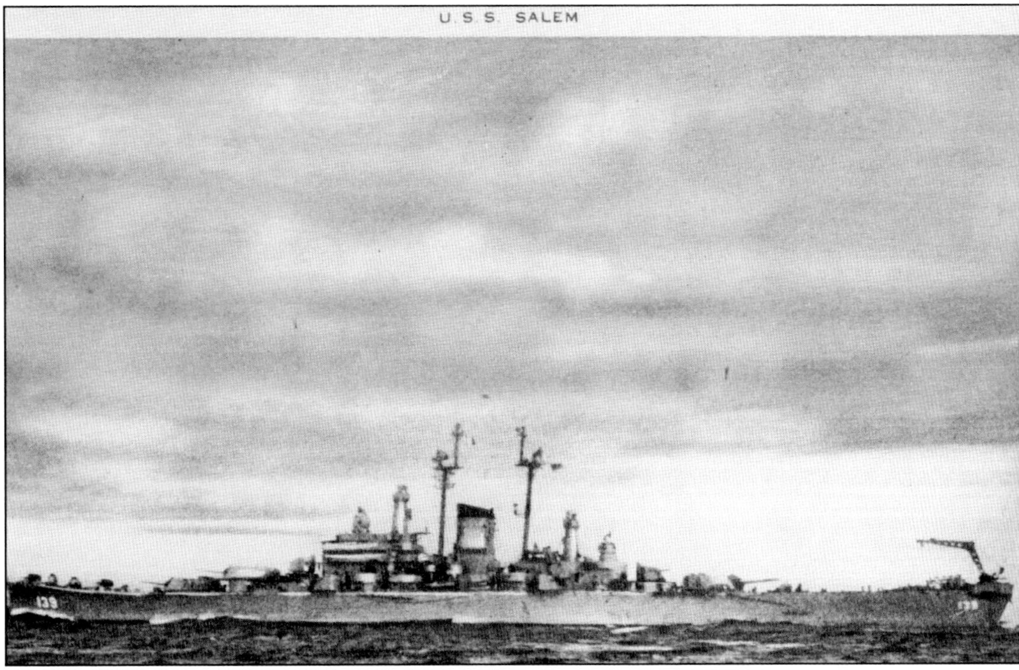

USS *Salem* (CA-139) is the only preserved heavy cruiser, moored at the Fore River Shipyard as the centerpiece of the US Naval Shipbuilding Museum. Commissioned in May 1949, she served as the flagship of the Sixth Fleet in the Mediterranean as well as the Second Fleet in the Atlantic. *Salem* and her sister ships *Des Moines* and *Newport News* were the first surface ships to be fully air-conditioned as well as the first to have large combat information centers built into the original design. Decommissioned in 1959, *Salem* was held in reserve at Philadelphia, Pennsylvania, until returning to Quincy in 1994. Museum programs include opportunities to sleep overnight in the same bunks that sailors did in 1958.

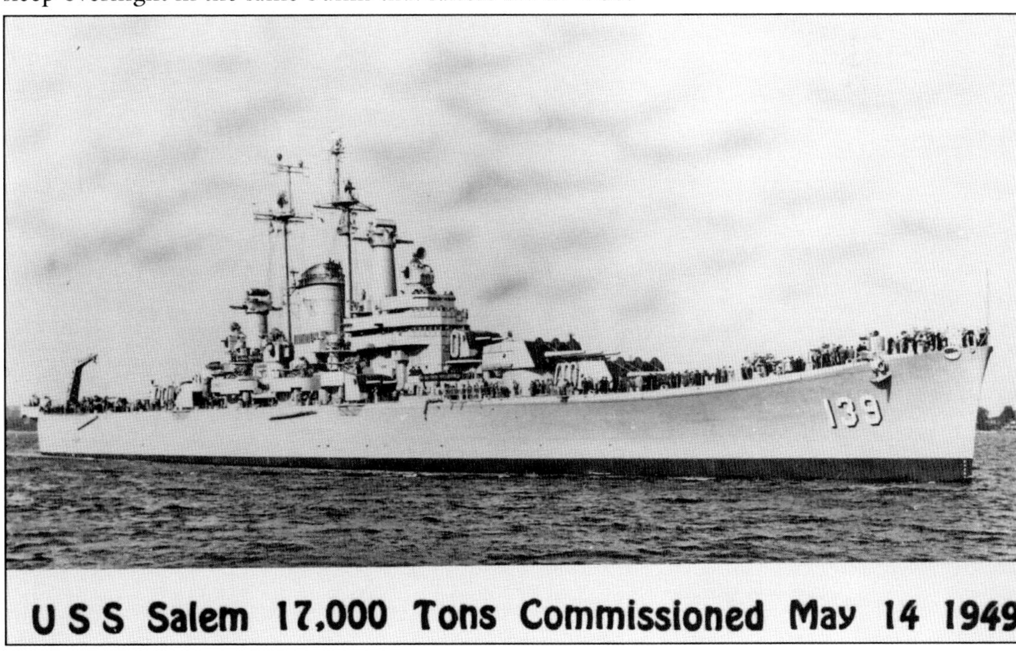

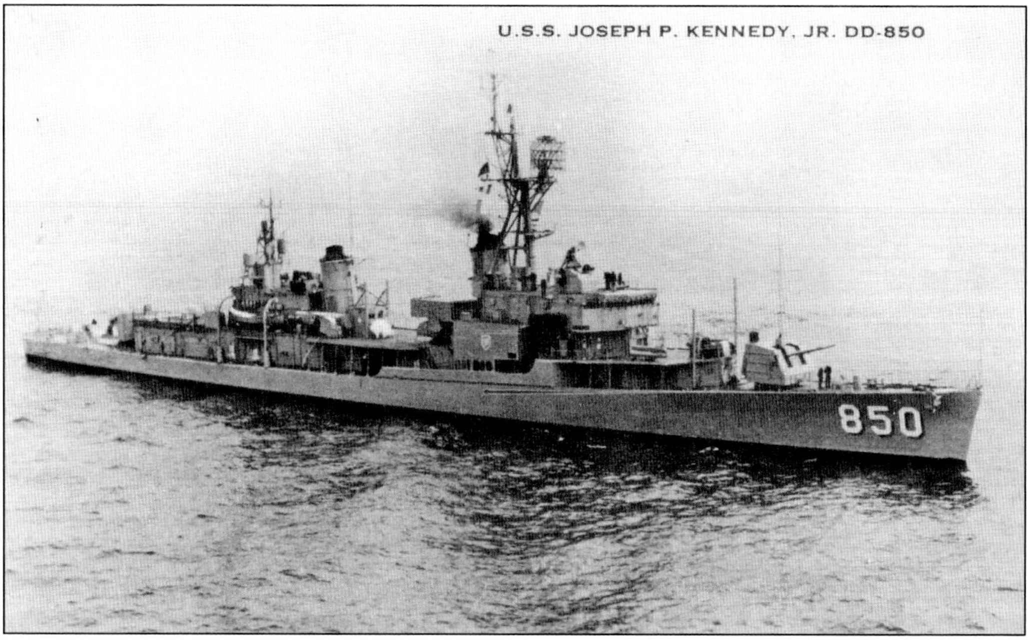

USS *Joseph P. Kennedy Jr.* (DD-850) and USS *Rupertus* (DD-851) were Gearing class destroyers, commissioned in December 1945 and March 1946, respectively. *Kennedy* was named after Pres. John F. Kennedy's older brother, a US Navy pilot who was killed in action in 1944. During the 1962 Cuban Missile Crisis, *Kennedy* took part in the blockade of Cuba. She was also a recovery ship for NASA during the Gemini program. Today, one can visit the ship at Battleship Cove Museum in Fall River, Massachusetts. *Rupertus* saw action in the Korean War, earning seven battle stars. She also served in the Vietnam War in the 1960s. She was decommissioned in 1973 and transferred to the Greek navy as HNS *Kountouriotis* (D-213), serving until 1994.

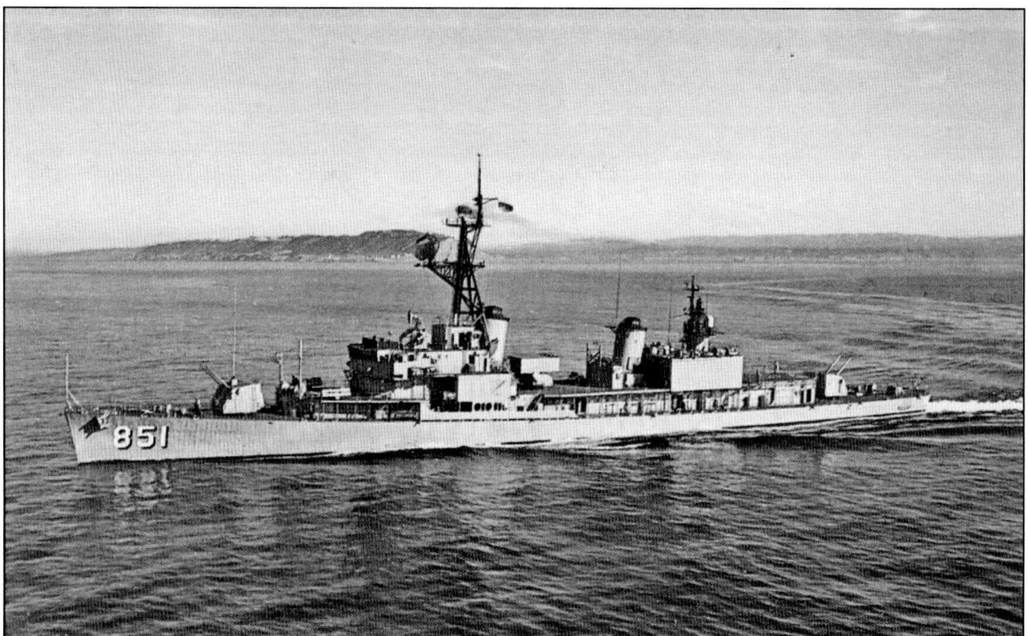

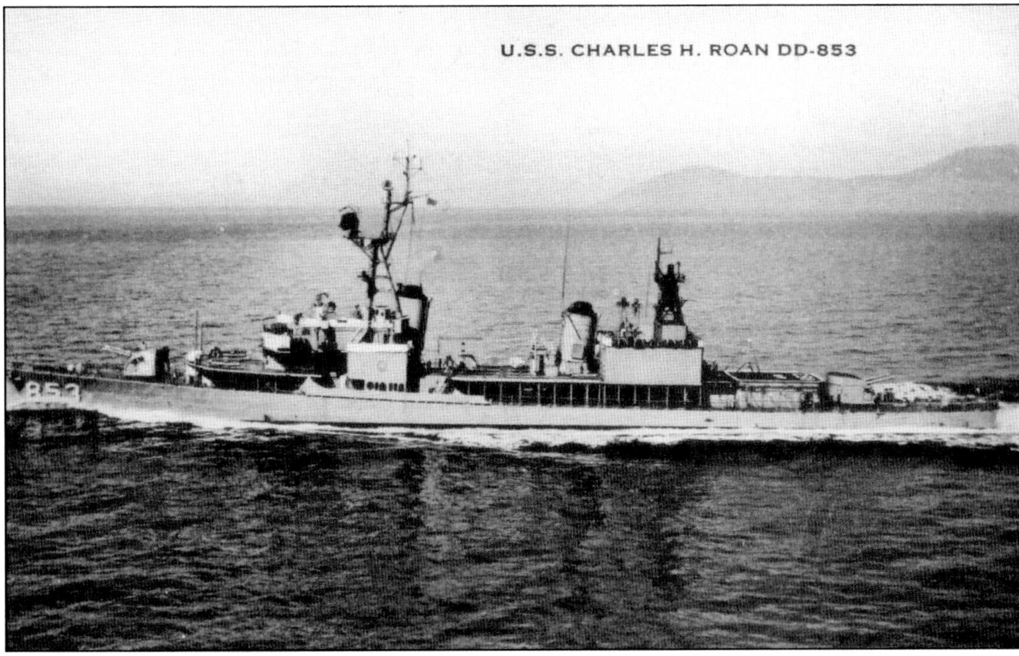

Commissioned in September 1946, Gearing class destroyer USS *Roan* (DD-853) operated in the Mediterranean during the 1956 Suez Canal crisis. In 1958, she took part in the dedication of the Saint Lawrence Seaway, becoming one of the first US Navy ships to pass through the seaway and into the Great Lakes. In 1973, *Roan* was transferred to the Turkish navy, serving as TCG *Maresal Fevzi Cakmak* until 1995.

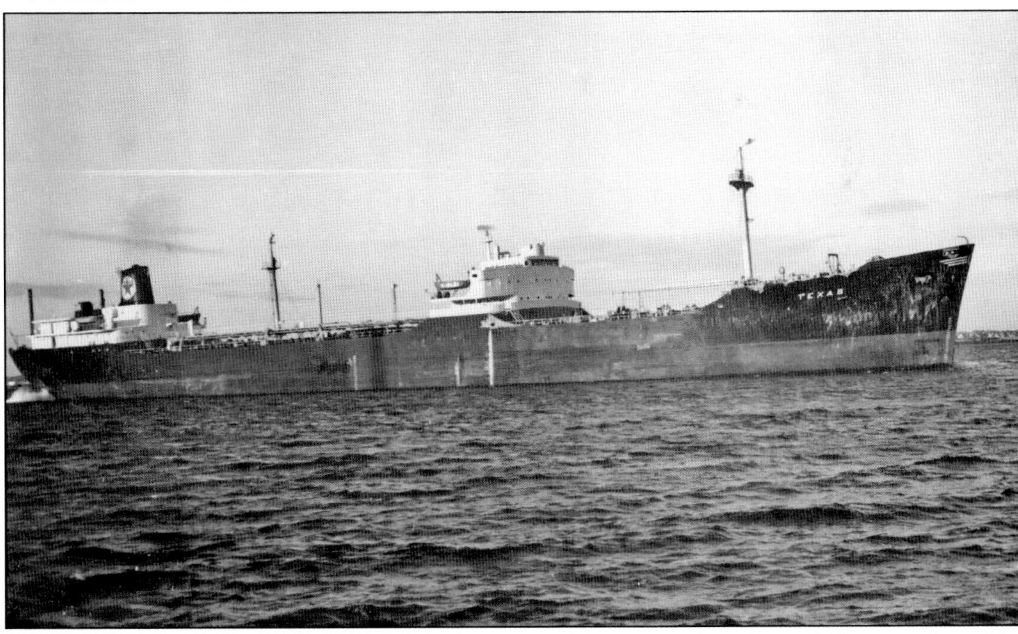

In 1949, the shipyard constructed its first post–World War II oil tankers, delivering four ships to Texaco. In addition to SS *Texas*, the shipyard simultaneously constructed SS *Ohio*, SS *Pennsylvania*, and SS *Kentucky*. The tankers were 624 feet long, and each could safely carry 28,000 deadweight tons. All four tankers were scrapped in 1985–1986.

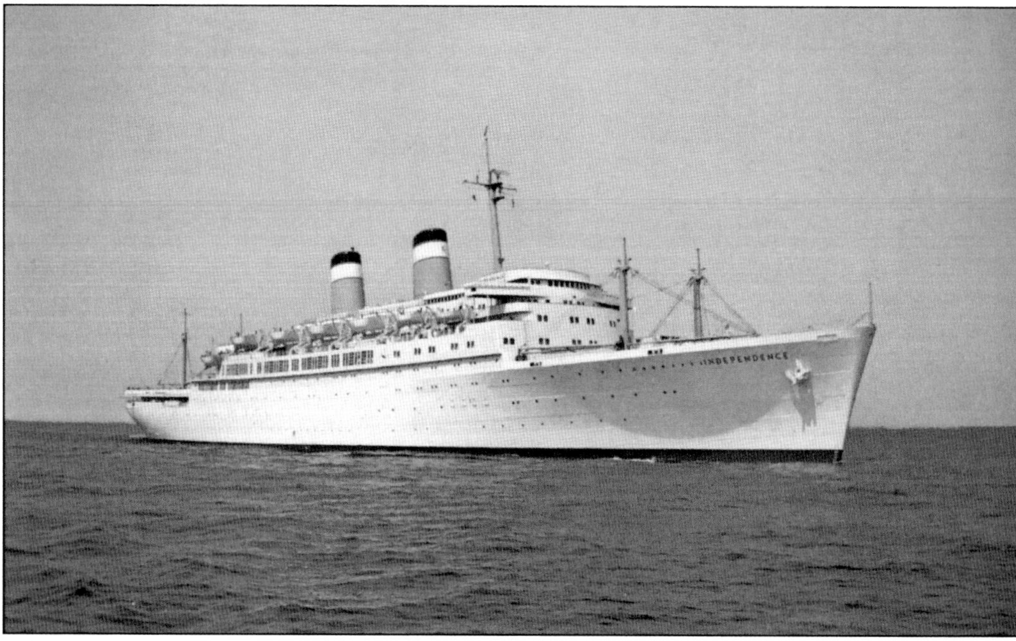

When completed in January 1951, SS *Independence* was 66-percent longer than the first cruise ship built at the shipyard in 1907 (SS *Creole*). She was 682 feet long and could accommodate 1,000 passengers on transatlantic voyages. *Independence* was also built to US Navy standards with potential troop transportation in mind and could have been quickly retrofitted to accommodate 5,000 men and equipment.

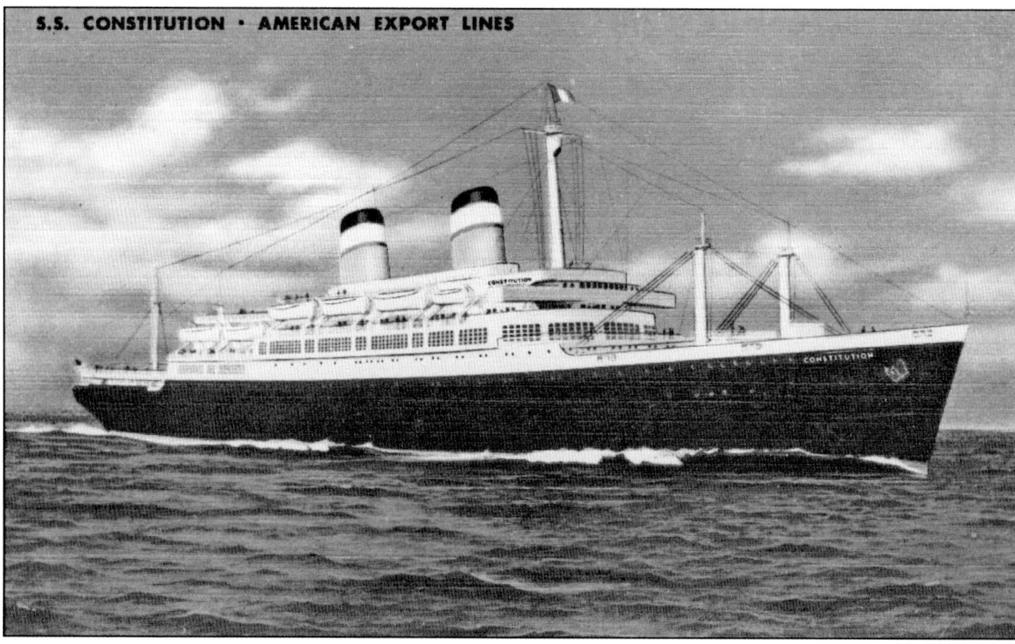

SS *Constitution* is notable as the last cruise ship built at the shipyard, delivered in June 1951 for American Export Lines. During her 44 years of service, *Constitution* appeared in episodes *of I Love Lucy* and *Magnum P.I.* as well as the movie *An Affair to Remember.* In 1956, Grace Kelly sailed the *Constitution* to Monaco for her wedding to Prince Rainier.

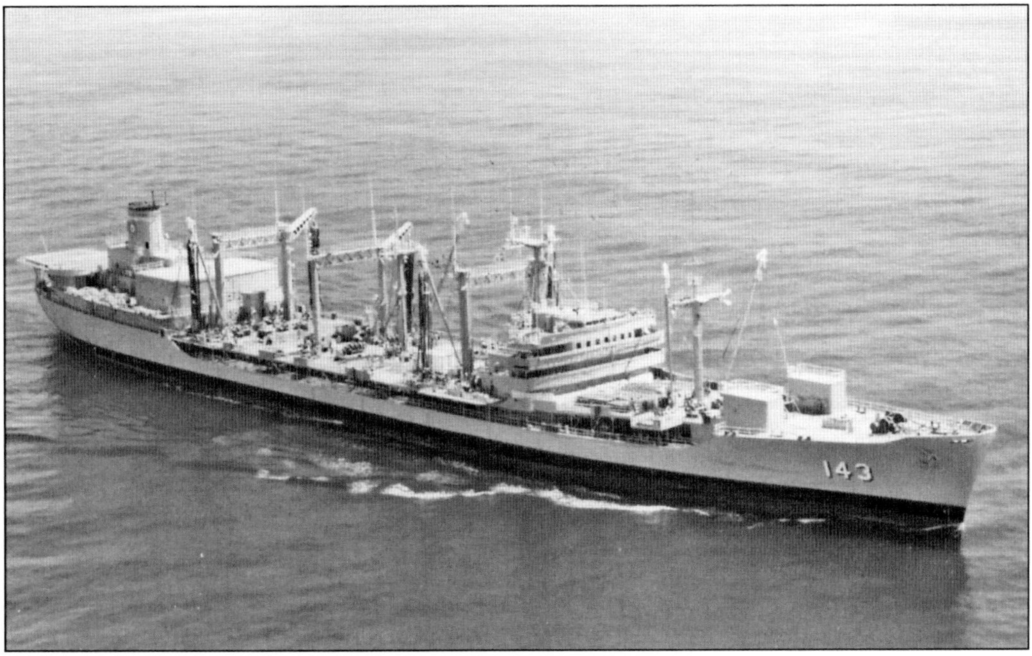

Commissioned in September 1954, USS *Neosho* (AO-143) served as the lead ship of a new class of fleet oilers, built for large capacity as well as speed. She proved invaluable by replenishing ships at sea during the 1956 Suez Crisis, the 1962 Cuban Missile Crisis, and the 1965 Dominican Republic Invasion. (Courtesy of Atlantic Fleet Sales.)

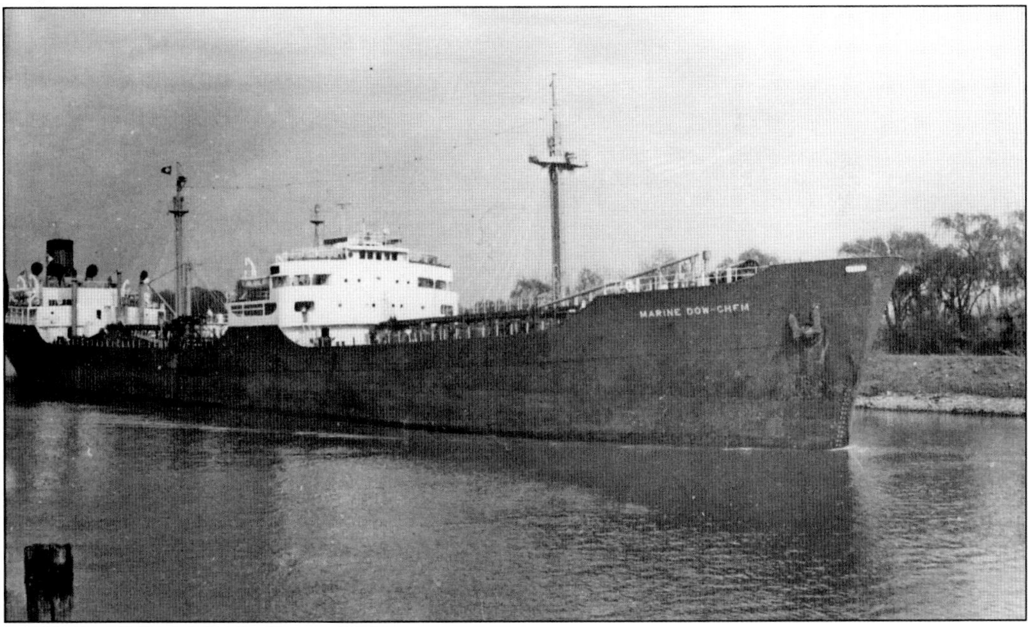

Marine Dow-Chem resulted from a collaboration between Bethlehem Shipbuilding and Dow Chemical, which sought to transport caustic chemicals at a constant temperature. Delivered in March 1954, she was the first tanker designed from the keel up to carry liquid chemicals and could carry up to 11 different chemicals at once. The hull was equipped with cathodic protection and the storage tanks and pipes lined to eliminate the possibility of corrosion.

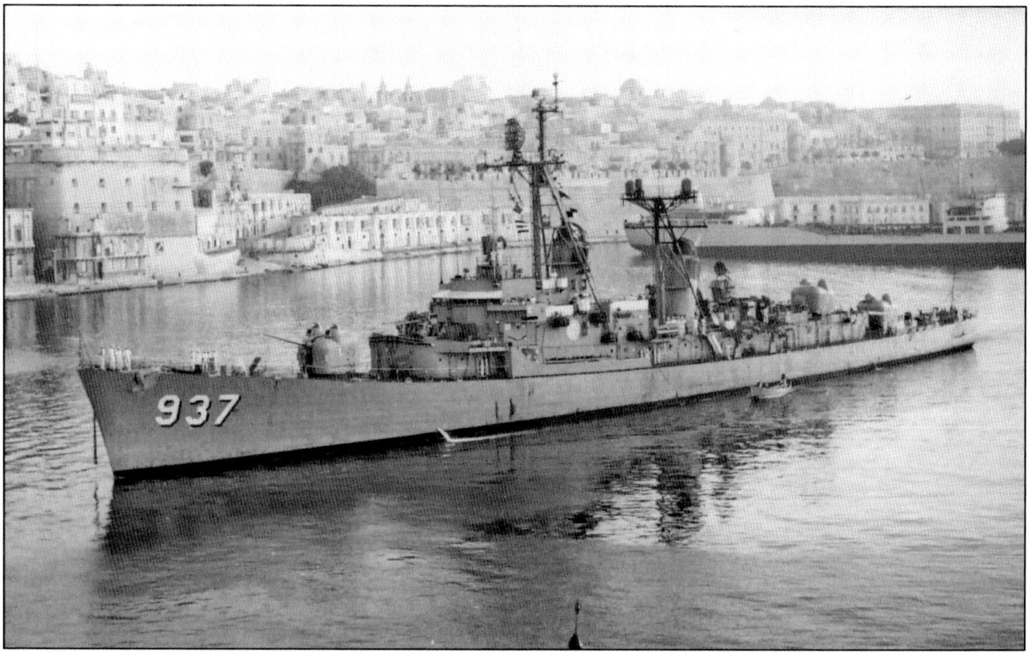

Forrest Sherman class destroyer USS *Davis* (DD-937) was commissioned in February 1957. This photograph was taken in June 1967 at Valetta Harbor in Malta. A week earlier, *Davis* was instrumental in saving USS *Liberty* from sinking, after Israeli planes off the coast of Israel mistakenly attacked *Liberty* during the Six-Day War. (Courtesy of Wright and Logan, National Museum of the Royal Navy.)

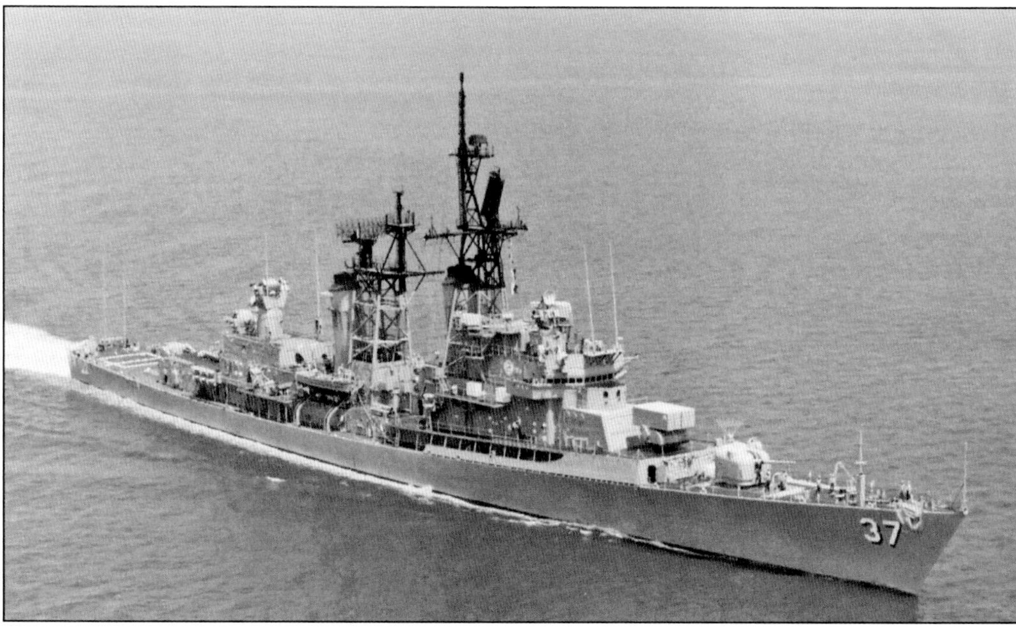

Named for the US Navy's first admiral, David Glasgow Farragut, USS *Farragut* (DLG-6) was launched in July 1958 as a guided missile frigate. She was reclassified as a guided missile destroyer in 1975 (DDG-37). *Farragut* operated with the Sixth Fleet in the Mediterranean, including the bombing of Libya by the United States in 1986. (Courtesy of Atlantic Fleet Sales.)

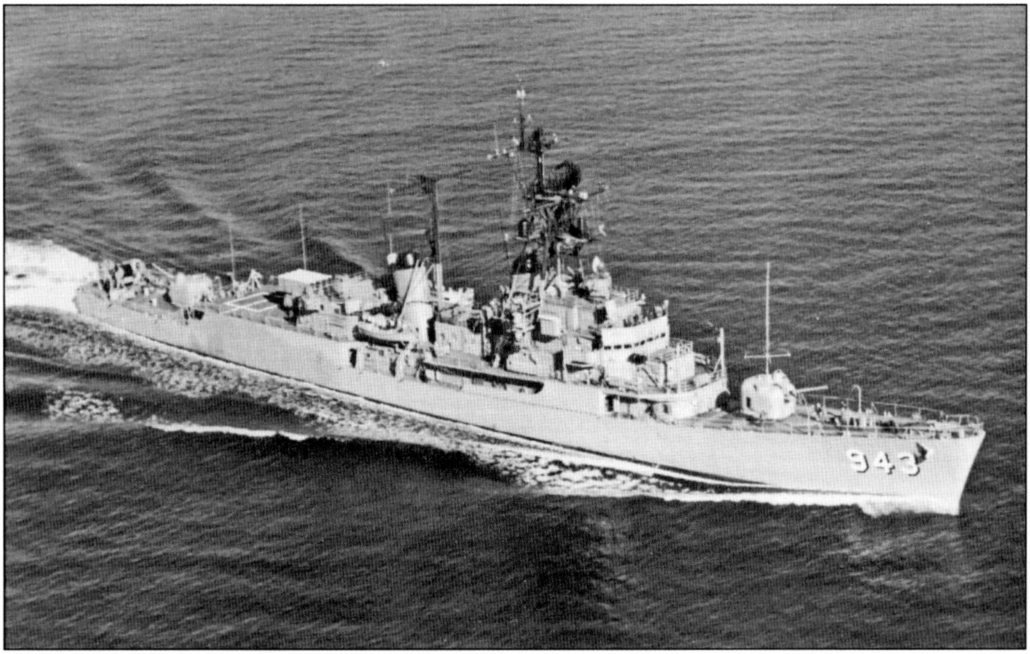

USS *Blandy* (DD-943) and USS *Mullinix* (DD-944) were Forrest Sherman class destroyers, commissioned in November 1957 and February 1958, respectively. During the 1962 Cuban Missile Crisis, *Blandy* forced a Russian submarine to the surface. In 1968, while operating off the coast of Vietnam, *Blandy* fired 27,428 rounds at the enemy, a record for a destroyer. Her guns collapsed three North Vietnamese bridges and damaged 11 more. *Mullinix* was the last destroyer built in Quincy. In 1966, *Mullinix* served off the coast of South Vietnam, providing gunfire support. Decommissioned in 1983, *Mullinix* was sunk as a target in 1992. (Both, courtesy of Atlantic Fleet Sales.)

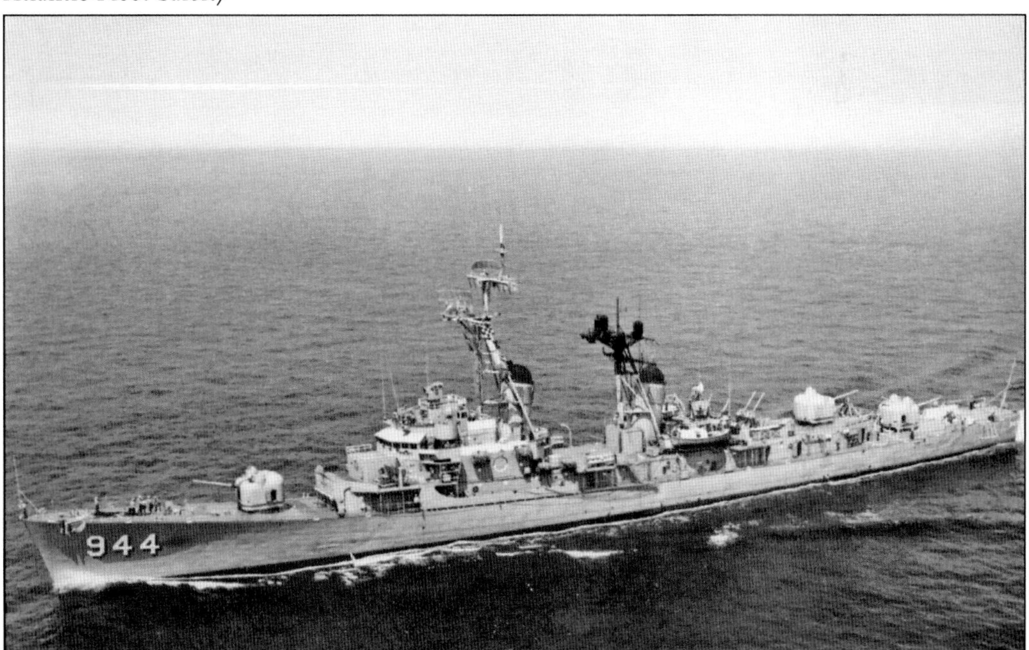

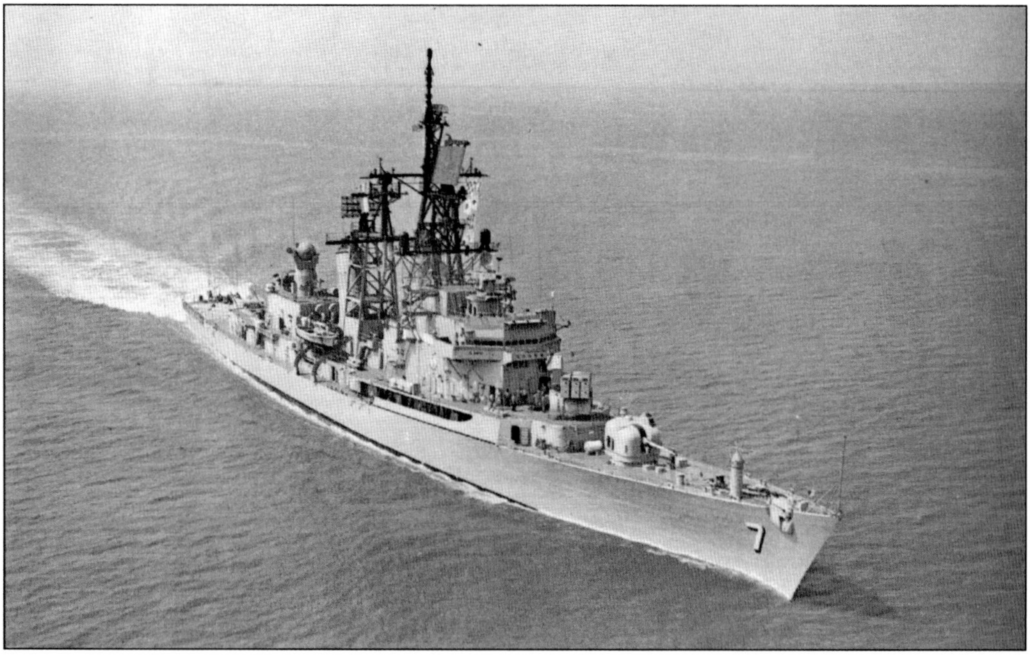

Named for Admiral Luce, the founder of the Naval War College in Newport, guided missile frigate USS *Luce* (DLG-7) was commissioned in May 1961. In January 1966, while docked at the Mayport Naval Station, *Luce* reported an "actual nuclear incident" when a nuclear warhead separated from the missile and dropped onboard the ship. Luckily, there were no casualties. (Courtesy of Marine Photos of San Diego.)

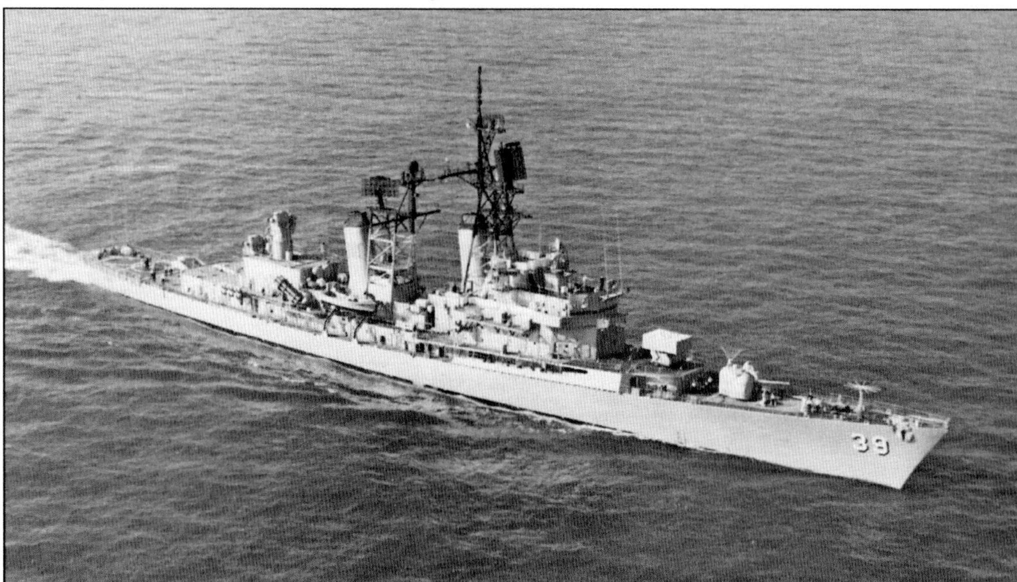

USS *Macdonough* (DLG-8) served as flagship for Cruiser-Destroyer Flotilla Six of the Atlantic Fleet during the 1962 Cuban Missile Crisis. She was commissioned as a Farragut class guided missile frigate in November 1961 and reclassified as a guided missile destroyer (DDG-39) in 1975. *Macdonough* was awarded the Kuwait Liberation Medal for service during Operation Desert Storm in 1991. (Courtesy of Atlantic Fleet Sales.)

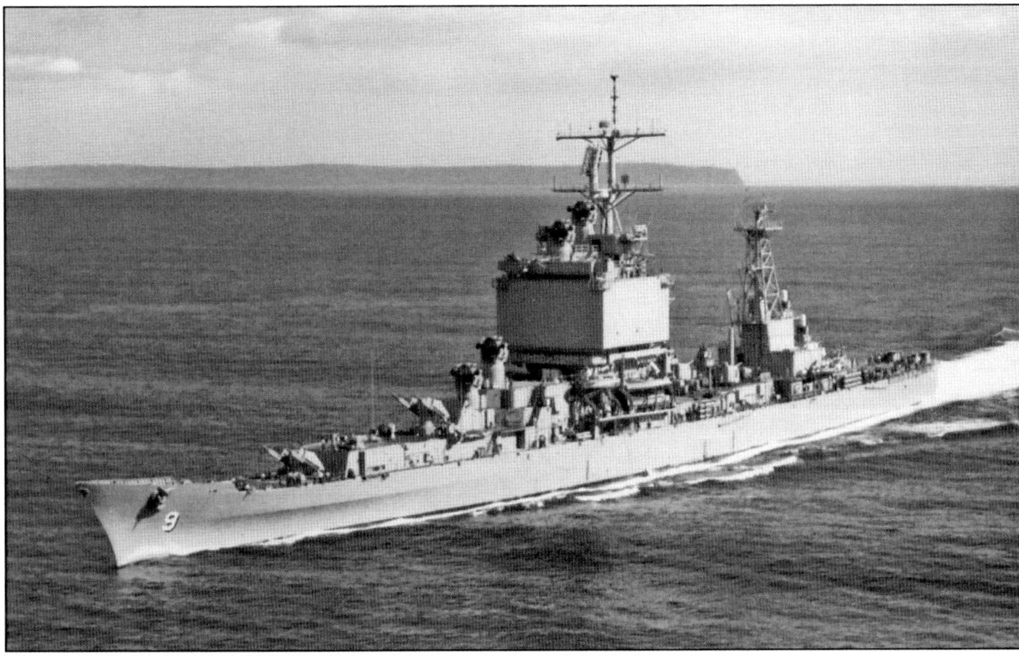

USS *Long Beach* (CGN-9) won fame as the world's first nuclear guided missile cruiser. Commissioned in September 1961, she served several tours in Vietnam between 1966 and 1973. *Long Beach* scored the first naval surface-to-air missile combat kill on May 23, 1968, when her Talos missiles downed a MiG fighter from a distance of 65 miles. (Courtesy of Marine Photos of San Diego.)

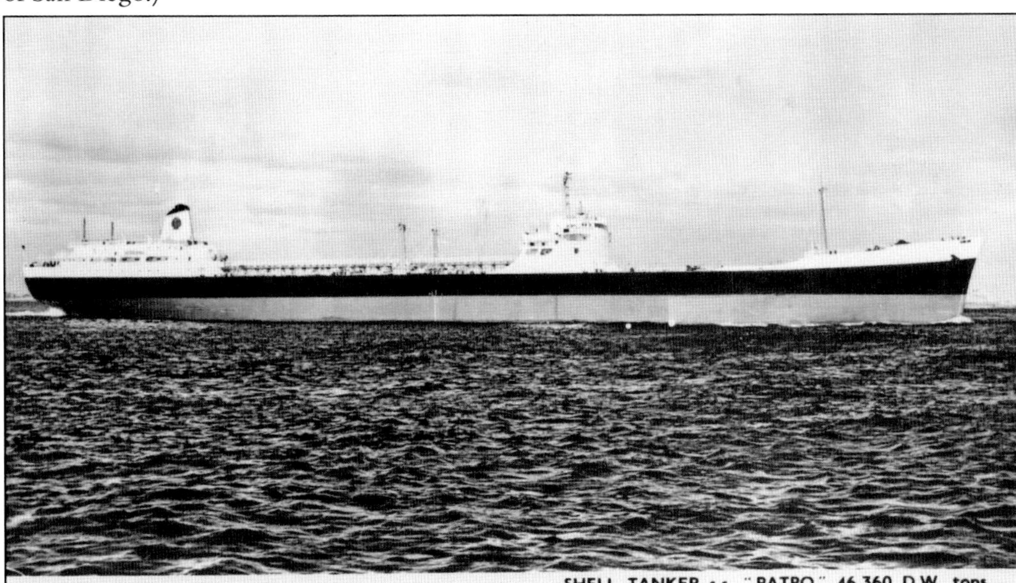

The shipyard was at the forefront of tanker development, constructing several 736-foot tankers in the late 1950s. These tankers could carry over 50-percent more tonnage than tankers delivered just five years earlier. Oil tanker SS *Patro* was capable of carrying 46,360 deadweight tons. Completed in February 1959, she was serving Shell Oil when this real-photo postcard was taken.

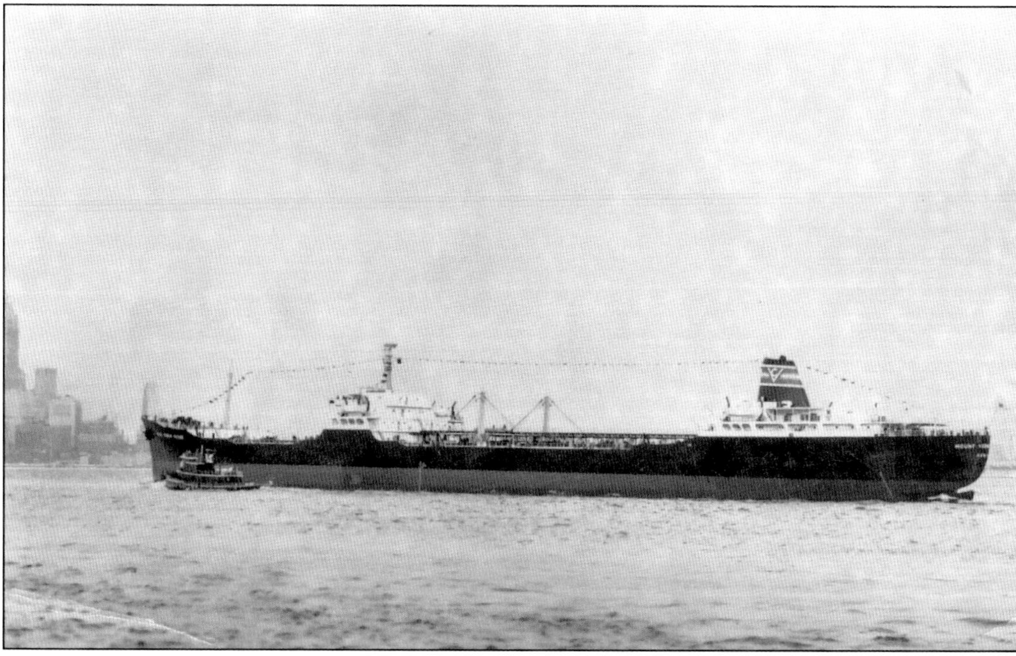

This real-photo postcard shows the *Mount Vernon Victory* on her maiden voyage to New York City. Delivered in January 1961 to Mount Vernon Tanker Company, she was owned by Greek shipping magnate Aristotle Onassis. The shipyard built several tankers for Onassis with the help of a controversial subsidy program in which the US government held mortgages on the ships.

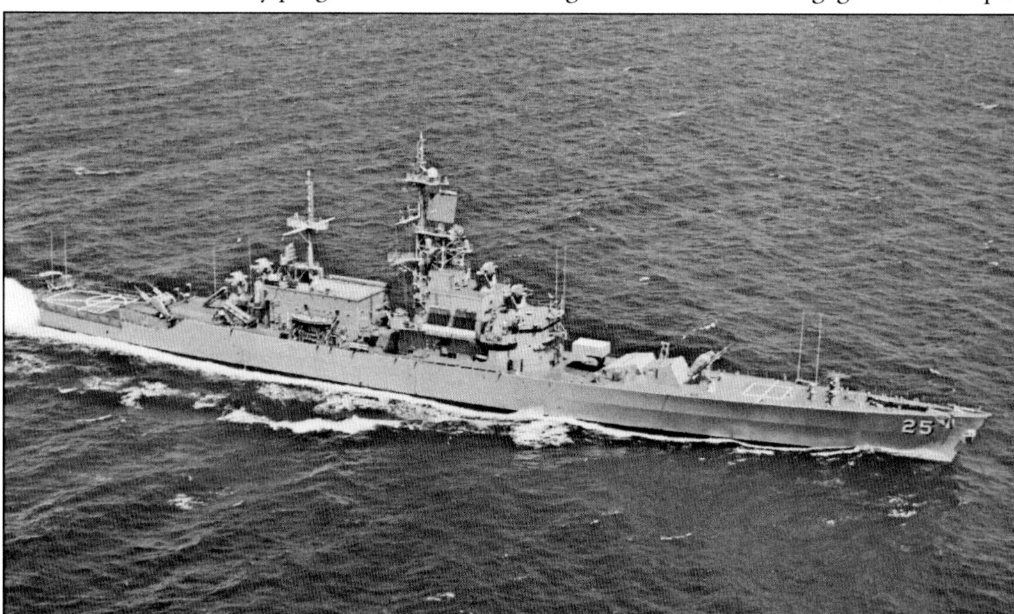

USS *Bainbridge* (DLGN-25) was commissioned in October 1962 as the first nuclear-powered guided missile frigate. Built with twin reactors that provided continuous power, she was capable of speeds in excess of 30 knots. In 1964, she was a member of Operation Sea Orbit, a two-month cruise around the world without refueling. *Bainbridge* earned eight battle stars for Vietnam service. (Courtesy of Marine Photos of San Diego.)

Ten

General Dynamics Era 1964 to 1986

Bethlehem Steel's 50-year ownership in Quincy came to a close in 1964 when the shipyard was sold to General Dynamics, a large defense contractor based in St. Louis, Missouri. Ironically, General Dynamics owned the Electric Boat Company (EBC). Between 1904 and 1924, the Fore River Shipyard built 80 submarines for EBC as a subcontractor before EBC built its own shipyard in Groton, Connecticut, in 1924.

General Dynamics immediately embarked on a $23 million modernization program to improve the competitiveness of the 175-acre facility, now reorganized as the Quincy Shipbuilding Division. Many of the buildings were upgraded, a new paint shop was added, and the shipyard's cranes were updated. A noteworthy landmark at the shipyard was the 328-foot Goliath crane, which arrived in 1975. It was the largest crane in North America, weighing 1,200 tons. It was used to lift large prefabricated modular units onto ships.

In the mid-1970s, the shipyard diversified its client base by constructing liquefied natural gas (LNG) tankers. From 1977 to 1980, the shipyard delivered 10 tankers that were 936 feet long and capable of carrying 125,000 cubic meters of LNG. Despite having half the capacity of many modern LNG tankers, Quincy's 10 tankers remain in service today.

The final contract at the shipyard was for five Maritime Prepositioning Ships for the Military Sealift Command. Upon delivery in 1985 and 1986, the ships were positioned in strategic locations around the world for fast delivery of Marine Corps equipment and supplies. These ships continue their valuable work over a quarter century after construction.

Unfortunately, the tanker business dried up, and contracts with the US Navy were awarded to other shipyards. With few prospects for new ship construction, General Dynamics closed the Fore River Shipyard in 1986, thus ending the 23-year ownership by General Dynamics and 103 years of shipbuilding along the Fore River in Braintree and Quincy.

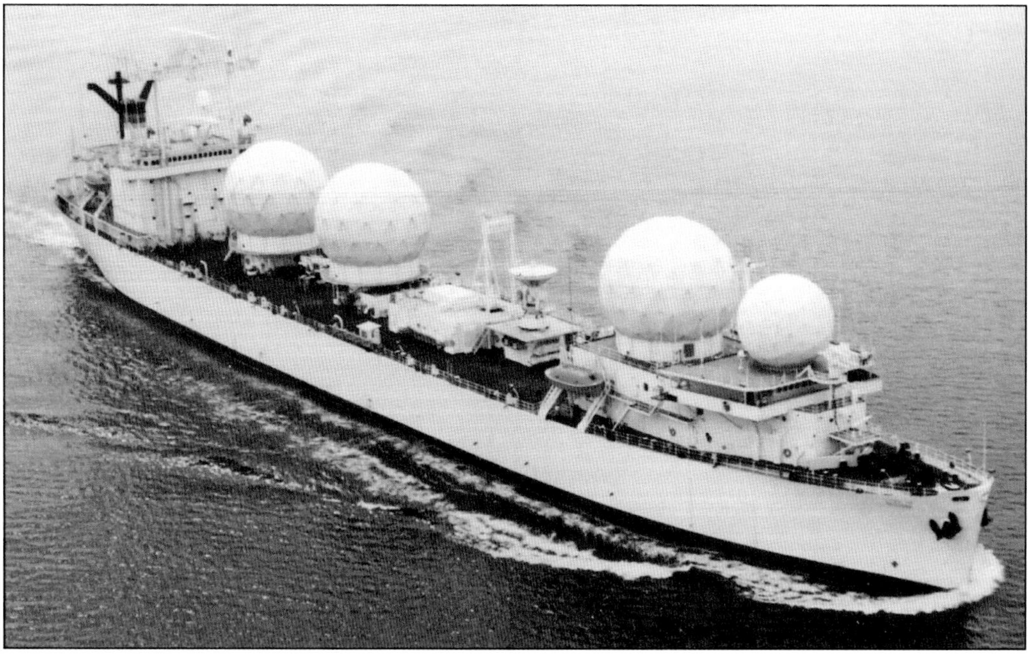

USNS *Redstone* (T-AGM-20) was originally built in 1943 as a fleet oiler. In 1964, General Dynamics won the contract to convert her to a Vanguard class range instrumentation ship. Operated by the Military Sealift Command, she was equipped with missile tracking and communications equipment that helped NASA track the early Apollo lunar missions. *Redstone* served from 1966 until 1993. (Courtesy of Atlantic Fleet Sales.)

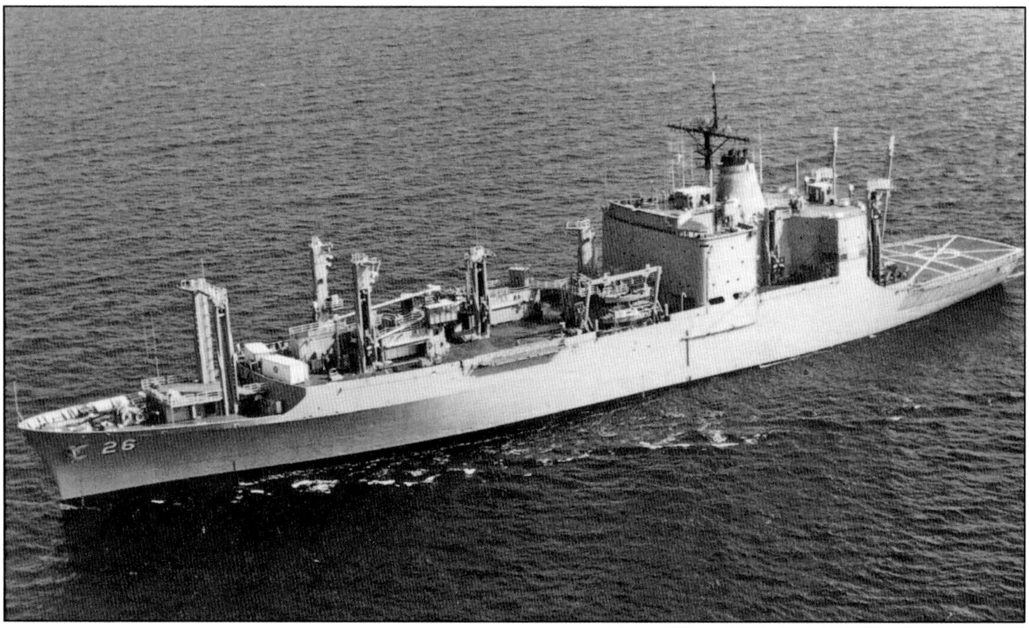

Commissioned in August 1968, ammunition ship USS *Kilauea* (AE-26) served in Vietnam from 1970 to 1972, earning four battle stars. Transferred to the Military Sealift Command in 1980, *Kilauea* operated with a civilian crew, deploying to the Persian Gulf in 1990–1991 for Operation Desert Shield and Operation Desert Storm. (Courtesy of Marine Photos of San Diego.)

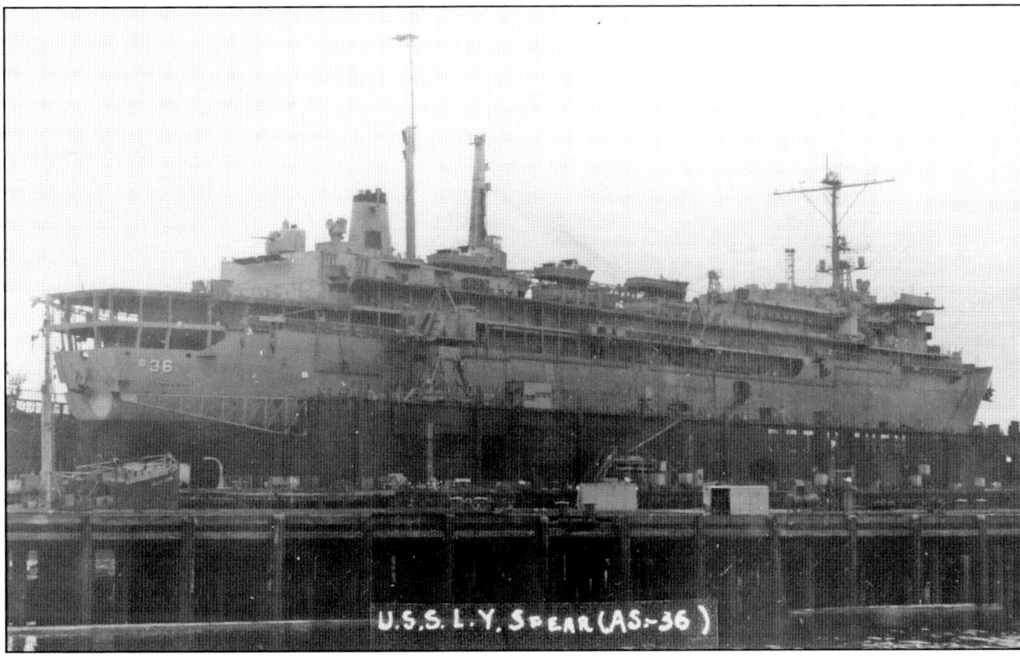

USS *L.Y. Spear* (AS-36) was the first ship in her class of submarine tenders. She was named after Lawrence Y. Spear, a pioneer in submarine construction in the early 1900s and president of the Electric Boat Company from 1942 to 1947. *Spear* could support a dozen nuclear attack submarines at sea and up to four simultaneously. This real-photo postcard shows the ship under construction in 1967.

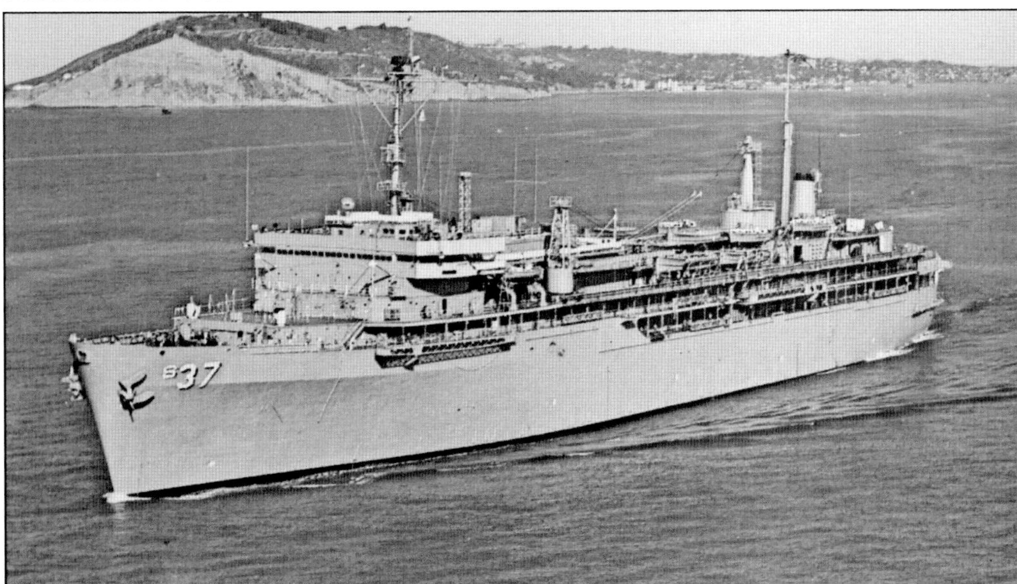

Submarine tender USS *Dixon* (AS-37) was named for George E. Dixon, Civil War commander of the Confederate submarine *H.L. Hunley*. Commissioned in August 1971, *Dixon* had full helicopter capability and was equipped with a diver recompression chamber. Decommissioned in 1995, *Dixon* was sunk as a bombing target in the Atlantic Ocean in 2003. (Courtesy of Marine Photos of San Diego.)

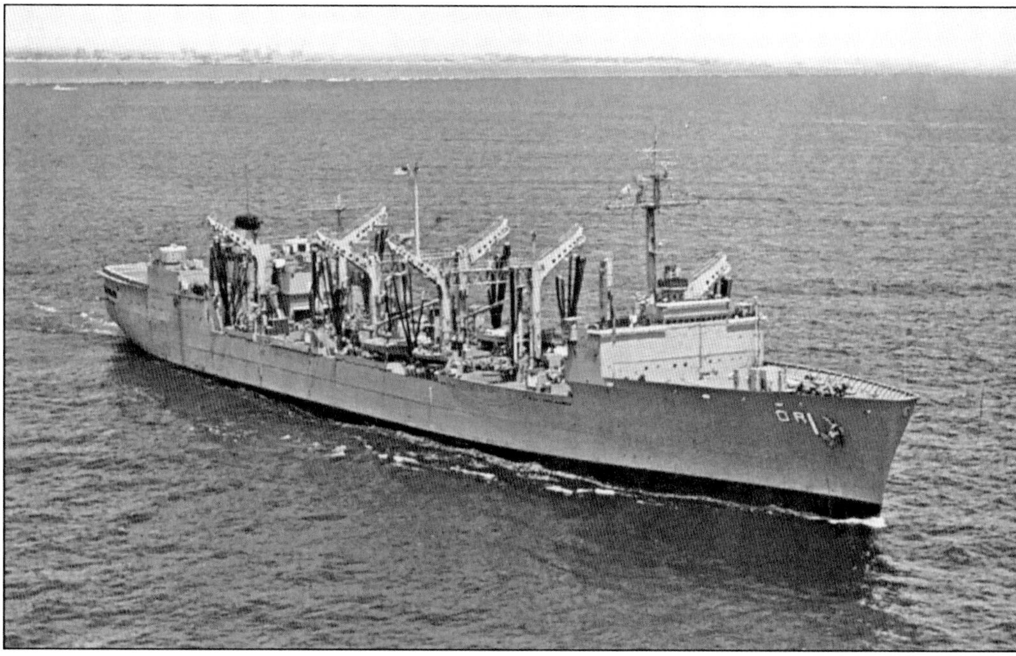

Commissioned in June 1969 as the lead ship of Wichita class replenishment oilers, USS *Wichita* (AOR-1) served in Vietnam from 1970 to 1973, earning four battle stars. She also received the Armed Forces Expeditionary Medal for replenishing a record 23 ships in 24 hours. *Wichita* was transferred to the US Maritime Administration in 1998. (Courtesy of Marine Photos of San Diego.)

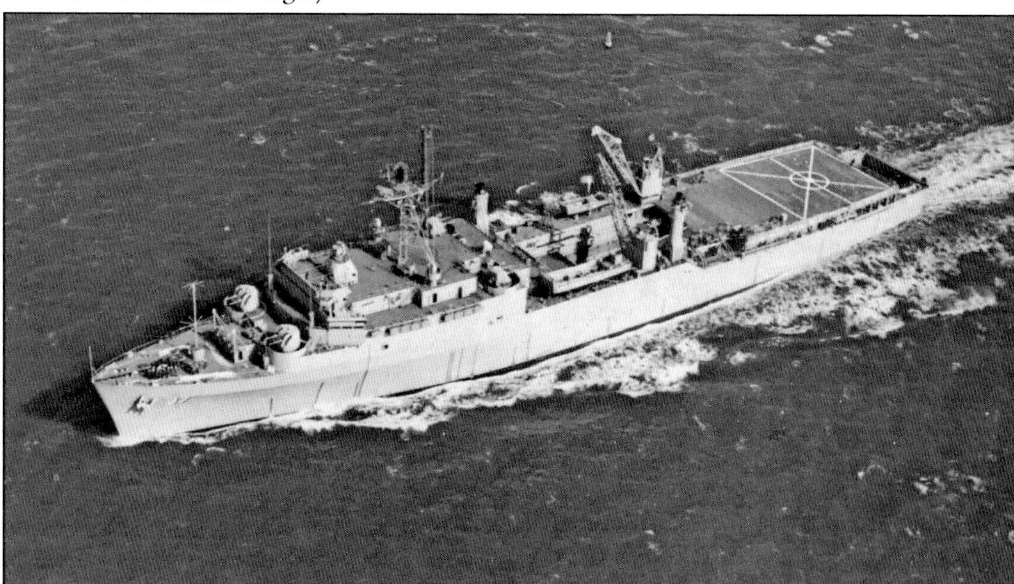

Commissioned in October 1970, USS *Portland* (LSD-37) served as an Anchorage class dock landing ship. The shipyard also built sister ships *Pensacola* (LSD-38), *Mount Vernon* (LSD-39), and *Fort Fisher* (LSD-40). These ships were capable of transporting and launching landing craft and amphibious vehicles. They were also equipped with a landing pad for helicopters. (Courtesy of Atlantic Fleet Sales.)

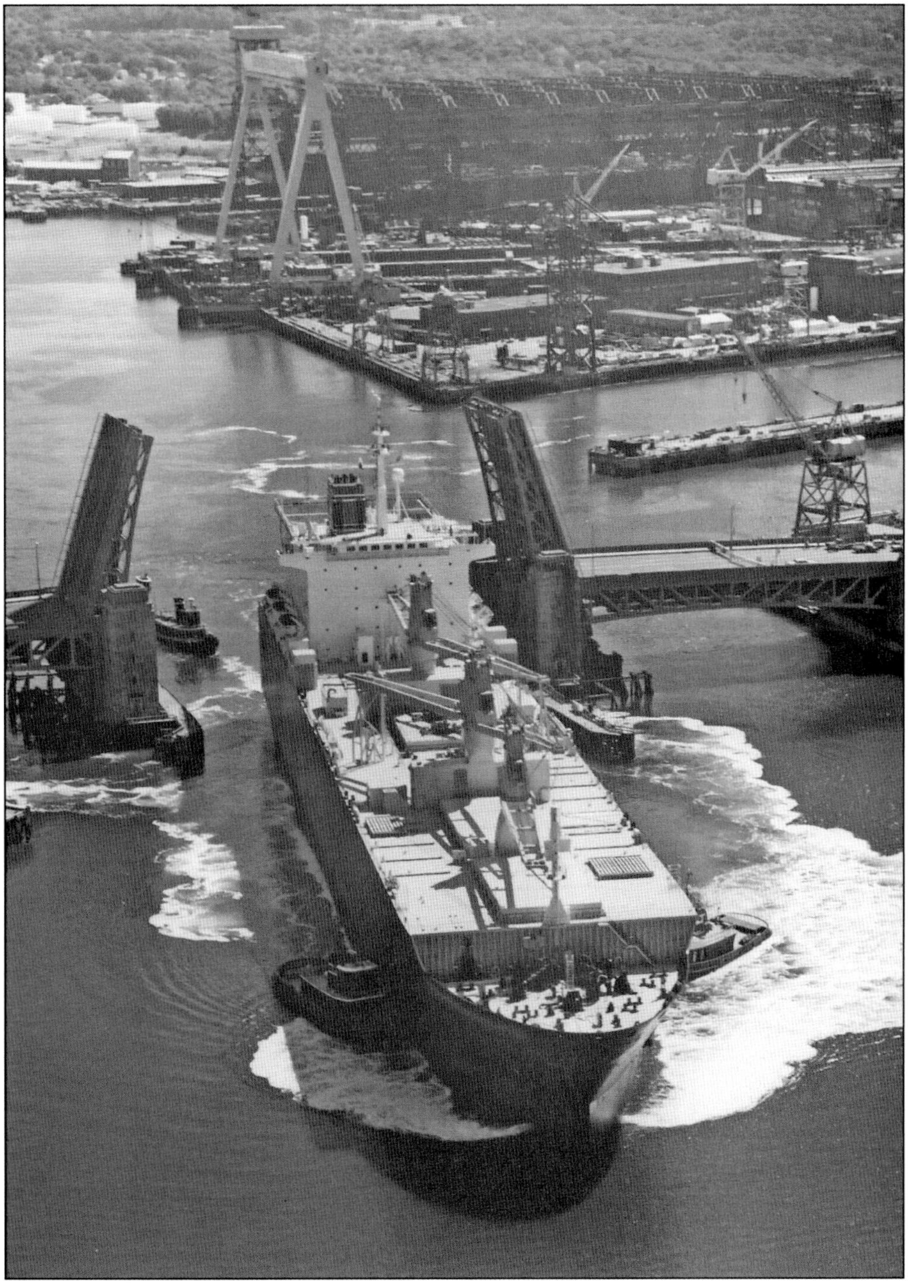

USNS *SGT William R. Button* (T-AK 3012) became the final ship built at the Fore River Shipyard, launched on May 22, 1986. ***Button*** is one of 12 prepositioning ships operating today for the Military Sealift Command. Capable of responding to a crisis anywhere in the world, these ships carry tanks, ammunition, food, water, hospital equipment, fuel, and spare parts in support of the US Marine Corps. When ***Button's*** keel was laid down in November 1984, few in Quincy would have believed their shipyard would close for good in two years. Although it has now been shuttered for over a quarter century, it is possible someday Quincy will again be home to a shipbuilding venture along the Fore River. For now, the memories of a job well done will have to do. (Courtesy of General Dynamics Corporation.)